The Rothbard Reader

The Rothbard Reader

JOSEPH T. SALERNO
MATTHEW McCAFFREY
EDITORS

MISESINSTITUTE
AUBURN, ALABAMA

Mises Institute
518 West Magnolia Ave.
Auburn, Ala. 36832
mises.org

paperback edition: 978-1-61016-661-4
large print edition: 978-1-61016-662-1
epub: 978-1-61016-663-8

Contents

Introduction

Few economists manage to produce a body of work that boasts a serious following twenty years after their deaths. Murray N. Rothbard is a rare exception. More than two decades since his passing, his influence lives on, both in the work of a new generation of social scientists, and among a growing number of the general public.

One reason for Rothbard's continuing popularity is his ability to reach across disciplines, and to connect them: unlike many contemporary economists, who specialize in increasingly narrow fields within the science, Rothbard's research agenda was expansive and interdisciplinary, covering most of the social sciences and humanities.

Some readers of this book will already be familiar with Rothbard's major works, such as his path-breaking treatise on economics, *Man, Economy, and State*. Yet Rothbard also produced hundreds of shorter works for both academic and popular audiences. Unfortunately, many lack the time to explore his writings; what's more, his *oeuvre* is so enormous it is often difficult to know where to begin.

This book aims to solve these problems by providing a window into Rothbard's achievements in the social sciences, humanities, and beyond. It includes introductory, intermediate, and advanced material, to ensure the book can be enjoyed by readers of all levels of understanding and familiarity with Rothbard's work. Therefore although it is intended primarily for newcomers, veteran readers will also find much to discover or re-discover in these pages.

The individual articles in this collection can be read in any order; with that in mind, we propose two ways to explore them. Those new to Rothbard's writing may want to begin with the shorter, more accessible chapters that interest them most, before continuing on to more difficult topics. However, we have intentionally arranged the articles and sections so that readers who prefer a systematic discussion, or who are already acquainted with Rothbard's ideas, can read the book cover to cover.

The volume begins with a personal look at Rothbard's life and work, as told in his own words. The opening section, "Rothbard: Man, Economist, and Anti-Statist," brings together three rare interviews, each highlighting different aspects of his unique personality and worldview. Readers will soon recognize an overarching theme running through Rothbard's life and work: a passion for liberty, a unifying principle in his thought, no matter the discipline.

This commitment can be seen further in the next section, "Foundations of Social Science and the Free Society." In the first essay, Rothbard stresses "The Discipline of Liberty" as the foundation for the study of humanity. This central interest serves as inspiration and foundation for the project that follows, namely, an outline of the human sciences and their primary method of investigation: praxeology.

Although Rothbard wrote on many subjects, his training—and heart —were in economics, and so too are the majority of the writings in this collection. The next two sections provide a concise exposition of economic theory, beginning with individual value and choice. They explore in turn Rothbard's insights into the "Principles of Economics and Government Intervention" and "Money, Banking, and the Business Cycle." Together, these chapters provide a brief overview of Rothbard's more comprehensive account of economic theory in *Man, Economy, and State*.

Austrian economists have always been fascinated by the history of their science, and Rothbard was no exception. In fact, his writings on the subject are among his most original and controversial. The section devoted to the "History of Economic Thought" surveys the contributions of many influential economists, outlining the development of economics from mercantilism to the modern Austrian school.

However, Rothbard's historical interests extended far beyond the history of economic doctrines. The section on "Economic History" illustrates how he consistently applied economic theory to historical experience in order to explain events like the American Revolution, the Progressive Era, and the rise of central banking in the United States.

Of course, no collection of Rothbard's major ideas could be complete without a section devoted to his political philosophy. Based firmly on the idea of property rights, Rothbard develops an account of the free society and its enemies, especially war and the state. These discussions are followed by Rothbard's assessment of the libertarian movement and its pitfalls, along with some of his views on effective strategies for creating a free society.

The collection ends on another personal note. Many of Rothbard's friends attest that when meeting him for the first time, they were stunned by the personality of the man they had previously known only through his academic work. Rothbard embodied a rare vigor and humor, and his love of liberty encompassed more than academic interests: he enjoyed the fruits of liberty as well. These included listening to jazz music and going to the movies, both of which he loved, although perhaps not as much as he delighted in writing about them. The final section, "Movie Reviews," collects some of Rothbard's most entertaining criticism through the years.

Joseph T. Salerno
Pace University

Matthew McCaffrey
University of Manchester

Section I

Rothbard:
Man, Economist, Anti-Statist

CHAPTER 1

Murray Rothbard

The Murray Rothbard wall poster depicts a graying professor pecking at a typewriter. His words rise magically from the machine and blend into a black flag of anarchy rippling above his head. Beneath the drawing is the caption: "Murray N. Rothbard—the greatest living enemy of the state." The poster, like almost everything else relating to politics, causes Rothbard to laugh. He has a penchant for humor that, in his younger days, let him to write an Off-Broadway play, *Mozart Was a Red*, which poked fun at the Ayn Rand cult of the individual. Today he still laughs very easily. If someone mentions the name of almost any establishment economist or political figure, Rothbard will respond with a nasal guffaw. Abe Beame, Jerry Ford, Hubert Humphrey, John Kenneth Galbraith, Alan Greenspan, Ronald Reagan—they all receive the same response: a laugh followed by a theoretical disputation in which Rothbard employs buzz-saw logic to rip into these persons he views as enemies of liberty, prosperity, and the common good.

Rothbard's freewheeling style and strong opinions have gradually earned him a public following. Today he is regarded as the chief theorist and spokesman for the new libertarian philosophy—a role he relishes after years of obscurity spent writing economic tomes and articles in scholarly periodicals. Now he frequently appears on national television, and he is

Reprinted from *Penthouse* (October 1976).

much in demand as a speaker on college campuses. His many books, some of which were long out of print, are reappearing in new editions issued by major publishers. And they have begun to sell. The first two volumes of Rothbard's five-volume history of Colonial America and the Revolution, *Conceived in Liberty*, have become "best-sellers" among scholarly books.

Of course, not everyone is pleased with the new interest in Rothbard's thought, which synthesizes both liberal and conservative ideas. Chief among his detractors are many of his professional economist colleagues, with whom Rothbard has been feuding for twenty-five years. The main outlines of the dispute are simple. Rothbard doesn't think that most of them know what they are talking about. They have retaliated by, so to speak, exiling him from his own profession. For a long time he has paid for his outspokenness by earning what must be regarded as a very narrow living for someone with a Ph.D. from Columbia. Instead of being invited to serve on a prestigious university faculty, he has had to settle for commuting by subway from his Manhattan home to the New York Polytechnic Institute in Brooklyn. Rothbard has also lost out on lucrative private consulting work, which makes economists rank among the highest paid of all professions. Instead of encouraging firms and government agencies to hire him, Rothbard wrote books and articles disputing the value of most economic advice. His contention that the charts and graphs and tables are mostly misleading dampened the demand for his services. Only one firm —a mushroom factory—has called on him for consulting advice in the past twenty years.

Although Rothbard may have disputed the commercial application of his work, others, such as Harry Browne (see the *Penthouse* interview with Browne, February 1975), have made fortunes in the financial-advice field by popularizing concepts developed in Rothbard's early books on depressions, such as *The Panic of 1819* and *America's Great Depression*. Browne and many lesser prophets of "doom and gloom" are earning thousands of dollars per day telling clients to "head for the hills" because the government-controlled economy is doomed to fail. What does Rothbard think of such advice? Not much. He refuses to comment directly on Browne to avoid the appearance of personal animosity. But his general feeling about dropping out is that taking such a step would be disastrous. "Besides," Rothbard says, "there aren't that many hills to fly to."

Penthouse interviewer Jim Davidson questioned Professor Rothbard about his controversial views. The conversation shows why the fifty-year-old economist has been described as the one political theorist who is "to the Left and the Right of everybody." Attacking the current political leadership and virtually every element of government policy, Rothbard explains why he still has confidence in the future of America.

———————

Penthouse: If you had a magic wand for correcting what's wrong in America, what would you do?

Rothbard: I would get the government out of the lives and the properties of all American citizens. I would first repeal all the legislation that's been undertaken and all the administrative edicts of the last century or so.

Penthouse: Even the laws have been designed to help the poor, to protect consumers, and to provide for the young, the ill, and the aged?

Rothbard: Yes. The laws to help the poor are phony. The poor don't really benefit from the welfare state.

Studies were made of a ghetto district in Washington, D.C. After estimating the taxes those people paid to the federal government and balancing that figure against the money the federal government gives back to them, it turned out that they are getting less from the government than they are giving. They're paying for the welfare state just as much as everybody else! The money is simply siphoned off into the military-industrial complex, into bureaucratic salaries, and so forth.

Penthouse: If welfare programs don't benefit the needy, why are they continued?

Rothbard: Because they build up a constituency of government employees for the rulers of the country, for the state apparatus, and for the people who benefit from it. Also they build up a façade of altruism, behind which the people who actually benefit from the state—the people who get the contracts and the subsidies and the monopoly privileges and so forth—are able to operate.

Penthouse: Can you be more specific?

Rothbard: For example, the Civil Aeronautics Board, which regulates the airline industry, was created because of lobbying pressure from the big airlines: Pan Am, United, and others. It was created in order to raise the rates, not to benefit the consumer. And that is how the CAB has functioned. It creates monopolies, restricts airline service on various key routes, and keeps rates up. The result has been the inefficiency and the high costs that the consumer has had to live with. The CAB put out of business quite a few small airlines that were operating very efficiently and very safely but that were undercutting the rates of the big airlines. The CAB just stopped issuing them "certificates of convenience and necessity," I think they're called. That's just one example of the sort of thing the government does on the federal, state, and local levels.

Penthouse: Then you are advocating that all governmental functions be abolished.

Rothbard: I think all these functions could be performed considerably better by voluntary means—financed by the consumers who actually use these services, not by taxpayers who are forced to pay for something they don't personally receive. The income of the policemen, the firemen, and the civil servants should be equivalent to the efficiency of their service to the consumers, not based on political manipulation and coercive taxation. Then they wouldn't be an entrenched bureaucracy anymore. Government employees would have to shape up like everybody else. All other goods and services are provided by businesses or individuals who receive their compensation because they have efficiently supplied a product that consumers want. The government supplies services through coercive taxation and therefore doesn't have to be efficient.

Penthouse: But how could the free market provide such services as the police?

Rothbard: There is no difference between saying that and saying, "How can the free market provide shoes?" In the present society, wealthy people can hire private guards—and they do just that, it's the poor people who have no choice but to rely on the public police.

Right now almost everybody has some kind of medical insurance, Blue Cross and that sort of thing. I see no reason why police insurance would be more costly than that. People would pay premiums every year for having police on retainer, so to speak, in case anything happened.

Those people who couldn't afford such payments would still be provided police aid. We now have legal-aid societies that provide indigent prisoners with free legal counsel, and in a libertarian society the same thing would happen regarding police protection.

Penthouse: If you did away with government and every service was provided by free enterprise, how would the poor be able to survive?

Rothbard: Well, in the first place the poor are only helped by free enterprise. It is private-capital investment and private entrepreneurship that have raised the standard of living from what it was in pre-industrial times to what we have today. This has all been done through private investment, not by government. The government is a drag on the system; it is an impoverishing devise and a parasitic burden on the productive system, not the opposite. Government doesn't help the poor; it hurts them.

Penthouse: We had private charity up through the nineteenth century. Dickens described the horrors it caused. Is that what you wish to return to?

Rothbard: No, the guiding aim of private charity has always been to get people on their feet so they wouldn't have to depend on charity. And private charity was largely successful in doing that. Today the Mormon church has a system of private aid, so that no Mormons are on welfare. The same is true of other ethnic groups that are opposed to any kind of welfare dependency. Albanian Americans in New York are very poor. They're virtually on the lowest income level, and yet none of them is on welfare because they think it's demeaning and degrading and they help each other out, voluntarily.

Penthouse: But if private charity is to work, the economy must be healthy; and many economists feel that an unhampered free market leads to recessions and depressions, which are cured only by government intervention.

Rothbard: Depressions and recessions are not brought about by a free-enterprise system. They are brought about by the government and its process of inflationary counterfeiting. It's the government's banking system that creates inflation, recession, and depression. The government distorts the economy and creates unsound investments. These investments have to be liquidated, and the result is a period of depression. Then the more the government intervenes in the depression—as it did in the 1930s—the longer the depression lasts. In a truly free market system, there would be no depressions.

Penthouse: So the New Deal actually prolonged the depression of the 1930s?

Rothbard: Exactly. Before the New Deal was instituted, there was a federal policy not to intervene once a depression was under way. As a result, depressions didn't last more than one or two years. But when the 1929 crash came, President Hoover, and then President Roosevelt, intervened extensively in a misguided attempt to keep wages and prices up and to shore up unsound companies with federal aid and with other kinds of assistance. The result was to prolong the depression for eleven years, a duration unprecedented in American history. We got out of it only because of World War II, which is a heck of a way to get out of depression.

Penthouse: What's the difference between your position and that of the conservatives, who for years have been talking against big government?

Rothbard: Well, the conservatives and President Ford often employ free-market rhetoric, but people's actions speak louder than their words. President Ford, when his actions are fully scrutinized, comes up with a deficit of about $75 billion in fiscal year 1976, although Arthur Anderson and Company made an accounting of the government finances and have arrived at the conclusion that the deficit is really nearer to $150 billion. Also, President Ford, despite all of his talk about eliminating or reducing government intervention, has proposed a $100 billion subsidy for private-energy sources.

The conservatives tend to favor subsidies to corporations, especially in the military-industrial complex. They tend to favor military expenditures. The same conservatives who would call for a $2 billion cut in welfare, let's say, would also favor a $20-billion expansion of wasteful military spending. They have a blind spot regarding militarism. They tend to be in favor of high tariffs. In a broader area, they tend to be opposed to personal liberty—religious, civil, and so forth. So their rhetoric is totally divorced from their actions. Their libertarian credentials are fairly suspect if you look at the whole picture.

Penthouse: How does the libertarian position differ from that of the liberals, of whom you are so critical?

Rothbard: Well, the libertarian position, basically, is that no person or group should be allowed to use force or violence against any person or his property. Everybody should have complete freedom in all activities of his life, both personal and economic. So this means that libertarians are in favor of economic freedom. Laissez-faire capitalism seems close to the conservative position in many ways. But we're also in favor of complete civil liberty, which, in many ways, is close to the liberal position. Liberals, however, are almost as inconsistent regarding the civil-liberties questions as the conservatives are regarding the free market. Many liberals who favor personal liberty also favor incarcerating mental patients, supposedly for the patients' benefit. Or they favor compulsory seat-belt buzzers, which I personally found extremely obnoxious!

Penthouse: You have said that you are in favor of any sort of capitalist acts between consenting adults. Are you also in favor of any other acts between consenting adults?

Rothbard: Any actions, capitalist or personal or of any other nature, performed by consenting adults should be permitted. Whether any of us personally approves of them is another story and is really irrelevant to the political question of their legality. This goes across the board. Incidentally, many supposed civil libertarians who would favor legalization of drugs or legalization of liquor or alcohol—which I would favor—are somehow opposed to the legalization of cigarette advertising, which should be just as much a civil-liberties question as the other issues.

Penthouse: Don't you feel that the people have a right to make a decision about the form that society should take? Isn't this why we have elections?

Rothbard: I think a person should have the right to have whatever he wants just as long as he doesn't impose his wishes on somebody else. Now, if those people want to vote to support a certain system or a certain person, that's fine. However, the problem is that they're imposing this system and this person on the rest of us.

These elections do not *really* mean that the public gets together at some sort of town meeting and chooses a certain system or a certain group of politicians. As you know, what actually happens is, first, most of the eligible people don't even vote; and, second, they are getting a package deal, a very narrow choice between two parties, which are more or less indistinguishable in their policies and image and cannot be counted upon to honor their promises. Nobody sues a president or a congressman for fraud if he violates his campaign promises—it's considered part of the game. It's called campaign oratory, which nobody pays attention to. A consumer, on the other hand, votes all the time, in a sense. He votes for groceries or clothing or hi-fi sets or other things by buying or by refusing to buy. He's the complete master of his fate. He doesn't have to make a choice between only two products.

Penthouse: And what about you—will you vote in the next election?

Rothbard: I haven't voted for a long time.

Penthouse: If you don't vote, don't you deserve what you get?

Rothbard: Oh no! On the contrary. It's those who *do* vote for the winning candidate who may deserve what they get, not the ones who don't vote for anybody.

Penthouse: But isn't the government the people, in the sense that it is the only institution that represents everybody, as opposed to selfish interest groups?

Rothbard: No. It represents only a fraction of the people. Let's say 45 percent of the people vote. If there's a close election, it means that only 23 percent voted for the winning candidate. That's hardly all the people. So the government is not the people. The people are the rest of us who are *not* in government. They're not *us*. There is just a group of people out there who call themselves "the government." When we see a worker moving to a better job because he will make more money, or when we see a businessman moving into an area where he can make more profits, everybody says, "Oh, he's moving to another job or he's going to another industry to make a higher income." And yet when somebody becomes a *government* employee, suddenly we assume that his objective is completely different. His motivation suddenly becomes "the public interest," "the common good," "national security," or whatever other cliché's are handed out. It would be a very useful exercise for everybody to think about the government, not as purveyors of the public good, but as people are bureaucrats trying to maximize their own income. Then see what kind of coherent explanation of the world you then come up with.

Penthouse: Can you give us examples of the way government officials act to "maximize their own incomes"?

Rothbard: For one thing, every government official increases his income in proportion to the number of people who are working under him. So the tendency is to increase the number of people working in one's organization. And this then leads to an increased budget. Suppose that the official doesn't really need 80 percent of his budget. He can't afford to spend only 2 percent, because Congress will cut his budget next year. So he has to spend at least as much as the budget allows. That's how the bureaucracy becomes a cancerous growth on the system.

Penthouse: Isn't there bureaucracy in private life and on the free market? Why criticize only the government?

Rothbard: Yes, there's bureaucracy in private life, too, but there are a couple of key differences. First, private bureaucracy is limited by profit and loss. If a firm doesn't make a profit and suffers losses, it will go out of business. The government doesn't have to make profits or avoid losses. The government can peg along at the most inefficient rate possible, creating deficits because we the taxpayers, pick up the tab. Because there's no profit-and-loss test for the government bureaucracy, it can proliferate *ad infinitum*.

Penthouse: Many people would probably agree that the government is too large and that it's doing many things poorly. However if we just chop off government programs and services with one swoop, that would create enormous hardships. Many persons depend on jobs that would not exist in the free market. So how would the adjustment to a free society be carried out?

Rothbard: The only way is to allow the free society to operate without government interference. For example, when we demobilized after World War II, more than 10 million people were released from the armed forces. Most economists predicted a massive depression and massive unemployment. How could the economy adjust to all these people suddenly thrown on the labor market? Well, what happened? There was no massive unemployment, and within six months the adjustments had been made very smoothly. If you allow the free market to operate, it works with remarkable speed and efficiency. If you try to tax the public more, supposedly to ease the adjustment, you're going to have a lingering, chronic disease instead of a short, swift end to the problem.

Also, you're going to perpetuate the vested interests, and they're going to be more and more in a position to try to continue their rule and to continue the "emergency" aid forever. We'd never get rid of it. It's very much as if you had sort of a short, brief surgical operation rather than allowing a chronic cancerous disease to continue along on its lethal course.

If government interference were eliminated, private citizens would have the money that has been taken away from them—expropriated by the state—and they would spend the money on what they wanted. Instead of more extensions to the Pentagon, there would be more hi-fi sets, more clothing, and other consumer goods. There would be more jobs in the private sector. The transition would be very rapid.

Penthouse: Many analysts have argued that big government is necessary to provide leadership in foreign policy. What do you say to that?

Rothbard: Big government is no more beneficial in foreign policy than it is in domestic affairs. It is precisely because the world economy and the world society are interconnected and interdependent that individual governments mixing in the situation create conditions leading to war and conflict.

When the government tried to subsidize foreign investments or grab raw materials or correct the so-called balance of power, it creates conditions of conflict that cause war and mass murder.

Penthouse: What about the argument that if the United States did not provide protection, dictators would impose their systems upon peoples and tyranny would enslave the world?

Rothbard: We've been going along with this idea of interventionist foreign policy since about the time of Woodrow Wilson's administration. We began by going to war to make the world "safe for democracy," as Wilson put it. After five or six decades of ubiquitous government intervention, we have a world that is much *less* free than ever before. Obviously, something must be wrong with this kind of policy.

The Vietnam War has shown that in the long run we cannot prevent the people of the world from controlling their own affairs, whether they're doing so badly or not. Whether they have dictatorships or not is their own business. It's not the business of the United States to deplete our treasures and sacrifice the lives of citizens in order to impose our solution on these countries.

Penthouse: Eldridge Cleaver has recently said that critics of American military and America's foreign policy have been mistaken and do not understand the nature of communism. What about that?

Rothbard: Well, I think Eldridge Cleaver has just about as much wisdom in his present incarnation as he had in his previous one—not very much. The danger is statism. I don't think communism is any particular danger *except* insofar as it is statism. We've got enough statism to try to roll back here, and part of that rolling back is the sort of foreign policy and anti-military policy that I advocate. I don't think that anybody really thinks Russia or China or Albania are out to conquer us militarily. If you press the cold warriors hard enough, they will admit that. But they're worried about so-called subversion. I other words, they're worried about *internal* communism, either here or abroad. And what I'm saying is that the internal problem we have to worry about is statism. The main objection I have to communism is that communism is statism. And American statism is what's oppressing us.

Penthouse: If American statism were abolished, wouldn't that action enable an enemy to move in and completely subjugate the American people?

Rothbard: I don't think there's any real threat of conquest. Conquest and wars evolve from reciprocal conflicts. In other words, one state threatens another state or moves in on another state, and the one reacts to the transgression. If you didn't have a state apparatus in this country, it would remove that kind of provocation for attack. Second, if any country did attack us, it would find that a voluntary defense, a free-market defense, would be much more efficient than a state defense. When the state army is conquered, the conquering army can run the system through the defeated but still existent state apparatus. Britain ran India—despite the fact that the British population was much smaller than the Indian—by simply conquering the army of the Indian monarchs and then giving orders to the monarchy. If there's no American state apparatus to give orders to, what's the occupying force going to do? It would have to set up an entirely new state apparatus in the United States, which is almost impossible, considering the size of the country.

And third, private defense is much more efficient than government defense because the military is prone to making blunders. It is not subject to any kind of market test to efficiency.

Penthouse: The present American military budget is in excess of $100 billion. What amount of money would be needed to defend the country through your free-market system?

Rothbard: Well, I'm really not a military expert, but as I understand it, we could do without the rather enormous overkill, which would enable us to destroy the entire Russian population many, many times over. I also understand that all we really need to defend the country against a nuclear attack is the Polaris submarines. If that's so, we can scrap all the spending on everything else. I don't know how much the reduction of the budget would be, but I imagine it would be enormous.

Penthouse: Marxists have said that excessive military spending proves that capitalism doesn't work. How do you react to that argument?

Rothbard: Of course, state capitalism, or statism, has failed. But the free-market hasn't failed. If you look at the history of Marxist economies, there is no evidence that they have anything which is an improvement over the free market. Not only have Marxist planners caused uncounted murders, tortures, and the expropriation of untold sums, but also they haven't delivered the goods, even in the sense of running a viable economic system. One of the reasons why they are able to accomplish anything is the vast black-market network. Despite planning policies in Russia and Eastern Europe, there's still an enormous black-market that manages to deliver goods and services, though in a crippling way, despite all the state can do.

Penthouse: What about environmental arguments against growth?

Rothbard: The answer is that the pollution of the environment has not been caused by the free market. The culprit is conscious government activity. For example, during the 1950s and perhaps the 1960s too, the Department of Agriculture was spraying vast areas of farmland with DDT from helicopters even though individual farmers objected. You also have municipal government sewage-disposal units dumping sewage into the rivers and onto land areas, polluting those areas without any kind of check. So much of all environmental damage has been done by the government itself. Also, the government hasn't fulfilled its supposed function of defending property rights. It has allowed the invasion of private property by other firms or individuals. An example of this is the smoke that destroys orchards. Under the common law or any kind of libertarian legal code, this would not be permitted. But the government has consciously allowed it for a hundred years or more.

Penthouse: Without strict environmental pollution standards established by the government, isn't there a danger that nuclear power plants would pollute the environment?

Rothbard: Well, in the first place, nuclear power plants are subsidized by the government; so if you eliminate the subsidies much of the problem might disappear. Second, the government subsidizes the *insurance* of nuclear power plants, against liability. If that were eliminated, it might reduce the nuclear power problem to manageable proportions. But, in general, I think the point is that the government shouldn't set any kind of standards in advance of activity, in advance of production and sale, because the government doesn't know much about what standards should be set and doing so inhibits the voluntary actions of people. Also, much of the time this means the standards of goods and services will be worse than they would be if the government had kept its hands off. Quality tends to go down to the lowest allowable minimum, to the government standard. Also, people tend to get lured into thinking that because the government sets the standard, everything is safe and acceptable. This is often not the case. What should happen is that if any kind of product injures the consumer—let's say you buy something and it turns out to be poison—then the consumer should be able to go to the courts and sue the seller or manufacturer for severe damages. But what tends to happen now is that if, for example, a building is certified as safe by a government inspector and then collapses and injures somebody, the victim *can't* sue, because the structure has already been certified as safe! The best solution, I think, would be to go through the regular court system to recover damages for injury.

Penthouse: What about efforts to socialize medicine in America?

Rothbard: That would be a monstrous development. In countries with socialized medicine, for instance, Britain, the result has been a tremendous decline in the quality of the medical service and a huge burden of taxes on the public and on the economy. The usual advance estimates of how much socialized medicine would cost are always extrapolated from the current number of people going to doctors and other statistics. What most people don't realize is that if a visit to a doctor were free, then many people would consult a doctor all the time. There would be an enormous increase in demand for medical services, most of it unnecessary, and then the doctor's time would have to be rationed in some way and the quality of medical care would decrease. That happened in England, with the result that the people who can afford to do so avail themselves of private medical care. They have to do this in order to get decent treatment.

The current government intervention in the medical field in the United States has created most of the problems that now exist. By creating licensing requirements—state regulations restricting the number of doctors and medical schools—the government creates a medical monopoly and increases the cost of medicine. In the last decade or so, the government has created the Medicaid-Medicare program, which has enormously increased the cost of doctors and hospitals by an almost indiscriminate disbursement of money to doctors. At first everybody thought the program would be a big bonanza. "Now we'd be able to get most of our medical bills paid," they thought. But what actually happened? Medical bills simply increased, and so we're really no better off than we were before.

In fact, we're worse off. Any further government intervention would compound the damage. And I advocate the elimination of licensing requirements for doctors and hospitals and the loosening of restrictions on other aspects of medicine. The cost of drugs could be cut by eliminating the requirement for prescriptions, which creates a pharmacy monopoly so that people have to go to licensed pharmacies in order to get their drugs. I don't think there's any real need for that.

Penthouse: You're saying that anybody, whether he has gone through medical school or not, should be able to put up a shingle and say, "I'm practicing medicine" or, "I'm a healer," or some similar form of quasi-medical self-advertisement.

Rothbard: Right. Of course, now you can be a *spiritual* healer without a license, but you can't say you're engaging in medical service. You can't employ medical techniques. I think that if I had a hangnail, I should be able to go to a local old crone on the corner and pay fifty cents or so to have the hangnail removed. I shouldn't have to go to a Park Avenue doctor and spend something on the order of fifty-five dollars to have it removed.

There are all sorts of degrees of injury and illness. Each individual should be able to decide for himself who he wants to administer to him, whether licensed or unlicensed—whether an old crone or a Park Avenue physician.

Penthouse: Do you see it as a major problem that many people have a vested stake in the state system and would be quite reluctant to see the regulations and subsidies removed?

Rothbard: Yes, there is a whole network of vested interests. And you're stepping on corns when you try to reduce their power. On the other hand, the mass of the public is not tied up in vested interests. They're the ones who are being exploited by the system. So, really, we would have a majority of the public on our side if they became interested and aware of this exploitation.

Penthouse: Do you believe the vested interests in America form a "ruling class," in the Marxist sense?

Rothbard: Yes, there is a ruling class that runs the state apparatus at the expense of the rest of us, who are the *ruled* classes. But I think the Marxists are definitely wrong in believing that all *businessmen* or *employers* are part of the ruling class, whether or not they have a leading role in the state. Simply hiring someone does not make a person part of the ruling class. I would say that there is no rule involved in any kind of voluntary employer-employee relationship on the free market.

The element of rule begins—and with it exploitation—when someone, or a group, gets hold of the state and starts to operate it. It could be a big businessman—often it is—or some groups of big businessmen. And it also could be members of the Communist party or whatever. In other words, any group—whether businessmen, labor union, or a king and his retinue—any group that manages to get control of the state naturally becomes a ruling class because of that overall control.

Penthouse: Who, then, constitutes the ruling class in America today?

Rothbard: Well, I would say it's a coalition of several groups. Obviously, the ruling politicians and bureaucrats are part of it. And in it, too, are those particular big businessmen who are aligned as allies of the state. Now, clearly, the Rockefellers and corporations like General Dynamics, which get most of their income from the state, would be included. And, as junior partners, so to speak, the unions, like the AFL-CIO unions, are a part of this grouping, particularly the leadership of these unions. Those are the basic elements of our ruling class.

Penthouse: Do you think things will get better or worse, insofar as our system and its ruling class are concerned?

Rothbard: It's a paradoxical thing, but I think things will get better *because* they're getting worse. In other words, we're now in such a crisis because of big government, because of government intervention, that the only way we can get out of it is through eliminating, or vastly reducing, government intervention.

I'm optimistic that we will do that. The public will see clearly now. I think that big government has caused us to get into this whole mess and can't get us out of it; therefore, there must be some other way out—and the only way is the libertarian way. So, I'm optimistic because we're in such a bad fix.

Penthouse: Is there any prospect that there will ever be another American Revolution, one which could get us out of the "bad fix" you talk about?

Rothbard: Well, the Founding Fathers were libertarians, basically. And recent histories have shown, incontrovertibly, that they were animated by libertarian visions. Jefferson said that if the American government became too tyrannical, another revolution would be needed to overturn it.

One would hope that as the American public becomes apprised of the situation in this country and becomes increasingly, sufficiently libertarian, peaceful measures will be sufficient to reduce or eliminate the power of the government.

CHAPTER 2

A Conversation with Murray N. Rothbard

*A*EN: How did *Man, Economy, and State* come to be?

Rothbard: It ended up totally different from the way it started. After Mises had written *Human Action*, the Volker Fund—which promoted classical liberal and libertarian scholarship—was looking for a college textbook that would boil it down and spell it out. Mises hardly knew me at the time since I had just started attending his seminar. I wrote a sample chapter, "Money: Free and Unfree." They showed it to Mises and he gave his endorsement. I then received a many-year grant to work on it. I thought it was going to be a textbook. But it grew and grew. New material kept coming in. As I kept going, I found ideas Mises had left out, or steps that were implicit in Mises that needed to be spelled out. I gave periodic reports to the Volker Fund. Finally they asked me: "Look, is this going to be a textbook or a treatise?" When I delivered a 1,900-page manuscript, they knew the answer. *Power and Market* was the final chapter called "The Economics of Violent Intervention." They asked me to cut it out because it was too radical. It was published separately years later by the Institute for Humane Studies.

AEN: Did you write the book in sequence?

Reprinted from the *Austrian Economics Newsletter* 2, no. 2 (Summer 1990).

Rothbard: Yes. I started on page one with methodology and it wrote itself.

AEN: Did anything get left out of the final version?

Rothbard: I took chapter 5 out of *Man, Economy, and State*, which included the usual cost-curve analysis. I wrote the whole chapter before I realized my approach was nonsense. So I started over.

AEN: Is there any doubt that Mises was your primary influence?

Rothbard: I didn't think so, but Joseph Salerno once gave a talk in which he said *Man, Economy, and State* is more Böhm-Bawerk-oriented than Mises's *Human Action*. I never thought of it that way, but it may be true. When I was spelling out capital theory, I used Böhm-Bawerk primarily. I didn't think about it since I thought Mises was a Böhm-Bawerkian and didn't see any contradiction. I would like to see Professor Salerno explore this. It's an example of the way an historian of economic thought can show something about a person's work that he himself didn't realize.

AEN: How many years did it take to complete *Man, Economy, and State*?

Rothbard: This is complicated. I received the grant in 1952, but shortly afterward I had to finish my doctoral thesis under Arthur Burns.[1] From 1953–56 I was working partly on both. I finally finished *Man, Economy, and State* in 1960 and it was published in 1962.

AEN: How was your dissertation, *The Panic of 1819*, received?

Rothbard: Very well. In fact, much better than any other of my books. Maybe that's because I didn't analyze the causes. I only wrote about how people wanted to cure it. I could have done much more work on it, and there is still more to say, but I am pleased with it. Plus, it remains the only book on the subject.

AEN: Were scholars anticipating the publication of *Man, Economy, and State*?

Rothbard: Not really. Very few were even interested, except the Mises-seminar people and FEE people like Larry Fertig and Henry Hazlitt. Most were non-economists or friends and admirers of Mises. They were

---

[1]Editor's note: Rothbard's dissertation adviser was Joseph Dorfman.

caterers, lawyers, clothing manufacturers. Other than Kirzner, Spadaro, Sennholz, Raico, Reisman, and Percy and Bettina Greaves, there was no Austrian movement to speak of.

AEN: Did you ever get discouraged and say "Why am I doing this?"

Rothbard: No. Any chance to write a book or meet new people was terrific. But I was lonely. Mises was in his sixties, Hayek and Machlup were in their fifties, and I was in my twenties. There was nobody in between. With the possible exception of Baldy Harper, who was a libertarian, but whose Austrian knowledge was limited, there was a missing generation. It had been wiped out by the New Deal.

AEN: If we do an *It's a Wonderful Life* experiment—the state of Austrian economics without *Man, Economy, and State*—it looks pretty grim.

Rothbard: That's an interesting point. Of the economists, Sennholz became a real-estate speculator, Spadaro didn't write much, Reisman became a Ricardian, and Hayek had drifted into philosophy and social thought. Kirzner was doing good work on entrepreneurship, but nobody was doing methodology, monetary theory, capital theory, or much else.

AEN: What were your thoughts on Mises's review of *Man, Economy, and State* when it appeared in the *New Individualist Review*?

Rothbard: I liked it, but he didn't say much about the book. I would have preferred him to go into more depth.

AEN: Was he bothered by some of your corrections of his theories?

Rothbard: I don't know because he never said. Mises and I had only two friendly arguments. One was on monopoly theory where he wound up calling me a Schmollerite. Although nobody else in the seminar realized it, that was the ultimate insult for an Austrian. The other argument was on his utilitarian refutation of government intervention. I argued that government officials can maximize their own well-being through economic interventionism, if not those of the public. He in turn argued that those kinds of politicians wouldn't survive popular vote, thus changing the terms of debate.

AEN: Was there a difference on foreign policy?

Rothbard: In all the years I attended his seminar and was with him, he never talked about foreign policy. If he was an interventionist on foreign affairs, I never knew it. It would have been a violation of Rothbard's law, which is that people tend to specialize in what they are worst at. For example, Henry George is great on everything but land, so therefore he writes about land 90 percent of the time. Friedman is great except on money, so he concentrates on money. Mises, however, and Kirzner too, always did what they were best at.

AEN: Did Hayek ever attend Mises's seminar in the US?

Rothbard: No. They had a very strange relationship. Hayek began making very arcane anti-Misesian comments in his books, but nobody knew it, not even Mises. For example, it turns out that the anti-Walras footnote in *Individualism and Economic Order* was really an anti-Mises footnote, as Hayek admitted a few years later. When Mises read the article, he called Hayek up and said he liked it as an attack on formalism and equilibrium. He didn't realize that some of it was directed against himself. Gradually, Hayek became more and more anti-Misesian without actually refuting what he had to say. Yet Mises and Hayek are still linked in academic minds.

AEN: What happened in the twelve years between *Man, Economy, and State* and Hayek winning the Nobel Prize?

Rothbard: Very little. There were various informal meetings, with Walter Block, and R.J. Smith. During the fifties, we had a whole group in New York, but it disbanded when Hamowy, Raico, and Liggio went to graduate school. There was another group coming up in the sixties, students of Robert LeFevre's Freedom School and later Rampart College. At one meeting, Friedman and Tullock were brought in for a week. I had planned to have them lecture on occupational licensing and on ocean privatization, respectively. Unfortunately, they spoke on these subjects for thirty minutes and then rode their hobby horses, monetary theory and public choice, the rest of the time. Friedman immediately clashed with the Rothbardians. He had read my *America's Great Depression* and was furious that he was suddenly meeting all these Rothbardians. He didn't know such things existed.

AEN: What happened to the Volker Fund?

Rothbard: The Volker Fund collapse in 1972 destroyed a major source of funding for libertarian scholarship. The president was a follower of R.J.

Rushdoony, who at the time was a pre-millenialist Calvinist, later converting to post-millenialism. He had sent me a Rushdoony book, which I blasted. Combined with other reviews, he became convinced he was surrounded by an atheist, anarchist, pacifist conspiracy to destroy Christianity. So he closed the Volker Fund in early 1972. It was a great tragedy. IHS [Institute for Humane Studies] was supposed to be established with the $17 million from the Volker Fund as an endowed think tank—publishing books, sponsoring students, funding research, and holding conferences. Instead, Baldy Harper had to start from scratch.

AEN: How did the *Ethics of Liberty* come about?

Rothbard: I received a Volker Fund grant to write it. It was supposed to be a reconciliation of libertarianism with conservative culture and personal ethics, what is called paleolibertarianism today. But as I worked on it, it turned into an anarcho-libertarian treatise. By the early sixties, conservatives had become pro-war and the whole idea of reconciling us with them had lost its attraction for me.

AEN: What about *Conceived in Liberty*?

Rothbard: After the Volker Fund collapsed, I got a grant from the Lilly Endowment to do a history of the US, which I worked on from 1962–66. The original idea was to take the regular facts and put a libertarian assessment on everything. But once I started to work on it, I found many facts that had been left out, like tax rebellions. So it got longer and longer. It turned into the five-volume *Conceived in Liberty*, covering the colonial period to the Constitution. I don't like to completely chart out my research in advance. I go step by step and it always seems to get longer than anticipated. After Arlington House published volume four, they went out of business. Volume five, on the Constitution, was written longhand and no one can read my handwriting.

AEN: What about conferences during the early seventies?

Rothbard: The first was conducted at Cornell, the summer of 1973. Forrest McDonald and myself were giving papers. At the 1974 conference, we added Garrison, Rizzo, O'Driscoll, Salerno, Ebeling, Hutt, Grinder, and others. It was held in a tiny town in Vermont, which we called a Walrasian-General-Equilibrium town because there was no action, no competition, no interest rates. In 1976, we had a wonderful conference at Windsor Castle, but after that there was nothing.

AEN: Just so that we're clear, between the 1940s and the early 1970s, you were practically the only one that did serious scholarly work in Austrian economics?

Rothbard: Well, Henry Hazlitt did some excellent work. But then he was un-credentialed. Hutt did some, but it wasn't really Austrian. Kirzner had written some serious articles. But basically the tradition had stagnated. By the late seventies, Austrian economics was considered Hayekian, not Misesian. Without the founding of the Mises Institute, I am convinced the whole Misesian program would have collapsed.

AEN: How is your history-of-thought book coming?

Rothbard: Fine. I start with Aristotle, but don't spend much time on the Greeks. I leap to the early Christians. Economic theory became pretty advanced in the Middle Ages and only started falling apart later. Most history of thought assumes linear growth. But I am trying to show that there is slippage.

Unfortunately, there is a hole in my book. I got to the English mercantilists and Francis Bacon, which took me to 1620, but then bogged down and leaped ahead. This summer I am going to repair the hole. Aside from the hole, I have just finished the laissez-faire French school. The next step is to cover the pre-Austrians of the mid-nineteenth century.

AEN: There seems to be a lengthening pattern to your projects.

Rothbard: Maybe so. What is happening to my history of thought is the same thing that happened to *Man, Economy, and State* and *Conceived in Liberty*. It was originally going to be a short book on the history of thought, taking the same people the orthodox people do, reversing the judgment, and giving the Austrian view. Unfortunately I couldn't do that since Smith was not the beginning of economics. I had to start with Aristotle and the Scholastics and work up. I found more and more people that couldn't be left out.

AEN: How many volumes have been completed so far?

Rothbard: I can never estimate things like that, but probably two or more. And I keep underestimating how much work I have to do. I thought I could finish off Marx in one chapter, but it took five. So I cannot give a projected date for finishing.

AEN: You have apparently taken an interest in religion as it affects the history of thought.

Rothbard: Religion was dominant in the history of thought at least through Marshall. The Scholastics emerged out of the Catholic doctrine. And John Locke was a Protestant Scholastic. I am convinced that Smith, who came from a Calvinist tradition, skewed the whole theory of value by emphasizing labor pain, typical of a Puritan. The whole objective-cost tradition grew out of that.

AEN: Why has all this been overlooked?

Rothbard: Because the twentieth century is the century of atheistic, secular intellectuals. When I was growing up, anyone who was religious was considered slightly wacky or even unintelligent. That was the basic attitude of all intellectuals. This is the opposite of the attitudes of earlier centuries when everyone was religious.

The anti-religious bias even shows up in the interpretations of the history of art, for example, in the secularist and positivist interpretation of Renaissance painting. When Jesus is painted as a real person, they assume that means it is a secular work. Whereas the real point of the Renaissance was to emphasize the Incarnation, when God became flesh. Even if art historians aren't interested in theology, they should realize that the people they study were. The same is true for economics. In doing history, you cannot read your own values into the past.

AEN: The anti-socialist revolution seems to be the fulfillment of everything Austrians have worked for.

Rothbard: That's right. We are living through revolutionary times. It's like living through the French or American Revolution and being able to watch it on television every night. Now the difference between the United States and the Eastern Bloc is that the United States still has a communist party.

AEN: This seems to be a vindication for your article, "Left, Right: the Prospects for Liberty."

Rothbard: Damn right. Western conservatives cannot take credit for this. They always argued that socialist totalitarianism couldn't reform from within. Only the libertarians considered and gloried in this possibility.

AEN: Did you see the seeds of anti-socialist revolt when you visited Poland several years ago?

Rothbard: Yes. At the first conference I attended, several dissident Marxists were there. But the next year, the organizers said they didn't need them. We went expecting dissident socialists and we found followers of Hayek, Friedman, Mises, and Rothbard. The economists and journalists that I met with had read many of my books and were publishing underground books on free markets.

AEN: Now that Marxism is dead where it has been tried, is there anything that is useful and important that should be remembered or kept?

Rothbard: There is one good thing about Marx: he was not a Keynesian. I recently asked Yuri Maltsev, former soviet economist, why is it that things seem to have fallen apart so rapidly in the Soviet Union in the last twenty years. He said in the last twenty years, the leaders of the Soviet Union have relaxed the money supply and have used inflation to solve short-term problems. That spelled doom for the system.

AEN: What about the prospects for liberty and a freer economy in the United States?

Rothbard: Everything is getting worse, and very rapidly. Few favor central planning, but the battleground has shifted to interventionism. There are three areas of interventionism which are the big issues, now and in the future: (1) Prohibitionism and the attempt to eliminate all risk. If, for example, automobiles cause accidents, they should be eliminated. (2) Egalitarianism and the idea that victim groups should get special treatment for the next 2,000 years for previous oppression. (3) Environmentalism or antihumanism. The implicit idea is that man is the lowest creature and every creature or inanimate thing has rights.

AEN: How are things in Las Vegas?

Rothbard: Great. Every semester we get more students, and the Austrians are at the top of their classes. We have a *Human Action* study group. I'm teaching a graduate seminar in Austrian economics this term and Hoppe will be teaching a seminar in the spring.

AEN: What in Austrian economics is most and least advanced?

Rothbard: In methodology, we are pretty advanced, thanks to the work of Hans Hoppe. But we can always use more since that is what sets us apart from the rest of the profession. And Joe Salerno is going great work on calculation.

Banking theory, however, has taken a very bad turn with free banking. We have to show that this is the old Currency and Banking school argument rehashed. They have adopted the Banking school doctrine, that the needs of business require an expansion of the money supply and credit. Moreover, the free banking people violate the basic Ricardian doctrine that every supply of money is optimal. Once a market in money is established, there is no longer a need for more money. That is really the key point.

CHAPTER 3

Murray Rothbard in
The New Banner

Managing Editor's Note: Having never met Murray Rothbard prior to this interview I was only aware of his scholarly side—through his writings; I had no conception of the type of personality which I was to encounter. Donald Stone, editor of the libertarian newsletter *Pegasus* and friend of *The New Banner*, who accompanied me and assisted in the interview, had only briefly met Murray Rothbard on one occasion a year before. We were both quite pleased, therefore, to discover that his esteemed reputation as a scholar was matched by his joviality and candor as a host and conversationalist. *The New Banner* is confident that with this interview, it has made available to its readers an up-to-date view of the libertarian struggle by the man who stands today as perhaps the foremost libertarian.

New Banner: In the no. 7 issue of the *Ayn Rand Letter*, Miss Rand admonishes her readers, "Do not join ... libertarian hippies who subordinate reason to whims and substitute anarchism for capitalism." Do you think that this remark was directed at you and other advocates of free market alternatives to government institutions, and do you think this remark is in keeping with Miss Rand's oft-stated principle of "defining your terms"?

Reprinted from *The New Banner: A Fortnightly Libertarian Journal*, 25 February 1972.

Rothbard: Well, it's hard to say, because you notice there are very few specific facts in her discussion. There is one sentence covering "libertarian hippies." Who are they? Where are they?

The movement that I'm in favor of is a movement of libertarians who do not substitute whim for reason. Now some of them do, obviously, and I'm against that. I'm in favor of reason over whim. As far as I'm concerned, and I think the rest of the movement, too, we are anarcho-capitalists. In other words, we believe that capitalism is the fullest expression of anarchism, and anarchism is the fullest expression of capitalism. Not only are they compatible, but you can't really have one without the other. True anarchism will be capitalism, and true capitalism will be anarchism.

As for her remark being in keeping with the principle of defining one's terms—well, obviously not. I don't think she has ever defined the term "anarchism," as a matter of fact.

New Banner: Do you see a possible future for libertarian retreatism or do you see it as a blow against an effective political development of the movement?

Rothbard: I don't think it's a blow, because there are not going to be many retreatists. How many people are going to retreat to their own island or their own atoll! Obviously, half a dozen people go out there, if they do, and it might be fine for them. I wish them well, but personally I wouldn't do it. I'm not going to go off to some damn island or some damn atoll! Ha. I think that most libertarians or most Americans won't do it either.

This might be a personal out for these individual people, but it is hardly a solution for the country. It's not a solution for me or for anybody else that I know of. And so I just think that they are interesting to read about, but they're irrelevant—to use a much clichéd term—to the current concerns of myself or the rest of the public.

Even if it were feasible—even if the government didn't crack down on it as a "hazard to navigation" or whatever, which it undoubtedly would, even if they could get it off the ground, who is going to go there?

Some of the retreatists, by the way, are philosophically very bad. You might know of this fellow Tom Marshall who is the big retreatist and nomad leader. He has this view that in order to be free you have to be a nomad. In other words, any ties to a place or a career injures your freedom. I think this is an evil philosophical error—which all too many people have.

New Banner: The American people seem on the whole to be passively if not actively supporting Phase II [of Nixon's price controls].[1] Conservatives are more concerned with law and order than with economic freedom; liberals are calling for more restrictions after this recent taste of controls. The rest the country apparently will resign itself to any situation after so many years of Orwellian double-talk. Where does this leave the libertarian? Alone for the next generation?

Rothbard: Well, not necessarily, because I think what's happened is that a vacuum of leadership has developed in the country about Phase I and Phase II. In other words, libertarians have been the only people who have been against Phase I and II from the beginning and on principle. Some of the labor union leaders are against it because they didn't get enough share of the pie. They obviously were not against it on principle. Libertarians were the only ones from the very beginning to establish this record and to go out to the public and attack it. I know that I've spent an enormous amount of time attacking it, debating Herb Stein and so forth. But I think it's useful also strategically, because Phase II is going to fall apart. It's already beginning to crack-up. As it cracks-up libertarians will be the only ones who have established a record of opposition to it. I think in a sense we can fill the vacuum. This might be a very good thing for the libertarian movement. As the thing falls apart people will begin to turn to us for leadership. "Well, here are these guys who've been prophetic. When everybody else was going along with it they realized it wasn't going to work."

New Banner: Some libertarians have recommended anti-voting activities during the 1972 election. Do you agree with this tactic?

Rothbard: I'm interested to talk about that. This is the classical anarchist position, there is no doubt about that. The classical anarchist position is that nobody should vote, because if you vote you are participating in a state apparatus. Or if you do vote you should write in your own name, I don't think that there is anything wrong with this tactic in the sense that if there really were a nationwide movement—if five million people, let's say, pledged not to vote, I think it would be very useful. On the other hand, I

---

[1]Editor's note: Rothbard is referring to the phases of the Economic Stabilization Act of 1970, which, among other things, imposed wage and price controls on the US economy from 1971 to April 1974.

don't think voting is a real problem. I don't think it's immoral to vote, in contrast to the anti-voting people.

Lysander Spooner, the patron saint of individualist anarchism, had a very effective attack on this idea. The thing is, if you really believe that by voting you are giving your sanction to the state, then you see you are really adopting the democratic theorist's position. You would be adopting the position of the democratic enemy, so to speak, who says that the state is really voluntary because the masses are supporting it by participating in elections. In other words, you're really the other side of the coin of supporting the policy of democracy—that the public is really behind it and that it is all voluntary. And so the anti-voting people are really saying the same thing.

I don't think this is true, because as Spooner said, people are being placed in a coercive position. They are surrounded by a coercive system; they are surrounded by the state. The state, however, allows you a limited choice—there's no question about the fact that the choice is limited. Since you are in this coercive situation, there is no reason why you shouldn't try to make use of it if you think it will make a difference to your liberty or possessions. So by voting you can't say that this is a moral choice, a fully voluntary choice, on the part of the public. It's not a fully voluntary situation. It's a situation where you are surrounded by the whole state which you can't vote out of existence. For example, we can't vote the Presidency out of existence—unfortunately, it would be great if we could—but since we can't why not make use of the vote if there is a difference at all between the two people. And it is almost inevitable that there will be a difference, incidentally, because just praxeologically or in a natural law sense, every two persons or every two groups of people will be slightly different, at least. So in that case why not make use of it. I don't see that it's immoral to participate in the election provided that you go into it with your eyes open —provided that you don't think that either Nixon or Muskie is the greatest libertarian since Richard Cobden!—which many people, of course, talk themselves into before they go out and vote.

The second part of my answer is that I don't think that voting is really the question. I really don't care about whether people vote or not. To me the important thing is, who do you support. Who do you hope will win the election? You can be a non-voter and say "I don't want to sanction the state" and not vote, but on election night who do you hope the rest of the voters, the rest of the suckers out there who are voting, who do you hope they'll elect. And it's important, because I think that there is a difference.

The Presidency, unfortunately, is of extreme importance. It will be running or directing our lives greatly for four years. So, I see no reason why we shouldn't endorse, or support, or attack one candidate more than the other candidate. I really don't agree at all with the non-voting position in that sense, because the non-voter is not only saying we shouldn't vote: he is also saying that we shouldn't endorse anybody. Will Robert LeFevre, one of the spokesmen of the non-voting approach, will he deep in his heart on election night have any kind of preference at all as the votes come in. Will he cheer slightly or groan more as whoever wins? I don't see how anybody could fail to have a preference, because it will affect all of us.

New Banner: What other activities would you consider appropriate for libertarians during the election?

Rothbard: Well, as I tried to indicate—supporting candidates. I think there will be two main groups of libertarians this year. One group will be the non-voting group. The other group will be the Dump Nixon group of which I am an enthusiastic member. I almost take the position—anybody but Nixon. Dump him! Punish him! Smash him! Retire him to the private life which he so richly deserves. Get him out! I think there are all sorts of reasons why, if you want to pursue it, why Nixon should be dumped.

I do not support Ashbrook, but I think it is a very interesting development, because there is a possibility that the extremists in the conservative camp are hoping that Ashbrook will run on a fifth party ticket in the general election, which is the important thing. Because, if he runs in Ohio, California, etc., he can break Nixon by just getting 10 percent of the conservative vote. That is, if he has the guts to run in a general election.

New Banner: At the outset, your newsletter, *Libertarian Forum*, was co-edited by Karl Hess. He has since departed. What ideological differences led to this split?

Rothbard: First of all, he wasn't the editor, he was the Washington editor, which meant that he wrote a column. He did not have anything to do with the editorial policy of the paper. The concrete split came when I made a very tangential attack on the Black Panthers. He got very upset about this. He thought, one, it was a terrible thing to attack the Panthers, and two, since his name was on the masthead, the Panthers might think he was a part of the party which was attacking them. He felt at that time that it was very important to work with the Panthers. I consider the Panthers a bunch of hooligans and I don't see any reason for supporting them—either in regard to whatever criminal activities they participate in or their free breakfast program. You know the Salvation Army has been giving away breakfast for many years, and I don't see anything particularly revolutionary in that. At any rate, at that time he was very committed to the Panthers and that was really the split.

But more deep than that is the fact that Karl after having been an anarcho-capitalist for some time shifted over to become an anarcho-communist or anarcho-syndicalist. I don't really see any basis for collaboration between the two groups, because even if we are both against the existing state, they would very quickly come up with another state. I don't think you can be an anarcho-communist or an anarcho-syndicalist. You know if the commune runs everything, and decides for everything, whether it is a neighborhood commune or a mass country commune—it really does not matter in this case, somebody's got to make the communal decision. You can't tell me that you'll have participatory democracy and that everybody is going to equally participate. There is obviously going to be a small group, the officiating board or the statistical administrative board or whatever they want to call it, whatever it's going to be, it's going to be the same damn group making decisions for everybody. In other words, it's going to be a coercive decision for the collective property. It will be another state again, as far as I can see. So I really can't see any basis for collaboration. That is really part of a broader analysis of the communist versus the individualist position.

You see, I was one of the people who originated the idea of an alliance with the New Left. But I didn't think of it in these terms. I didn't think of an alliance with the New Left as living in communes with the Black Panthers. I thought of it as participating with the New Left in anti-draft actions or in opposition to the war. I conceived of a political rather than an ideological alliance. While we are both against the draft, let's have joint rallies to attack it, or something like that. This is a completely different sort of thing.

This incidentally has been a problem with libertarians for a long time. Both in the old days when they were always allied with the right-wing and now when they tend to be allied with the left. You start allying yourself with a group and pretty soon you find yourself as one of the group. In other words, the alliance slips away. Start with the idea that we are going to work with either conservatives or radicals for specific goals and somehow they start spending all their time with these people and they wind up as either conservatives or radicals. The libertarian goal drops away and the means become the ends. This is a very difficult problem because you don't want to be sectarian and have nothing to do with anybody. Then you're never going to succeed at all. I think that one of the answers to it is to have a libertarian group which is strong enough to keep reinforcing the libertarianism of our members.

New Banner: David Nolan is forming a Libertarian Party. Its membership has indicated an interest in nominating you for its Presidential candidate in 1972. What is your response to this overture?

Rothbard: Ha, ha, ha (prolonged laughter). I really don't think, as lovable as third parties are, that a libertarian party at this stage of our development is anything but foolhardy. There are just not that many libertarians yet. There's no finances, there's no people, there's nothing. Maybe eventually we will have a libertarian political party.

New Banner: What would be the purpose of a libertarian party?

Rothbard: I think if there were a libertarian party—and I don't want to make it seem as if this is a realistic thing at this time—if there ever were a strong libertarian party it could do several things. Tactically, we could have a balance of power. Even better as an educational weapon. If we had ten guys in Congress, let's say, each of whom are constantly agitating for libertarian purposes—voting against the budget, etc., I think it would be very useful.

Also, we have a long-range problem which none of us has ever really grappled with to any extent. That is, how do we finally establish a libertarian society? Obviously ideas are a key thing. First off you have to persuade a lot of people to be anarchists—anarcho-capitalists. But then what? What is the next step? You certainly don't have to convince the majority of the public, because most of the public will follow anything that happens. You obviously have to have a large minority. How do we then implement this? This is the power problem. As I've expressed this in other places, the government is not going to resign. We are not going to have a situation where Nixon reads *Human Action*, *Atlas Shrugged*, or *Man, Economy and State* and says "By God, they're right. I'm quitting!" I'm not denying the philosophical possibility that this might happen, but strategically it's very low on the probability scale. As the Marxists put it, no ruling class has ever voluntarily surrendered its power. There has to be an effort to deal with the problem of how to get these guys off our backs. So, if you really have a dedicated group in Congress or the Senate, you can start voting measures down or whatever. But I don't think this is the only way. I think maybe there will be civil disobedience where the public will start not paying taxes or something like that. If you look at it, there are several possible alternatives in dismantling the state. There is violent revolution, there is non-violent civil disobedience and there is the political action method. I don't know which of these will be successful. It's really a tactical question which you can't really predict in advance, it seems to me that it would be foolhardy to give up any particular arm of this.

It's incumbent upon people to come up with some sort of strategic perspective to dismantle the state. For example, Bob LeFevre somehow works it out that it's almost impossible to get rid of the state—from his own point of view. He is against violent revolution—okay, now that is a very respectable position; he's also against voting; he's against political parties—it becomes very difficult to really see how one can get to the state at all with this kind of procedure. I don't see why we should give up something like political parties. It might be a route eventually to dismantling the state or helping to dismantle it.

New Banner: In the February, 1971, *Libertarian Forum* you stated that the movement was "taking off." In the perspective of the last year would you change your opinion?

Rothbard: No, I think it's taking off. It's growing very rapidly, and it's getting a lot of publicity which is important. The recent New York Conference was very successful in many ways. We are still in pretty good shape. I don't know where to go from here, particularly. I'd like to see more strategic thinking on the part of the movement as to what to do next. For instance, should there be any organizational effort, if so, what? This sort of thing.

New Banner: Do you see any wisdom in anarcho-capitalists allying with today's New Left?

Rothbard: There is no New Left now. The New Left is really finished—there isn't any such animal anymore. One of the reasons that I liked the New Left in the old days, in the middle-60s, was that there were a lot of libertarian elements in the New Left. Not only was there opposition to the war and the draft, but also opposition to bureaucracy, central government, and so forth. But all that seems to have dropped out. There is really nothing going on in the New Left now at all.

New Banner: Why do you think the New Left has never strongly supported the anti-draft movement? They seemed to have been more anti-war, but not concerned with anti-draft.

Rothbard: They were against the draft, but as you say, they didn't really have their heart in it. They really weren't against the draft. They are in favor of the People's Republic draft, when the People's Republic gets established. I remember when Castro first got in power in 1959. A lot of the more sincere Castro followers said that one of the great things about Castro was that he had abolished the draft. Of course, he had, but a couple years later it was back. So you see, they're against a draft by a reactionary government, but not by a people's government. Ha, ha.

New Banner: Do you agree with the proposal that libertarians overlook their philosophical differences in order to provide a unified front?

Rothbard: I don't think that question can really be answered flatly. I don't agree with the sectarian idea that you have to agree on everything before you can act on anything. In other words, that you have to agree on A is A, free will, modern art, or whatever. I don't buy that, I think it's unrealistic. On the other hand, simply saying that you will unite on anything if you agree on "Smash the State," on a couple of slogans, is very dangerous, too. It depends upon the goal of your action or activity. If you are engaging in an *ad hoc* sort of thing like an anti-draft rally, then I don't see anything wrong with having speakers or common activity with all anti-draft people regardless of their original premises. If you are going to have a libertarian organization carrying on all sorts of activities, conferences, journals, and things like that, you will want to have much more full agreement.

Of course, in the libertarian movement you have a pretty wide spectrum, which I think however, fortunately is narrowing. I think we are getting a situation in which the extreme left and the extreme right, so-called, are sort of mellowing into a central position, which gives us more basis for cooperation. The "rip off Amerika" group is beginning to calm down, and the Randians are beginning to get more wary about the Constitution, the Founding Fathers, and American foreign policy. So, I think that there is more agreement now than there was a year ago.

New Banner: In regard to the ongoing debate between you and the Friedmanites, David Friedman has made an accusation. He has accused you of having not read what his father Milton Friedman has written, misquoting or quoting out of context what you have read, and further has accused you of being a mediocre economist who is jealous of all the attention accorded Milton. Any comments?

Rothbard: Ha, ha, ha. As for misquoting, of course, you can always say that nobody has fully read the works of other people.

I don't think Milton, for example, knows anything about the Austrian school. Obviously, Milton is more of an expert on his own writings than anyone else. As for being jealous of attention, that's like saying that I am jealous of Keynes or Galbraith. Let me put it this way, I think that they are getting over-deserved attention. It seems to me that Galbraith is getting a lot more attention than he deserves, and I think the same is true of Milton.

But I think it is also very clear that you don't have to be an expert on Friedman's writings to realize that Milton is in favor of the absolute control of the money supply by the state, that he is in favor of a 3 or 4 percent increase in the money supply (the numbers keep changing all the time) by the state every year, that he favors a negative income tax which is essentially a guaranteed annual income by the state, and that he favors a voucher plan which would leave the state solidly in control of the educational system. These things are quite blatant; there is no secret about it. I think it is pretty clear that Friedman is a statist. I mean, if you are in favor of the state having control of the money supply, control of the education system, and a guaranteed annual income, that's it. There is not much more that can be said. The fact that the Friedmanites are against price control is all very well, and I hail that, but the fundamental aspects of the state remain. The state still commands the highposts of the economy.

This is one of the problems with Friedmanites—they have no political theory of the nature of the state. They think of the state, and this is true of Milton and the whole gang as far as I can see, as another social instrument. In other words, there is the market out here and then there is the state, which is another friendly neighborhood organization. You decide on which thing, which activity, should be private and which should be state on the basis of an *ad hoc*, utilitarian kind of approach. "Well, let's see, we'll feed the thing through the computer. We find that the market usually wins out, that the market is usually better." So, most of the time they come out in favor of the market on things like price control or government regulations, but they really think of the state as just another social instrument. And so when they come out in favor of the state, they go all out. In other words, there is no limitation. Well, they say, the state will do this. The state will run the educational system or whatever the cop-out happens to be. So, they feed the thing in—we'll have controls for a while and then they will die out—it's not very important anyway. You see, they really think they can put through Friedmanism, let's say, just by educating Nixon. The sort of thing I said before jocularly, about Nixon reading *Atlas Shrugged* and being converted. That is really the sort of theory of social change the Friedmanites have. You see the President once in a while, you talk to him and you convince him that there shouldn't be price controls, the ICC should be eliminated, or whatever—and then he goes ahead and does it. But it just doesn't work that way. They have no realization that the state is essentially a gang of thieves and looters. That they are exploiting the public, that they have a whole bureaucratic apparatus of exploitation, and that they are not just going to give it up. In other words, there is the whole problem of power involved which the Friedmanites refuse to face. They don't realize that the state is not a social instrument. It's an inimical organization which is hostile to society, plundering it, which has to be confined, whittled away, reduced and hopefully ultimately abolished. They have no conception of that at all. They just think of it as another friendly, corner grocer kind of thing which you either use or don't use.

New Banner: Federal Reserve Chairman Arthur Burns said recently that he would expand the money supply at a rate that would insure a "vigorous" expansion of the US economy. At the same lime, the Price Commission will be permitting only limited price increases. What do you think the net result of these policies will be?

Rothbard: The net result will be further inflation, with black markets and with people losing out. Those people who haven't got the political muscle at the Price Commission or Pay Board won't get their increases, while those who do have that muscle will get it.

All sorts of monstrous situations will occur. Decline in quality, for example. We will find that there will be more air in the Baby Ruth—you can't find the Baby Ruth anymore anyway. There will be less chocolate in the chocolate. There is no way the state can police this, of course. And it's very harmful to the public.

And the real root of inflation, which is the money supply, well, the tap is being turned on. It's unfortunate, but a lot of people including conservatives and libertarians even, have been great fans of Arthur F. Burns. I've never been able to see that. He's always been an inflationist, a statist, and a pragmatist.

New Banner: Nixon is supposed to push for a value-added tax (VAT), a move which he will probably reveal soon. What might be the results of such a tax?

Rothbard: Well, it's a national sales tax. It is one thing that has not been tapped yet. I think Chodorov said that the principle of taxation that the government always uses is the same principle as the highwayman: Grab them where they are—if it moves, tax it! If you can find something that hasn't been taxed yet, well, tax it. VAT is a new gimmick which hasn't been imposed yet in the United States.

Income tax is obviously reaching a critical limit. It would be difficult for them to increase that. The property tax is fortunately going by the board. And with the whole education question—well, they need a new tax to finance it. It's a sales tax, so it will tax the poor more than the wealthy. Also, it's a hidden tax, so the public wouldn't realize it. It's a value added tax which is paid by each manufacturer as they go down the list.

It also injures turnovers. If a product is made eight times, if it turns over eight times before it gets to the consumer, it is going to be taxed twice as much as if it turns over four times. This will restrict what the Austrians call "the longer process of production" which will injure capital investment a great deal. Incidentally, only the Austrians have dealt with this whole question of the period of production. It will also bring about vertical integration—mergers—which the government claims are monopolistic. If the thing turns over it means that you pay an extra tax, but if the two firms merge they won't have to pay any tax on that phase of it. So, it will encourage mergers.

New Banner: In the light of your past record of accurate predictions, what will be the nature of Phase III?

Rothbard: I don't claim to be a great predictor or forecaster. It is in the nature, incidentally, of Austrian economic theory that the economist can't really forecast perfectly at all. I'm not sure about Phase III. A lot depends upon whether Nixon gets reelected or not. As in all cases of government intervention you are presented with two alternatives as the sun sinks in the west—as Phase II begins to crack up as it already is.

Already the Pay Board has granted increases to some groups and shut off increases to other groups. So, as this thing becomes increasingly unworkable, then the government will be faced with the question—either we scrap the thing altogether and go back to the free market or we tighten the controls, get people who really believe in it, get Galbraith instead of Stein, and we have a rigorous program. It could go either way. Who knows how Nixon is going to go? You can't tell from one day to the next what Nixon is going to do anyway. The summer of last year, Nixon would have been equally likely *a priori* to either drop a bomb on China or else form an agreement with it. There is no way of predicting which path he is going to take.

You have the curious situation now where the economists in charge of the Phase II program almost exclusively are against it. They all say, "Well of course we're against control and are in favor of the free market, but we have to do this anyway." In this kind of self-contradictory situation, who knows what they're going to do?

New Banner: In February, 1971, Senator Mark Hatfield made some interesting but vague comments in praise of your book *Power and Market*. Have you had any contact with the senator concerning his ostensible sympathy with libertarianism?

Rothbard: I've only met the senator personally once—in the summer of 1969. At that time he was very friendly toward libertarianism and said he had committed himself to the cause of libertarianism. Now, I've had a couple of contacts with him since then by mail. But, obviously his voting record is not particularly libertarian. It's very good on foreign policy and the draft, but it's not too great on other things.

What the reason for this is I really don't know. However, he has been very good in introducing legislation for tax credits and for the right to own gold. I really don't have that much contact with the Hatfield staff. In the abstract, at least, he is very favorable to libertarianism.

He seems to understand it. I also understand that one member of the Hatfield staff is an anarchist who was converted by the Tannehill book—this is the rumor I get.

New Banner: I understand that you have written two other major manuscripts that have yet to be published; *The Ethics of Liberty* and *The Betrayal of the American Right*.

Rothbard: *The Betrayal of the American Right* is not really a major manuscript. It is a pleasant enough thing. It's fairly short. It's sort of a combination personal and general history of the right-wing from Mencken and Nock in the Twenties and going into the World War II period and then up to the present. That's not going to be published so far, because Ramparts Press, which was originally supposed to publish it, didn't like it, and it has now been turned into a reader. Right now the idea is that they are going to come out with a reader of Old Right stuff like Mencken and Nock, and I'll be picking the readings and doing the introduction. So, as for that manuscript, after the reader comes out, I guess I'll look around for a publisher for the original *Betrayal of the American Right*.

The ethics book has only been partially finished, so that's the problem with that.

Right now I'm working on a libertarianism book for Macmillan. The tentative title is *For a New Liberty*. It will be sort of a general book. It is a rather difficult book to write, because I can't be as scholarly as I'd like to be, and yet on the other hand I can't be too mass oriented. So, I have to pick my spots. I've started off with a description of the movement discussing who is in it, the spectrum in it, and then I go into the philosophy of the movement—the central core of libertarian philosophy. Then I go on to the applications of that philosophy. I just finished the chapter on education and next I'll go on to welfare. After I finish that I'll start working on the ethics book, which is really my favorite. So far I have written in *Power and Market*, etc., on the "value free," praxeological aspects of liberty and I have not really tackled the ethical position in print. One thing which I find exciting in it is that I'm going to try to deduce the ethics like I do the economics from a Robinson Crusoe and Friday situation—a Crusoe political philosophy. I'll show what happens when Crusoe and Friday engage in voluntary trade and exchange as opposed to coercion and then bring in the whole coercion versus liberty issue. Then work from there on up.

I also have another manuscript which is a very long-term thing—that being a history of the United States. In that I have written up to the Constitution. It will be a history of the United States from a libertarian point of view. It is very difficult to write that, because the thing is we don't know what has happened—a lot of the facts have been buried. Orthodox histories don't give many facts; a lot of facts are just left out.

New Banner: Is it intended to be a textbook?

Rothbard: No, not really. It's just a libertarian history of the United States. It could be used as a textbook, I hope. You know, *Man, Economy, and State* was originally supposed to be a textbook and wound up as a giant treatise. I think this might be the same thing.

New Banner: Dr. Rothbard, on behalf of our readers and our staff, I would like to thank you for this most informative interview.

Rothbard: You are quite welcome.

Section II

Foundations of Social Science
and the Free Society

CHAPTER 4

The Discipline of Liberty

Probably the most common question that has been hurled at me—in some exasperation—over the years is: "Why don't you stick to economics?" For different reasons, this question has been thrown at me by fellow economists and by political thinkers and activists of many different persuasions: Conservatives, Liberals, and Libertarians who have disagreed with me over political doctrine and are annoyed that an economist should venture "outside of his discipline."

Among economists, such a question is a sad reflection of the hyper-specialization among intellectuals of the present age. I think it manifestly true that very few of even the most dedicated economic technicians began their interest in economics because they were fascinated by cost curves, indifference classes, and the rest of the paraphernalia of modern economic theory. Almost to a man, they became interested in economics because they were interested in social and political problems and because they realized that the really hard political problems cannot be solved without an understanding of economics. After all, if they were really interested mainly in equations and tangencies on graphs, they would have become professional mathematicians and not have devoted their energies to an economic theory that is, at best, a third-rate application of mathematics. Unfortunately, what usually happens to these people is that as they

Excerpt from "Introduction" to *Egalitarianism as a Revolt Against Nature*, 1974.

learn the often imposing structure and apparatus of economic theory, they become so fascinated by the minutiae of technique that they lose sight of the political and social problems that sparked their interest in the first place. This fascination is also reinforced by the economic structure of the economics profession (and all other academic professions) itself: namely, that prestige, rewards, and brownie points are garnered not by pondering the larger problems but by sticking to one's narrow last and becoming a leading expert on a picayune technical problem.

Among some economists, this syndrome has been carried so far that they scorn any attention to politico-economic problems as a demeaning and unclean impurity, even when such attention is given by economists who have made their mark in the world of specialized technique. And even among those economists who do deal with political problems, any consideration devoted to such larger extra-economic matters as property rights, the nature of government, or the importance of justice is scorned as hopelessly "metaphysical" and beyond the pale.

It is no accident, however, that the economists of this century of the broadest vision and the keenest insight, men such as Ludwig von Mises, Frank H. Knight, and F.A. Hayek, came early to the conclusion that mastery of pure economic theory was not enough, and that it was vital to explore related and fundamental problems of philosophy, political theory, and history. In particular, they realized that it was possible and crucially important to construct a broader systematic theory encompassing human action as a whole, in which economics could take its place as a consistent but subsidiary part.

In my own particular case, the major focus of my interest and my writings over the last three decades has been a part of this broader approach—libertarianism—the discipline of liberty. For I have come to believe that libertarianism is indeed a discipline, a "science," if you will, of its own, even though it has been only barely developed over the generations. Libertarianism is a new and emerging discipline which touches closely on many other areas of the study of human action: economics, philosophy, political theory, history, even—and not least—biology. For all of these provide in varying ways the groundwork, the elaboration, and the application of libertarianism. Some day, perhaps, liberty and "libertarian studies" will be recognized as an independent, though related, part of the academic curriculum.

CHAPTER 5

Value Implications of Economic Theory

Economics, as a science, attempts and claims to be purely value-free; that is, separate from the personal, valuational, or political proclivities of the economist. And yet economics and economists are continually making political pronouncements; economics *per se* is shot through with value-loaded assumptions, usually implicit, which then emerge as political conclusions and recommendations. It is my contention that this procedure is illegitimate and unscientific, and that it is incumbent on economic theory to purge itself of all vestiges of the unsupported value judgment. As a science, economics can and should stand apart from such value judgments. But since all political policy recommendations necessarily involve value judgments, does this mean that the economist must never make any policy recommendations or indeed, never use any terminology that is value-loaded? Not necessarily.

There are only two possible kinds of philosophical status for value judgments. *Either* they are all necessarily purely subjective and personal whims on the part of the valuer, in which case for the economist to remain a scientist he must indeed refrain from all policy recommendations whatever. *Or* these judgments may well be part of a general ethical system which is rationally and objectively demonstrable; in that case, it is perfectly legitimate

Reprinted from *The American Economist* (Spring, 1973): 35–39; reprinted in *Economic Controversies* (Auburn, Ala.: Mises Institute, 2011), chap. 12.

for the economist when he applies his scientific theory to public policy to use this ethical system to arrive at economic policy recommendations. Let us take an example from medicine. A "purely" scientific, value-free medical procedure enables a physician to say that Treatment X will cure disease Y. As an applied scientist, the physician can then take this knowledge and *combine* it with the ethical judgment that "cure of the disease is good" and indeed is the goal of his treatment, and then conclude with the "policy" conclusion that he should apply Treatment X. In this case both the patient and the physician are proceeding, implicitly or explicitly, on the basis of a deeply shared ethical system; their value judgments are neither personal nor arbitrary, but stem from a shared ethical system which pronounces health and life as great goods for man and death and disease as corresponding evils.[1]

The point is that in medicine all parties proceed from the basis of a deeply shared ethical system. In the case of economics, this is scarcely true; here there are many competing and clashing values and value-systems held in society. Hence, the applied economist is in a more difficult situation. If an economist does not have an ethical system, but only subjective and arbitrary values, then it is incumbent upon him as a scientist ruthlessly to keep them out of his work. In short, the economist who lacks an ethical system must refrain from any and all value-loaded or political conclusions. (This statement, of course, is itself a value judgment stemming from an ethical system which holds that science must confine itself strictly to the search for, and the exposition of, truth.) But suppose on the other hand that an economist *also* holds an ethical system. What then?

It must be emphasized that if ethics is a rational and demonstrable discipline, it is self-subsistent, that is, its principles are arrived at apart from economics or any other particular science except itself. As in the case of medicine, the applied economist would then have to take this ethical system and add it to his economic knowledge to arrive at policy conclusions and recommendations. But in that case it is incumbent upon the applied economist to state his ethical system fully and with supporting argument; whatever he does, he must not slip value judgments, *ad hoc*, unanalyzed, and unsupported, into the body of his economic theory or into his policy

---

[1]In some cases, of course, Treatment X may lead to other effects that both patient and physician may consider "harmful"; again both share a judgment stemming from a shared ethic about the evils of injury to the human organism. Both parties will then have to judge the treatment by weighing these contrasting effects.

conclusions. And yet this is precisely what the bulk of economists have been doing. They, and economic theory along with them, habitually make a host of value judgments which are smuggled into their analyzes, and which then permit them to make policy recommendations, implicit or explicit, without presenting or defending a coherent ethical system. Because they cannot, like physicians, work from a universally shared ethical system, it is incumbent upon economists to present a coherent and supported ethical system or forever hold their valuational and political peace.

There is no room here to cover more than a few of the outstanding examples of the smuggling of unsupported value judgments into economic analysis. In the first place, there is the familiar case of the "Pareto Optimum." If A and B trade two goods or services, they each do so because they will be, or rather expect to be, better off as a result of the trade. Surely it is legitimate then to say that A and B are both better off, and "therefore" that "society is better off," since no one demonstrably loses by the exchange. It is implicit, and even explicit from the use of the value-loaded term "optimal," that this exchange is therefore a "good thing." I am sympathetic to the view that this exchange is a good thing, but I do not believe that this can be concluded merely from the fact of exchange, as the Pareto Optimum does. In the first place, there might well be one or more people in existence who dislike and envy A or B, and who therefore experience pain and psychic loss because the object of their envy has now improved his lot. We cannot therefore conclude from the mere fact of an exchange that "everyone" is better off, and we can therefore not simply leap to the valuational idea of social utility. In order to pronounce this voluntary exchange as "good," we need another term to our syllogism: we must make the ethical pronouncement that envy is evil, and should not be allowed to cloud our approval of the exchange. But in that case we are back to the need for a coherent ethical system. I believe, as an "ethicist," that envy is evil, but I see no willingness among economists to admit the need for, much less set forth, any sort of coherent ethical position.

This brings me to the position of the bulk of free market economists, such as the Chicago school, who favor the free market but claim to do so not on ethical grounds, but purely on the grounds of "efficiency." I maintain that it is impermissible to advocate the free market without bolstering one's economic analysis with an ethical framework. Indeed, in some cases it is even *impossible* to set forth a coherent free-market approach without taking a frankly ethical position, and a position which goes beyond the almost universally-held utilitarian viewpoint of economists. Let us ponder our above-mentioned voluntary exchange between A and B. The free market economist advocates a world where such exchanges are legitimate and not interfered with. But any exchange implies an exchange of titles to private property. If I buy a newspaper for fifteen cents, what has happened is that I have ceded my ownership of the fifteen cents to the newsdealer, who in turn has granted his ownership of the newspaper to me. But this means that to *advocate* our right to make this exchange, means *also* to advocate the propriety, and hence the justice, of the existing property titles in the first place. To pronounce it "good" for myself and the newsdealer to have the right to make the exchange, means also to pronounce it "good" and just for each of us to own the fifteen cents and the newspaper to begin with. Yet economists are not willing to make this extension, for to do so would mean adopting a systematic concept of justice in property titles, which would involve the adoption of a system of political ethics. Economists have generally regarded such ethical systems as beyond their province; but if so, it is illegitimate for them to advocate a free market at all.

Let us illustrate: suppose that in our presumed exchange between A and B, A has sold to B a watch which he has stolen from a third party, C. Here it becomes clear that it is illegitimate to cheer this voluntary exchange from the sidelines. For since A had stolen the watch, it was not his legitimate property, and therefore he had no right to keep it or sell it; the watch was not in his legitimate title to do with as he wished. But if this is true in the case of the watch, then it would also be true in other less directly flagrant cases of unjust property titles.

Furthermore, not only is it illegitimate for the economist to *advocate* a free market without also adumbrating a theory of justice in property titles; he cannot even *define* a free market without doing so. For even to define and expound upon the free-market model, the economist is describing a system in which property titles are being exchanged, and therefore he must also define and expound upon how these titles are arrived at in the first place; he must have a theory of original property and of how property comes into being.

This problem of justice in property titles also exposes a fatal flaw in the concept of the "Unanimity Principle" as a supposedly value-free guide for the applied economist. Thus, Professor James Buchanan and others have declared that it is legitimate and presumably value-free for the economist to advocate a public policy, provided that everyone can agree on such a policy. Once again, and even more than in the case of the Pareto Optimum, this position is scarcely self-evident when subjected to analysis.

For the implicit assumption of the Unanimity Principle is that all existing property titles are just. The Unanimity Principle would mean, for example, that it would be illegitimate to confiscate A's watch *even though* he had stolen it from C. But if we regard A's property title as illegitimate, then we must say that A's watch *should be* confiscated and returned to C. Once again, our ethical systems intrude ineluctably into the discussion.

The well-known Compensation Principle, adopted by most economists as a supposedly value-free route for making political recommendations, is in even worse straits than the pure Unanimity Principle. (*A fortiori*, the "weak" version of the Compensation Principle—that compensation does not *actually* have to be made but only be conceptually possible—seems to me to have no rational foundation whatever.) For the Compensation Principle assumes also that it is conceptually possible to measure losses and thereby to compensate the losers. But "utility" is a purely subjective and unmeasurable concept, and being purely psychic, it cannot be measured, either conceptually or in practice. If I buy the newspaper, all that can be known is that my utility from the newspaper is greater than from the fifteen cents, and vice versa for the newsdealer. There is no way of measuring these utility gains, for utility is not a quantity, but a rank order of subjective valuation.

Let us take, for example, the hypothetical proposition that the imposition of a tariff on zinc is "good" or socially useful because the gainers can (and even do) take their gains from the tariff, recompense the losers, and still have monetary gains left over. But suppose that I, as a convinced adherent of free trade and opponent of tariffs, declare that my psychic loss from the imposition of a zinc tariff is so great that no feasible monetary compensation could compensate me for that disutility. No one can say to me nay, and therefore the Compensation Principle falls to the ground. Conversely, the same could be true for the idea that *repeal* of the tariff on zinc could be advocated in some sort of value-free manner on compensation grounds. Once again, I might be such a dedicated protectionist that I could not feasibly be compensated for my psychic loss stemming from repeal of the tariff. The Compensation Principle falls in either case.

The relation between the Compensation Principle (as well as the related Unanimity Principle) and theories of justice can be starkly demonstrated from the example of slavery. During the debates in the British Parliament in the early nineteenth century on abolition of slavery, the early adherents of the Compensation Principle were maintaining that the masters must be compensated for the loss of their investment in slaves. At that point,

Benjamin Person, a member of the Manchester school, declared that "he had thought it was the slaves who should have been compensated."[2] Here is the stark example of the need, in advocating public policy, of an ethical system, of a concept of justice. Those of us who hold that slavery is unjust would always oppose the idea of compensating the masters, and indeed would think rather in terms of reparations of the masters compensating the slaves for their years of oppression. But what is there here for the *wertfrei* economist to say?

A similar argument applies to the Coase-Demsetz analysis of property rights and external cost. Coase-Demsetz declare that "it doesn't matter" from the point of view of allocation of resources whether, for example, a railroad is given the property right to pour smoke onto the land of neighboring farmers, or the farmers are given the property right to require compensation for invasion of their land by the railroad. The implication is that the effect is "only" a matter of distribution of wealth. In the first place, of course, the decision "matters" a great deal to the railroad and the farmers. I contend that it is totally invalid to dismiss such "distribution effects" as somehow unworthy of consideration by the economist, even though it is clear that ethical considerations are directly relevant to any treatment of such distribution. But apart from this, the Coase-Demsetz analysis is not even correct for short-run allocational problems (setting aside its validity or invalidity for long-run allocation) if we realize that social costs are psychic to the individual and therefore cannot be measured in monetary terms. One or more of the farmers, for example, may love his land so deeply that no feasible monetary compensation for the smoke loss could be made by the railroad. As soon as we admit these psychic costs into the picture, the Coase-Demsetz analysis becomes invalid even for the short-run allocation of resources. This is apart from another consideration: that in law, an invasion of property can be stopped completely by court injunction and not merely be compensated after the fact.

This brings us to the entire analysis of neighborhood effects in the economic literature. It is simply assumed without adequate support, for example, that external economies *should* be internalized. But why? What is the ethical groundwork for this position? Let us take an example of an external economy which no economist has suggested we internalize— not out of logical consistency but simply from empirical convenience.

---

[2]William D. Grampp, *The Manchester School of Economics* (Stanford, Calif.: Stanford University Press, 1960), p. 59.

Women, let us say, purchase and use cosmetics; this use has a great deal of external spillover effects in conferring psychic benefits among a large part of the population; and yet these males are "free riders"; they are not paying for the cosmetics. The neighborhood effect theorist, to be consistent, must claim that "too little" cosmetics are being used; that men are free riders on the female use of cosmetics and therefore should be taxed to subsidize females in their use. There are, of course, many problems with this doctrine, apart from those that we have already stated. The "internalizing" theorist must assume illegitimately that he can measure, even conceptually, how much men are being benefited, and gauge the precise amount of tax and subsidy. But apart from the conceptual impossibility of doing this, there are other grave problems involved in all attempts to apply such a principle for governmental action. One is that some men may dislike cosmetics intensely, and that *they* are therefore being penalized still further by the subsidy program. And furthermore, the very use of government implies a whole host of questionable political value judgments: for example, that government action *per se* involves neither psychic costs nor ethical injustice.

But there is a flaw even more directly germane to the concept of internalizing external economies. For by what ethical standard is the production and use of cosmetics "too low"? Too low for whom, and by what ethical standards? The very concept of "too low" is a value judgment which is by no means self-evident and arrives here unsupported by any sort of ethical system.

Professor Demsetz goes on to advocate an allocation of property rights in accordance with whichever allocation involves lower total social transaction costs, such as costs of enforcing the given property right.[3] But once again, there are two grave flaws in this position. One, since social costs embody psychic costs or disutilities for each individual, it is impossible to measure and hence to add them up interpersonally. But apart from this, such a gauge for the allocation of property rights brusquely sets aside any consideration of the justice of property titles. But this *itself* is an ethical position unsupported by the economist. In the case of slavery, for example, it might well be found that the monetary cost of enforcing slave titles is lower than the monetary cost of each freed slave defending himself from

[3]Thus, see Harold Demsetz, "When Does the Rule of Liability Matter?" *Journal of Legal Studies* 1, no. 1 (1971): 25–28; and Demsetz, "Some Aspects of Property Rights," *Journal of Law and Economics* (October 1966): 66.

reenslavement. For those of us who claim that slavery is unjust, such considerations would be piddling as compared to the dictates of justice. But for an economist to try to decide such questions as the allocation of property rights by discarding considerations of justice must be totally unscientific and illegitimate.

There is only space here to touch very briefly on a few other examples of the illegitimate use of implicit value assumptions in economics. One example is the long-standing aim of the Chicago school—at least until Milton Friedman's recent essay on the "Optimum Quantity of Money"—to achieve a constant price level, either in the short or the long run. But little has been written to justify this goal. The value of the goal is scarcely self-evident, particularly when we consider the fact that a growing, unhampered economy will lead to secularly falling prices and costs, with the resulting higher living standards spread throughout the ranks of the consumers. And if falling prices would be a consequence of an increased demand for money, then again it is surely not self-evident that it is the business of government deliberately to thwart the desire of the public for a higher level of real cash balances—any more than it is the business of government to thwart the desires of consumers for any other goods or services.

Another example is the problem of rational pricing for governmental services. Thus, in recent years, much valuable work has been done advocating market-clearing prices for such services as streets, roads, and subways; for example, that pricing be graduated in accordance with peak hours and the degree of congestion on the roads. All this makes a great deal of sense, but one vital assumption is missing: that there is nothing wrong with the fact that an increased amount of revenue will thereby accrue to the coffers of government. The implicit value assumption is that there is nothing wrong economically or ethically with an increased amount of social resources being siphoned off to government. For those of us who do not take such a sanguine ethical view of government, this consideration must be an important factor in our policy conclusions.

In the area of government, indeed, there has been much discussion of the difficulties of national product accounting, but little has been said of the implicit—and scarcely self-evident—value assumption at the heart of the treatment of government. The blithe assumption that government expenditure on its own salaries can in any way measure government's contribution to the national product encapsulates what some of us would consider a highly naïve view of the functions and operations of government—

indeed a view that places one's ethical *imprimatur* on every one of the government's activities. In these days of military overkill, and of pyramid-building on a grand scale, there are not very many people who would still automatically accept Lord Keynes's famous dictum that building pyramids is just as productive an expenditure as anything else. In fact, anyone who believes that government expenditure contains at least 51 percent waste—surely not a very unreasonable assumption by anyone's reckoning—would construct national product accounts by *subtracting* government expenditures as a burden upon production and upon society, rather than adding it as a productive contribution.

Finally, there is the generally held view that an economist can provide technical advice to his client while remaining purely value-free. I submit, on the contrary, that servicing a client's ends thereby commits the economist to the ethical value of the end itself. Often it is held that by simply furnishing advice on the pursuit of goals or values held by the majority of the public, the economist remains uncommitted to values. But surely value-freedom means free of values, period; and the fact that the majority of the public might have such values does not make commitment to them any less value-laden. To take a deliberately dramatic example, let us suppose that an economist is hired by the Nazis to advise the government on the most efficient way of setting up concentration camps. I submit that by doing so, the economist has, willy-nilly, adopted a pursuit of "better," that is, more efficient, concentration camps as a goal. And he would be doing so even if this goal were heartily endorsed by the great majority of the German public. To underscore this point, it should be clear that an economist whose value system led him to oppose concentration camps might well then give such advice to his clients as to make the concentration camps as *inefficient* as possible, that is, to sabotage their operations. In short, whatever advice he gives to his clients, the economist's value-commitment, for or against the clients' project, is inescapable. But if this is true for concentration camps, it is true also for the myriad of other and usually less significant projects that his clients have in mind.

I would like to cite a passage on this question from the last essay of the great Italian economist Luigi Einaudi. Einaudi wrote that the economic advisors to government "indispensable, extremely learned, extremely informed, the experts, the only people who know the jargon, have become … one of the seven plagues of Egypt, a disgrace to humanity." A "plague," Einaudi wrote, because of the typical economist's view that "I have performed my duty fully when I have decided whether the proposed means or other alternatives are consistent with the end prosecuted by the politician." Einaudi then commented:

> No. The economist has failed in that case to perform the essential part of his task. ... The economist ... has not the right to be neutral or to hide under an unreal distinction between means and ends. He must declare himself for that end to which he is closest; and must prove what he assumes.[4]

It is important to stress what this paper is *not* saying: I am *not* taking the position, now fashionable in many quarters, that there is no such thing as a value-free economics, that all economic analysis is inextricably shot through with value assumptions. On the contrary, I believe that the main body of economic analysis is scientific and value-free; what I *am* saying is that any time that economists impinge on political or policy conclusions, value-judgments have entered into their discussion. My conclusion, then, is that economists must either make their value judgments explicit and defend them with a coherent ethical system, or strictly refrain from entering, directly, or indirectly into the public policy realm.

---

[4]Luigi Einaudi, "Politicians and Economists," *Il Politico* (Pavia) (June 1962): 258, 262–63.

CHAPTER 6

Statistics:
Achilles' Heel of Government

Ours is truly an Age of Statistics. In a country and an era that worships statistical data as super "scientific," as offering us the keys to all knowledge, a vast supply of data of all shapes and sizes pours forth upon us. Mostly, it pours forth from government. While private agencies and trade associations do gather and issue some statistics, they are limited to specific wants of specific industries. The vast bulk of statistics is gathered and disseminated by government. The overall statistics of the economy, the popular "gross national product" data that permits every economist to be a soothsayer of business conditions, come from government. Furthermore, many statistics are by-products of other governmental activities: from the Internal Revenue bureau come tax data, from unemployment insurance departments come estimates of the unemployed, from customs offices come data on foreign trade, from the Federal Reserve flow statistics on banking, and so on. And as new statistical techniques are developed, new divisions of government departments are created to refine and use them.

The burgeoning of government statistics offers several obvious evils to the libertarian. In the first place, it is clear that too many resources are

Reprinted from *Essays on Liberty* (Irvington-on-Hudson, N.Y.: Foundation for Economic Education, 1961), vol. 8; reprinted in *The Logic of Action Two* (Cheltenham, U.K.: Edward Elgar, 1997), chap. 8; and *Economic Controversies* (Auburn, Ala.: Mises Institute, 2011), chap. 22.

being channeled into statistics-gathering and statistics-production. Given a wholly free market, the amount of labor, land, and capital resources devoted to statistics would dwindle to a small fraction of the present total. It has been estimated that the federal government alone spends over $48,000,000 on statistics, and that statistical work employs the services of over 10,000 full-time civilian employees of the government.[1]

THE HIDDEN COSTS OF COERCED REPORTING

Second, the great bulk of statistics is gathered by government coercion. This not only means that they are products of unwelcome activities; it also means that the true cost of these statistics to the American public is much greater than the mere amount of tax money spent by the government agencies. Private industry, and the private consumer, must bear the burdensome costs of record keeping, filing, and the like, that these statistics demand. Not only that; these fixed costs impose a relatively great burden on small business firms, which are ill-equipped to handle the mountains of red tape. Hence, these seemingly innocent statistics cripple small business enterprise and help to rigidify the American business system. A Hoover Commission task force found, for example, that:

> No one knows how much it costs American industry to compile the statistics that the Government demands. The chemical industry alone reports that each year it spends $8,850,000 to supply statistical reports demanded by three departments of the Government. The utility industry spends $32,000,000 a year in preparing reports for Government agencies ...
>
> All industrial users of peanuts must report their consumption to the Department of Agriculture. ... Upon the intervention of the Task Force, the Department of Agriculture agreed that henceforth only those that consume more than ten thousand pounds a year need report ...

---

[1]Cf. Neil Macneil and Harold W. Metz, *The Hoover Report, 1953–1955* (New York: Macmillan, 1956), pp. 90–91; Commission on Organization of the Executive Branch of the Government, *Task Force Report on Paperwork Management* (Washington, DC: June 1955); and idem, *Report on Budgeting and Accounting* (Washington, DC: February 1949).

If small alterations are made in two reports, the Task Force says one industry alone can save $800,000 a year in statistical reporting.

Many employees of private industry are occupied with the collection of Government statistics. This is especially burdensome to small businesses. A small hardware store owner in Ohio estimated that 29 per cent of his time is absorbed in filling out such reports. Not infrequently people dealing with the Government have to keep several sets of books to fit the diverse and dissimilar requirements of Federal agencies.[2]

OTHER OBJECTIONS

But there are other important, and not so obvious, reasons for the libertarian to regard government statistics with dismay. Not only do statistics gathering and producing go beyond the governmental function of defense of persons and property; not only are economic resources wasted and misallocated, and the taxpayers, industry, small business, and the consumer burdened. But, furthermore, statistics are, in a crucial sense, critical to all interventionist and socialist activities of government. The individual consumer, in his daily rounds, has little need of statistics; through advertising, through the information of friends, and through his own experience, he finds out what is going on in the markets around him. The same is true of the business firm. The businessman must also size up his particular market, determine the prices he has to pay for what he buys and charge for what he sells, engage in cost accounting to estimate his costs, and so on. But none of this activity is really dependent upon the *omnium gatherum* of statistical facts about the economy ingested by the federal government. The businessman, like the consumer, knows and learns about his particular market through his daily experience.

Bureaucrats as well as statist reformers, however, are in a completely different state of affairs. They are decidedly outside the market. Therefore, in order to get "into" the situation that they are trying to plan and reform, they must obtain knowledge that is not personal, day-to-day experience;

---

[2]Macneil and Metz, *The Hoover Report*, pp. 90–91.

the only form that such knowledge can take is statistics.[3] Statistics are the eyes and ears of the bureaucrat, the politician, the socialistic reformer. Only by statistics can they know, or at least have any idea about, what is going on in the economy.[4] Only by statistics can they find out how many old people have rickets, or how many young people have cavities, or how many Eskimos have defective sealskins—and therefore only by statistics can these interventionists discover who "needs" what throughout the economy, and how much federal money should be channeled in what directions. And certainly, only by statistics can the federal government make even a fitful attempt to plan, regulate, control, or reform various industries—or impose central planning and socialization on the entire economic system. If the government received no railroad statistics, for example, how in the world could it even start to regulate railroad rates, finances, and other affairs? How could the government impose price controls if it didn't even know what goods have been sold on the market, and what prices were prevailing? Statistics, to repeat, are the eyes and ears of the interventionists: of the intellectual reformer, the politician, and the government bureaucrat. Cut off those eyes and ears, destroy those crucial guidelines to knowledge, and the whole threat of government intervention is almost completely eliminated.[5]

---

[3]On the deficiencies of statistics as compared to the personal knowledge of all participants utilized on the free market, see the illuminating discussion in F.A. Hayek, *Individualism and the Economic Order* (Chicago: University Press, 1948), chap. 4. Also see Geoffrey Dobbs, *On Planning the Earth* (Liverpool: K.R.P. Pubs., 1951), pp. 77–86.

[4]As early as 1863, Samuel B. Ruggles, American Delegate to the International Statistical Congress in Berlin, declared: "Statistics are the very eyes of the statesmen, enabling him to survey and scan with clear and comprehensive vision the whole structure and economy of the body politic." For more on the interrelation of statistics—and statisticians—and the government, see Murray N. Rothbard, "The Politics of Political Economists: Comment," *Quarterly Journal of Economics* (November 1960): 659–65. Also see Dobbs, *On Planning the Earth.*

[5] Macneil and Metz, *Reports on Budgeting and Accounting*, pp. 91–92:

> Government policy depends upon much detailed knowledge about the Nation's employment, production, and purchasing power. The formulation of legislation and administrative progress. ... Supervision ... regulation ... and control ... must be guided by knowledge of a wide range of relevant facts. Today as never before, statistical data play a major role in the supervision of Government activities. Administrators not only make plans in the light of known facts in their field of interest, but also they must have reports on the actual progress achieved in accomplishing their goals.

Without Statistics Bureaucracy Would Wither Away

It is true, of course, that even deprived of all statistical knowledge of the nation's affairs, the government could still try to intervene, to tax and subsidize, to regulate and control. It could try to subsidize the aged even without having the slightest idea of how many aged there are and where they are located; it could try to regulate an industry without even knowing how many firms there are or any other basic facts of the industry; it could try to regulate the business cycle without even knowing whether prices or business activity are going up or down. It could try, but it would not get very far. The utter chaos would be too patent and too evident even for the bureaucracy, and certainly for the citizens. And this is especially true since one of the major reasons put forth for government intervention is that it "corrects" the market, and makes the market and the economy more rational. Obviously, if the government were deprived of all knowledge whatever of economic affairs, there could not even be a pretense of rationality in government intervention. Surely, the absence of statistics would absolutely and immediately wreck any attempt at socialistic planning. It is difficult to see what, for example, the central planners at the Kremlin could do to plan the lives of Soviet citizens if the planners were deprived of all information, of all statistical data, about these citizens. The government would not even know to whom to give orders, much less how to try to plan an intricate economy.

Thus, in all the host of measures that have been proposed over the years to check and limit government or to repeal its interventions, the simple and unspectacular abolition of government statistics would probably be the most thorough and most effective. Statistics, so vital to statism, its namesake, is also the State's Achilles' heel.

CHAPTER 7

Ludwig von Mises and the Paradigm for Our Age

U
nquestionably the most significant and challenging development in the historiography of science in the last decade is the theory of Thomas S. Kuhn. Without defending Kuhn's questionable subjectivist and relativistic philosophy, his contribution is a brilliant sociological insight into the ways in which scientific theories change and develop.[1]

Essentially, Kuhn's theory is a critical challenge to what might be called the "Whig theory of the history of science." This "Whig" theory, which until Kuhn was the unchallenged orthodoxy in the field, sees the progress of science as a gradual, continuous, ever-upward process; year by year, decade by decade, century by century, the body of scientific knowledge gradually grows and accretes through the process of framing hypotheses, testing them empirically, and discarding the invalid and keeping the valid theories. Every age stands on the shoulders of and sees further and more clearly than every preceding age.

---

[1]Philosophically, Kuhn tends to deny the existence of objective truth and therefore denies the possibility of genuine scientific progress. Thomas S. Kuhn, *The Structure of Scientific Revolutions*, 2nd ed. (Chicago: University of Chicago Press, 1970).

Written on the occasion of Mises's ninetieth birthday. Originally appeared in *Modern Age* (Fall, 1971); reprinted in *The Logic of Action One* (Cheltenham, U.K.: Edward Elgar, 1997), chap. 9; and *Economic Controversies* (Auburn, Ala.: Mises Institute, 2011), chap. 11, pp. 225–39.

In the Whig approach, furthermore, there is no substantive knowledge to be gained from reading, say, nineteenth-century physicists or seventeenth-century astronomers. We may be interested in reading Priestley or Newton or Maxwell to see how creative minds work or solve problems, or for insight into the history of the period; but we can never read them to learn something about science which we didn't know already. After all, their contributions are, almost by definition, incorporated into the latest textbooks or treatises in their disciplines.

Many of us, in our daily experience, know enough to be unhappy with this idealized version of the development of science. Without endorsing the validity of Immanuel Velikovsky's theory, for example, we have seen Velikovsky brusquely and angrily dismissed by the scientific community without waiting for the patient testing of the open-minded scientist, which we have been led to believe is the essence of scientific inquiry.[2] And we have seen Rachel Carson's critique of pesticides generally scorned by scientists only to be adopted a decade later.

But it took Professor Kuhn to provide a comprehensive model of the adoption and maintenance of scientific belief. Basically, he states that scientists, in any given area, come to adopt a fundamental vision or matrix of an explanatory theory, a vision that Kuhn calls a "paradigm." And whatever the paradigm, whether it be the atomic theory or the phlogiston theory, once adopted the paradigm governs all the scientists in the field without being any longer checked or questioned—as the Whig model would have it.

The fundamental paradigm, once established, is no longer tested or questioned, and all further research soon becomes minor applications of the paradigm, minor clearing up of loopholes or anomalies that still remain in the basic vision. For years, decades, or longer, scientific research becomes narrow, specialized, and always within the basic paradigmatic framework.

But then, gradually, more and more anomalies pile up; puzzles can no longer be solved by the paradigm. But the scientists do not give up the paradigm; quite the contrary, increasingly desperate attempts are made to modify the particulars of the basic theory so as to fit the unpleasant facts and to preserve the framework provided by the paradigm.

---

[2]On the sociology of the reception of Velikovsky in the scientific community, see Alfred de Grazia, "The Scientific Reception System," in *The Velikovsky Affair*, Alfred de Grazia, ed. (New Hyde Park, N.Y.: University Books, 1966), pp. 171–231.

Only when anomalies pile up to such an extent that the paradigm itself is brought into question do we have a "crisis situation" in science. And even here, the paradigm is never simply discarded until it can be replaced by a new, competing paradigm which appears to close the loopholes and liquidate the anomalies.

When this occurs, there arrives a "scientific revolution," a chaotic period during which one paradigm is replaced by another, which never occurs smoothly as the Whig theory would suggest. And even here, the older scientists, mired in their intellectual vested interests, will often cling to the obsolete paradigm, with the new theory only being adopted by the younger and more flexible scientists. Thus, of the codiscoverers of oxygen in the late eighteenth century, Priestley and Lavoisier, Joseph Priestley never—till the day he died—conceded that he had in fact discovered oxygen; to the end he insisted that what he had discovered was merely "dephlogisticated air," thus remaining within the framework of the phlogiston theory.[3]

And so, armed with Kuhn's own paradigm of the history of scientific theories, which is now in the process of replacing the Whig framework, we see a very different picture of the process of science. Instead of a slow and gradual upward march into the light, testing and revising at each step of the way, we see a series of "revolutionary" leaps, as paradigms displace each other only after much time, travail, and resistance.

Furthermore, without adopting Kuhn's own philosophical relativism, it becomes clear that, since intellectual vested interests play a more dominant role than continual open-minded testing, it may well happen that a successor paradigm is less correct than a predecessor. And if that is true, then we must always be open to the possibility that, indeed, we often know less about a given science now than we did decades or even centuries ago.

Because paradigms become discarded and are never looked at again, the world may have forgotten scientific truth that was once known, as well as added to its stock of knowledge. Reading older scientists now opens up the distinct possibility that we may learn something that we haven't known—or have collectively forgotten—about the discipline. Professor de Grazia states that "much more is discovered and forgotten than is known,"

---

[3]Kuhn, *The Structure of Scientific Revolutions*, pp. 53–56.

and much that has been forgotten may be more correct than theories that are now accepted as true.[4]

If the Kuhn thesis is correct about the physical sciences, where we can obtain empirical and laboratory tests of hypotheses fairly easily, how much more must it be true in philosophy and the social sciences, where no such laboratory tests are possible!

For in the disciplines relating to human action, there are no clear and evident laboratory tests available. The truths must be arrived at by the processes of introspection, "common sense" knowledge, and deductive reasoning; and such processes, while arriving at solid truths, are not as starkly or compellingly evident as in the physical sciences.

Hence, it is all the more easy for philosophers or social scientists to fall into tragically wrong and fallacious paradigms, and thus to lead themselves down the garden path for decades, and even centuries. For once the sciences of human action adopt their fundamental paradigms, it becomes much easier than in the physical sciences to ignore the existence of anomalies, and therefore easier to retain erroneous doctrines for a very long time.

There is a further well-known difficulty in philosophy and the social sciences which makes systematic error still more likely: the infusion of emotions, value judgments, and political ideologies into the scientific process. The angry treatment accorded to Jensen, Shockley, and the other theorists of inequalities of racial intelligence by their fellow scientists, is a case in point. For underlying the bulk of the scientific reception of Jensen and Shockley is the idea that even if their theories are true, they should not say so, at least for a century, because of the unfortunate political consequences that may be involved.

While this sort of stultifying of the quest for scientific truth has happened at times in the physical sciences, it is fortunately far less prevalent there; and whatever the intellectual vested interests at stake, there was at least no ideological and political buttressing for the phlogiston theory or the valence theory in chemistry.

Until recent decades, philosophers and social scientists harbored a healthy recognition of vast differences between their disciplines and the natural sciences; in particular, the classics of philosophy, political theory, and economics were read not just for antiquarian interest but for the truths that might lie there. The student of philosophy read Aristotle, Aquinas, or

---

[4]De Grazia, "The Scientific Reception System," p. 197.

Kant not as an antiquarian game but to learn about answers to philosophical questions. The student of political theory read Aristotle and Machiavelli in the same light. It was not assumed that, as in the physical sciences, all the contributions of past thinkers have been successfully incorporated into the latest edition of the currently popular textbook; and it was therefore not assumed that it was far more important to read the latest journal article in the field than to read the classical philosophers.

In recent decades, however, the disciplines of human action—philosophy and the social sciences—have been frantically attempting to ape the methodology of the physical sciences. There have been many grave flaws in this approach, which have increasingly divorced the social sciences from reality: the vain substitute of statistics for laboratory experimentation; the adoption of the positivistic hypothesis-testing model; and the unfortunate conquest of all of the disciplines—even history, to some extent—by mathematics, are cases in point.

But here the important point is that in the aping of the physical sciences, the social disciplines have become narrow specialties; as in the physical sciences, no one reads the classics in the field or indeed is familiar with the history of the discipline further back than this year's journal articles. No one writes systematic treatises anymore; systematic presentations are left for jejune textbooks, while the "real" scholars in the field spend their energy on technical minutiae for the professional journals.

We have seen that even the physical sciences have their problems from uncritical perpetuation of fundamental assumptions and paradigms; but in the social sciences and philosophy this aping of the methods of physical science has been disastrous. For while the social sciences were slow to change their fundamental assumptions in the past, they were eventually able to do so by pure reasoning and criticism of the basic paradigm.

It took, for example, a long time for "marginal utility" economics to replace classical economics in the late nineteenth century, but it was finally done through such fundamental reasoning and questioning. But no systematic treatise—with one exception to be discussed below—has been written in economics, not a single one, since World War I.

And if there are to be no systematic treatises, there can be no questioning of the fundamental assumptions. Deprived of the laboratory testing that furnishes the ultimate checks on the theories of physical science and now also deprived of the systematic use of reason to challenge fundamental assumptions, it is almost impossible to see how contemporary philosophy and social science can ever change the fundamental paradigms in which they have been gripped for most of this century.

Even if one were in total agreement with the fundamental drift of the social sciences in this century, the absence of fundamental questioning—the reduction of every discipline to narrow niggling in the journals—would be cause for grave doubts about the soundness of the social sciences.

But if one believes, as the present author does, that the fundamental paradigms of modern, twentieth-century philosophy and the social sciences have been grievously flawed and fallacious from the very beginning, including the aping of the physical sciences, then one is justified in a call for a radical and fundamental reconstruction of all these disciplines, and the opening up of the current specialized bureaucracies in the social sciences to a total critique of their assumptions and procedures.

Of all the social sciences, economics has suffered the most from this degenerative process. For economics is erroneously considered the most "scientific" of the disciplines. Philosophers still read Plato or Kant for insights into truth; political theorists still read Aristotle and Machiavelli for the same reason. But no economist reads Adam Smith or James Mill for the same purpose any longer.

History of economic thought, once required in most graduate departments, is now a rapidly dying discipline, reserved for antiquarians alone. Graduate students are locked into the most recent journal articles, the reading of economists published before the 1960s is considered a dilettantish waste of time, and any challenging of fundamental assumptions behind current theories is severely discouraged.

If there is any mention of older economists at all, it is only in a few perfunctory brush strokes to limn the precursors of the current Great Men in the field. The result is not only that economics is locked into a tragically wrong path, but also that the truths furnished by the great economists of the past have been collectively forgotten by the profession, lost in a form of Orwellian "memory hole."

Of all the tragedies wrought by this collective amnesia in economics, the greatest loss to the world is the eclipse of the "Austrian school." Founded in the 1870s and 1880s, and still barely alive, the Austrian school has had to suffer far more neglect than the other schools of economics for a variety of powerful reasons.

First, of course, it was founded a century ago, which, in the current scientific age, is in itself suspicious. Second, the Austrian school has from the beginning been self-consciously philosophic rather than "scientistic";

far more concerned with methodology and epistemology than other modern economists, the Austrians arrived early at a principled opposition to the use of mathematics or of statistical "testing" in economic theory. By doing so, they set themselves in opposition to all the positivistic, natural-science–imitating trends of this century. It meant, furthermore, that Austrians continued to write fundamental treatises while other economists were setting their sights on narrow, mathematically oriented articles. And third, by stressing the individual and his choices, both methodologically and politically, Austrians were setting themselves against the holism and statism of this century as well.

These three radical divergences from current trends were enough to propel the Austrians into undeserved oblivion. But there was another important factor, which at first might seem banal: the language barrier. It is notorious in the scholarly world that, "language tests" to the contrary notwithstanding, no American or English economists can really read a foreign language. Hence, the acceptance of foreign-based economics must depend on the vagaries of translation.

Of the great founders of the Austrian school, Carl Menger's work of the 1870s and 1880s remained untranslated into English until the 1950s; Menger's student Eugen von Böhm-Bawerk fared much better, but even his completed work was not translated until the late 1950s. Böhm-Bawerk's great student, Ludwig von Mises, the founder and head of the "neo-Austrian" school, has fared almost as badly as Menger. His classic *Theory of Money and Credit*, published in 1912, which applied Austrian economics to the problems of money and banking, and which contained the seeds of a radically new (and still largely unknown) theory of business cycles, was highly influential on the continent of Europe, but remained untranslated until 1934. By that time Mises's work was to be quickly buried in England and the United States by the fervor of the "Keynesian Revolution," which was at opposite poles from Mises's theory. Mises's book of 1928, *Geldwerstabilisierung und Konjunkturpolitik*, which predicted the Great Depression on the basis of his developed business cycle theory, remains untranslated to this day.[5]

Mises's monumental systematic treatise, *Nationalökonomie*, integrating economic theory on the grounds of a sound basic epistemology, was overlooked also from its being published in 1940, in the midst of war-torn

---

[5]Editor's note: This book was translated seven years later by Bettina Bien Greaves, and is now available as *The Causes of the Economic Crisis*.

Europe. Again its English translation as *Human Action* (1949) came at a time when economics had set its methodological and political face in a radically different direction and therefore Mises's work, as in the case of other challenges to fundamental paradigms in science, was not refuted or criticized but simply ignored.

Thus, while Ludwig von Mises was acknowledged as one of Europe's most eminent economists in the 1920s and 30s, the language barrier shut off any recognition of Mises in the Anglo-American world until the mid-1930s; then, just as his business cycle theory was beginning to achieve renown as an explanation for the Great Depression, Mises's overdue recognition was lost in the hoopla of the Keynesian Revolution.

A refugee deprived of his academic or social base in Europe, Mises emigrated to the United States at the mercy of his new-found environment. But while, in the climate of the day, the leftist and socialist refugees from Europe were cultivated, feted, and given prestigious academic posts, a different fate was meted out to a man who embodied a methodological and political individualism that was anathema to American academia. Indeed, the fact that a man of Mises's eminence was not offered a single regular academic post and that he was never able to teach in a prestigious graduate department in this country is one of the most shameful blots on the none-too-illustrious history of American higher education.

The fact that Mises himself was able to preserve his great energy, his remarkable productivity, and his unfailing gentleness and good humor in the face of this shabby treatment is simply one more tribute to the qualities of this remarkable man whom we now honor on his ninetieth birthday.

Agreed then that Ludwig von Mises's writings are the embodiment of a courageous and eminent man hewing to his discipline and to his vision, unheeding of shabby maltreatment. Apart from this, what substantive truths do they have to offer an American in 1971? Do they present truths not found elsewhere and therefore do they offer intrinsic interest beyond the historical record of a fascinating personal struggle?

The answer—which obviously cannot be documented in the compass of this article—is simply and startlingly this: that Ludwig von Mises offers to us nothing less than the complete and developed correct paradigm of a science that has gone tragically astray over the last half century. Mises's work presents us with the correct and radically divergent alternative to the flaws, errors, and fallacies which a growing number of students are sensing in present-day economic orthodoxy.

Many students feel that there is something very wrong with contemporary economics, and often their criticisms are trenchant, but they are ignorant of any theoretical alternative. As Thomas Kuhn has shown, a paradigm, however faulty, will not be discarded until it can be replaced by a competing theory. Or, in the vernacular, "you can't beat something with nothing." And "nothing" is all that many present-day critics of economic science can offer.

But the work of Ludwig von Mises furnishes that "something"; it furnishes an economics grounded not on the aping of physical science, but on the very nature of man and of individual choice. And it furnishes that economics in a systematic, integrated form that is admirably equipped to serve as a correct paradigmatic alternative to the veritable crisis situation—in theory and public policy—that modern economics has been bringing down upon us. It is not exaggeration to say that Ludwig von Mises is the Way Out of the methodological and political dilemmas that have been piling up in the modern world. But what is needed now is a host of "Austrians" who can spread the word of the existence of this neglected path.

Briefly, Mises's economic system—as set forth particularly in his *Human Action*—grounds economics squarely upon the axiom of action: on an analysis of the primordial truth that individual men exist and act, that is, make purposive choices among alternatives. Upon this simple and evident axiom of action, Ludwig von Mises deduces the entire systematic edifice of economic theory, an edifice that is as true as the basic axiom and the fundamental laws of logic.

The entire theory is the working out of methodological individualism in economics, the nature and consequences of the choices and exchanges of individuals. Mises's uncompromising devotion to the free market, and his opposition to every form of statism, stems from his analysis of the nature and consequences of individuals acting freely on the one hand, as against governmental coercive interference or planning on the other.

For, basing himself on the action axiom, Mises is able to show the happy consequences of freedom and the free market in social efficiency, prosperity, and development, as against the disastrous consequences of government intervention in poverty, war, social chaos, and retrogression. This political consequence alone, of course, makes the methodology as well as the conclusions of Misesian economics anathema to modern social science.

As Mises puts it,

Despots and democratic majorities are drunk with power. They must reluctantly admit that they are subject to the laws of nature. But they reject the very notion of economic law. Are they not the supreme legislators? ... In fact, economic history is a long record of government policies that failed because they were designed with a bold disregard for the laws of economics.

It is impossible to understand the history of economic thought if one does not pay attention to the fact that economics as such is a challenge to the conceit of those in power. An economist can never be a favorite of autocrats and demagogues. With them he is always the mischief-maker. ...

In the face of all this frenzied agitation, it is expedient to establish the fact that the starting point of all praxeological and economic reasoning, the category of human action, is proof against any criticisms and objections. ... From the unshakable foundation of the category of human action praxeology and economics proceed step by step by means of discursive reasoning. Precisely defining assumptions and conditions, they construct a system of concepts and draw all the inferences implied by logically unassailable ratiocination.[6]

And again,

The laws of the universe about which physics, biology, and praxeology [essentially economics] provide knowledge are independent of the human will, they are primary ontological facts rigidly restricting man's power to act.

Only the insane venture to disregard physical and biological laws. But it is quite common to disdain praxeological laws. Rulers do not like to admit that their power is restricted by any laws other than those of physics and biology. They never ascribe their failures and frustrations to the violation of economic law.[7]

---

[6]Ludwig von Mises, *Human Action* (New Haven, Conn.: Yale University Press, 1949), p. 67.

[7]Ibid., pp. 755–56. As Mises indicates, the revolt against economics as the harbinger of a free-market economy is as old as the classical economists whom Mises acknowledges as

A notable feature of Mises's analysis of "interventionism"—of government intervention in the economy—is that it is fundamentally what could now be called "ecological"; for it shows that an act of intervention generates unintended consequences and difficulties, which then present the government with an alternative: either more intervention to "solve" these problems, or repeal of the whole interventionist structure.

In short, Mises shows that the market economy is a finely constructed, interrelated web; and coercive intervention at various points of the structure will create unforeseen troubles elsewhere. The logic of intervention, then, is cumulative; and so a mixed economy is unstable—always tending either toward full-scale socialism or back to a free-market economy. The American farm-price support program, as well as the New York City rent-control program, are almost textbook cases of the consequences and pitfalls of intervention.

Indeed, the American economy has virtually reached the point where the crippling taxation; the continuing inflation; the grave inefficiencies and breakdowns in such areas as urban life, transportation, education, telephone, and postal service; the restrictions and shattering strikes of labor unions; and the accelerating growth of welfare dependency, all have brought about the full-scale crisis of interventionism that Mises has long foreseen.

The instability of the interventionist welfare-state system is now making fully clear the fundamental choice that confronts us between socialism on the one hand and capitalism on the other. Perhaps the most important single contribution of Mises to the economics of intervention is also the one most grievously neglected in the present day: his analysis of money and business cycles. We are living in an age when even those economists supposedly most devoted to the free market are willing and eager to see the state monopolize and direct the issuance of money. Yet Mises has shown that

---

his forebears. It is no accident, for example, that George Fitzhugh, the foremost Southern apologist for slavery and one of America's first sociologists, brusquely attacked classical economics as "the science of free society," while upholding socialism as "the science of slavery." See George Fitzhugh, *Cannibals All!*, C. Vann Woodward, ed. (Cambridge, Mass.: Harvard University Press, 1960), p. xviii; and Joseph Dorfman, *The Economic Mind in American Civilization* (New York: Viking Press, 1964), vol. 2, p. 929. On the statist and anti-individualist bias embedded deep in the foundations of sociology, see Leon Bramson, *The Political Context of Sociology* (Princeton, N.J.: Princeton University Press, 1961), esp. pp. 11–17.

- there is never any social or economic benefit to be conferred by an increase in the supply of money;

- the government's intervention into the monetary system is invariably inflationary;

- therefore, government should be separated from the monetary system, just as the free market requires that government not intervene in any other sphere of the economy.

Here Mises emphasizes that there is only one way to ensure this freedom and separation: to have a money that is also a useful commodity, one whose production is like other commodities subject to the supply and demand forces of the market. In short, that commodity money—which in practice means the full gold standard—shall replace the fiat issue of paper money by the government and its controlled banking system.[8]

Mises's brilliant theory of the business cycle is the only such theory to be integrated with the economists' general analysis of the pricing system and of capital and interest. Mises shows that the business cycle phenomenon, the recurring alternations of boom and bust with which we have become all too familiar, cannot occur in a free and unhampered market. Neither is the business cycle a mysterious series of random events to be checked and counteracted by an ever-vigilant central government. On the contrary, the business cycle is generated by government: specifically, by bank credit expansion promoted and fueled by governmental expansion of bank reserves.

The present-day "monetarists" have emphasized that this credit expansion process inflates the money supply and therefore the price level; but they have totally neglected the crucial Misesian insight that an even more damaging consequence is distortion of the whole system of prices and production.

Specifically, expansion of bank money causes an artificial lowering of the rate of interest, and an artificial and uneconomic overinvestment in capital goods: machinery, plant, industrial raw materials, and construction projects. As long as the inflationary expansion of money and bank credit continues, the unsoundness of this process is masked, and the economy can ride on the well-known euphoria of the boom; but when the bank

---

[8]Thus, see Ludwig von Mises, *The Theory of Money and Credit* (Irvington-on-Hudson, N.Y.: Foundation for Economic Education, 1971).

credit expansion finally stops, and stop it must if we are to avoid a runaway inflation, then the day of reckoning will have arrived.

For without the anodyne of continuing inflation of money, the distortions and misallocations of production, the overinvestment in uneconomic capital projects, and the excessively high prices and wages in those capital goods industries become evident and obvious. It is then that the inevitable recession sets in, the recession being the reaction by which the market economy readjusts itself, liquidates unsound investments, and realigns prices and outputs of the economy so as to eliminate the unsound consequences of the boom. The recovery arrives when the readjustment has been completed.

It is clear that the policy prescriptions stemming from the Misesian theory of the business cycle are the diametric opposite of the "post-Keynesian" policies of modern orthodox economics. If there is an inflation, the Misesian prescription is, simply, for the government to stop inflating the money supply.

When the inevitable recession occurs, in contrast to the modern view that the government should rush in to expand the money supply (the monetarists) or to engage in deficit spending (the Keynesians), the Austrians assert that the government should keep its hands off the economic system—should, in this case, allow the painful but necessary adjustment process of the recession to work itself out as quickly as possible.

At best, generating another inflation to end the recession will simply set the stage for another, and deeper, recession later on; at worst, the inflation will simply delay the adjustment process and thereby prolong the recession indefinitely, as happened tragically in the 1930s. Thus, while current orthodoxy maintains that the business cycle is caused by mysterious processes within the market economy and must be counteracted by an active government policy, the Mises theory shows that business cycles are generated by the inflationary policies of government and that, once underway, the best thing that government can do is to leave the economy alone. In short, the Austrian doctrine is the only consistent espousal of *laissez-faire*; for, in contrast to other "free market" schools in economics, Mises and the Austrians would apply *laissez-faire* to the "macro" as well as the "micro" areas of the economy.

If interventionism is invariably calamitous and self-defeating, what of the third alternative: socialism? Here, Ludwig von Mises is acknowledged to have made his best-known contribution to economic science: his demonstration, over fifty years ago, that socialist central planning was irrational since socialism could not engage in that "economic calculation" of prices indispensable to any modern, industrialized economy.

Only a true market, based on private ownership of the means of production and on the exchange of such property titles, can establish such genuine market prices, prices which serve to allocate productive resources—land, labor, and capital—to those areas which will most efficiently satisfy the demands of consumers. But Mises showed that even if the government were willing to forget consumer desires, it could not allocate efficiently for its own ends without a market economy to set prices and costs. Mises was hailed even by socialists for being the first to raise the whole problem of rational calculation of prices in a socialist economy; but socialists and other economists erroneously assumed that Oskar Lange and others had satisfactorily solved this calculation problem in their writings of the 1930s. Actually, Mises had anticipated the Lange "solutions" and had refuted them in his original article.[9]

It is highly ironic that no sooner had the economics profession settled contentedly into the notion that Mises's charge had been refuted, than the Communist countries of Eastern Europe began to find, pragmatically and much against their will, that socialist planning was indeed unsatisfactory, especially as their economies were becoming industrialized. Beginning with Yugoslavia's breakaway from state planning in 1952, the countries of Eastern Europe have been heading with astonishing rapidity away from socialist planning and toward free markets, a price system, profit-and-loss tests for enterprises, and so on. Yugoslavia has been particularly determined in its cumulative shift toward a free market and away even from state control of investments—the last government stronghold in a socialistic economy. It is unfortunate but not surprising that, neither in the East nor in the West, has Ludwig von Mises's name been brought up as the prophet of the collapse of central planning.[10]

---

[9]Mises's classic article was translated as "Economic Calculation in the Socialist Commonwealth," in *Collectivist Economic Planning*, F.A. Hayek, ed. (London: George Routledge and Sons, 1935), pp. 87–130. Mises's and other articles by Lange and Hayek are reprinted in *Comparative Economic Systems*, Morris Bornstein, ed., rev. ed. (Homewood, Ill.: Richard D. Irwin, 1969). An excellent discussion and critique of the whole controversy may be found in Trygve J.B. Hoff, *Economic Calculation in the Socialist Society* (London: William Hedge, 1949).

[10]On Yugoslavia, see Rudolf Bicanic, "Economics of Socialism in a Developed Country," in *Comparative Economic Systems*, M. Bornstein, ed., pp. 222–35; on the other countries of Eastern Europe, see Michael Gamarnikow, *Economic Reforms in Eastern Europe* (Detroit, Mich.: Wayne State University Press, 1968).

If it is becoming increasingly evident that the socialist economies are collapsing in the East, and, on the other hand, that interventionism is falling apart in the West, then the outlook is becoming increasingly favorable for both East and West to turn before very long to the free market and the free society. For this courageous and devoted champion of liberty, there could be no more welcome prospect in his ninetieth year.

But what should never be forgotten is that these events are a confirmation and a vindication of the stature of Ludwig von Mises, and of the importance of his contribution and his role. For Mises, almost single-handedly, has offered us the correct paradigm for economic theory, for social science, and for the economy itself, and it is high time that this paradigm be embraced, in all of its parts.

There is no more fitting conclusion to a tribute to Ludwig von Mises than the moving last sentences of his greatest achievement, *Human Action*:

> The body of economic knowledge is an essential element in the structure of human civilization; it is the foundation upon which modern industrialism and all the moral, intellectual, technological, and therapeutical achievements of the last centuries have been built. It rests with men whether they will make the proper use of the rich treasure with which this knowledge provides them or whether they will leave it unused. But if they fail to take the best advantage of it and disregard its teachings and warnings, they will not annul economics; they will stamp out society and the human race.[11]

Thanks in no small measure to the life and work of Ludwig von Mises, we can realistically hope and expect that mankind will choose the path of life, liberty, and progress and will at last turn decisively away from death and despotism.

---

[11]Mises, *Human Action*, p. 881.

Section III

Principles of Economics
and Government Intervention

CHAPTER 8

Fundamentals
of Value and Price

udwig von Mises (1881–1973) was born on September 29, 1881, in
the city of Lemberg (present day Ukraine), then part of the Austro-
Hungarian Empire, where his father, Arthur Edler von Mises, a distinguished construction engineer working for the Austrian railroads, was
stationed. Growing up in Vienna, Mises entered the University of Vienna
at the turn of the century to study for his graduate degree in law and economics. He died October 10, 1973, in New York City.

Mises was born and grew up during the high tide of the great "Austrian school" of economics, and neither Mises nor his vital contributions
to economic thought can be understood apart from the Austrian school
tradition which he studied and absorbed.

By the latter half of the nineteenth century, it was clear that "classical
economics," which had reached its apogee in England in the persons of
David Ricardo and John Stuart Mill, had foundered badly on the shoals of
several fundamental flaws. The critical flaw was that classical economics
had attempted to analyze the economy in terms of "classes" rather than the
actions of individuals. As a result, the classical economists could not find
the correct explanation of the underlying forces determining the values and

Reprinted from *The Essential von Mises* (1973); reprinted in *Scholar, Creator, Hero* (1988);
and *The Essential von Mises* (Auburn, Ala.: Mises Institute, 2009), pp. 3–11.

relative prices of goods and services; nor could they analyze the actions of consumers, the crucial determinants of the activities of producers in the economy. Looking at "classes" of goods, for example, the classical economists could never resolve the "paradox of value": the fact that bread, while extremely useful and the "staff of life," had a low value on the market; whereas diamonds, a luxury and hence a mere frippery in terms of human survival, had a very high value on the market. If bread is clearly more useful than diamonds, then why is bread rated so much more cheaply on the market?

Despairing at explaining this paradox, the classical economists unfortunately decided that values were fundamentally split: that bread, though higher in "use value" than diamonds, was for some reason lower in "exchange value." It was out of this split that later generations of writers denounced the market economy as tragically misdirecting resources into "production for profit" as opposed to the far more beneficial "production for use."

Failing to analyze the actions of consumers, classical economists earlier than the Austrians could not arrive at a satisfactory explanation of what it was that determined prices on the market. Groping for a solution, they unfortunately concluded (a) that value was something inherent in commodities; (b) that value must have been conferred on these goods by the processes of production; and (c) that the ultimate source of value was production "cost" or even the quantity of labor hours incurred in such production.

It was this Ricardian analysis that later gave rise to Karl Marx's perfectly logical conclusion that since all value was the product of the quantity of labor hours, then all interest and profit obtained by capitalists and employers must be "surplus value" unjustly extracted from the true earnings of the working class.

Having thus given hostage to Marxism, the later Ricardians attempted to reply that capital equipment was productive and therefore reasonably earned its share in profits; but the Marxians could with justice offer the rebuttal that capital too was "embodied" or "frozen" labor, and that therefore wages should have absorbed the entire proceeds from production.

The classical economists did not have a satisfactory explanation or justification for profit. Again treating the share of proceeds from production purely in terms of "classes," the Ricardians could only see a continuing "class struggle" between "wages," "profits," and "rents," with workers, capitalists, and landlords eternally warring over their respective shares.

Thinking only in terms of aggregates, the Ricardians tragically separated the questions of "production" and "distribution," with distribution a matter of conflict between these combating classes. They were forced to conclude that if wages went up, it could only be at the expense of lower profits and rents, or vice versa. Again, the Ricardians gave hostages to the Marxian system.

Looking at classes rather than individuals, then, the classical economists not only had to abandon any analysis of consumption and were misled in explaining value and price; they could not even approach an explanation of the pricing of individual factors of production: of specific units of labor, land, or capital goods. As the nineteenth century passed its mid-mark, the defects and fallacies of Ricardian economics became even more glaring. Economics itself had come to a dead end.

It has often happened in the history of human invention that similar discoveries are made at the same time purely independently by people widely separated in space and condition. The solution of the aforementioned paradoxes appeared, purely independently and in different forms, in the same year, 1871: by William Stanley Jevons in England; by Léon Walras in Lausanne, Switzerland; and by Carl Menger in Vienna. In that year, modern, or "neo-classical," economics was born. Jevons's solution and his new economic vision was fragmented and incomplete; furthermore, he had to battle against the enormous prestige that Ricardian economics had accumulated in the tight intellectual world of England. As a result, Jevons had little influence and attracted few followers. Walras's system also had little influence at the time; as we shall see in what follows, it was unfortunately reborn in later years to form the basis of the fallacies of current "microeconomics." By far the outstanding vision and solution of the three neo-classicists was that of Carl Menger,[1] professor of economics at the University of Vienna. It was Menger who founded the "Austrian school."

Menger's pioneering work bore full fruition in the great systematic work of his brilliant student, and his successor at the University of Vienna, Eugen von Böhm-Bawerk. It was Böhm-Bawerk's monumental work, written

---

[1]See Carl Menger's *Principles of Economics*, James Dingwall and Bert F. Hoselitz, trans. (Glencoe, Ill.: The Free Press, 1950); reprinted 2007 (Auburn, Ala.: Ludwig von Mises Institute); original German edition, *Grundsätze der Volkswirtschaftslehre* (1871). See also Menger's *Problems of Economics and Sociology*, Francis J. Nock, trans. (Urbana: University of Illinois Press, 1963); original German edition, *Untersuchungen über die Methode der Socialwissenschaften und der Politischen Oekonomie insbesondere* (1883).

largely during the 1880s, and culminating in his three-volume *Capital and Interest*,[2] that formed the mature product of the Austrian school. There were other great and creative economists who contributed to the Austrian school during the last two decades of the nineteenth century; notably Böhm-Bawerk's brother-in-law, Friedrich von Wieser, and to some extent the American economist John Bates Clark; but Böhm-Bawerk towered above them all.

The Austrian, or Menger–Böhm-Bawerkian, solutions to the dilemmas of economics were far more comprehensive than those by the Ricardians, because the Austrian solutions were rooted in a completely contrasting epistemology. The Austrians unerringly centered their analysis on the *individual*, on the acting individual as he makes his choices on the basis of his preferences and values in the real world. Starting from the individual, the Austrians were able to ground their analysis of economic activity and production in the values and desires of the individual *consumers*. Each consumer operated from his own chosen scale of preferences and values; and it was these values that interacted and combined to form the consumer demands that form the basis and the direction for all productive activity. Grounding their analysis in the individual as he faces the real world, the Austrians saw that productive activity was based on the expectations of serving the demands of consumers.

Hence, it became clear to the Austrians that no productive activity, whether of labor or of any productive factors, could confer value upon goods or services. Value consisted in the subjective valuations of the individual consumers. In short, I could spend thirty years of labor time and other resources working on the perfection of a giant steam-powered tricycle. If, however, on offering this product no consumers can be found to purchase this tricycle, it is economically valueless, regardless of the misdirected effort that I had expended upon it. Value is consumer valuations,

---

[2]See Eugen von Böhm-Bawerk's three-volume *Capital and Interest*: vol. I, *History and Critique of Interest Theories*; vol. II, *Positive Theory of Capital*; vol. III, *Further Essays on Capital and Interest*, George D. Huncke and Hans F. Sennholz, trans. (Grove City, Penn.: Libertarian Press, 1959); this was the first complete English translation of the third and fourth German editions. German title for Böhm-Bawerk's *opus* is, *Kapital und Kapitalzins* (first edition of vol. I in 1884 and vol. II in 1889; second edition of vol. I in 1900 and vol. II in 1902; third and completely revised edition of vol. I in 1914 and part of vols. II and III in 1909; balance of vols. II and III in 1912; fourth (posthumous) edition, I, II, III in 1921).

and the relative prices of goods and services are determined by the extent and intensity of consumer valuations and desires for these products.[3]

Looking clearly at the individual rather than at broad "classes," the Austrians could easily resolve the "value paradox" that had stumped classicists. For no individual on the market is ever faced with the choice between "bread" as a class and "diamonds" as a class. The Austrians had shown that the greater the quantity—the larger the number of units—of a good that anyone possesses, the *less* he will value any given unit. The man stumbling through the desert, devoid of water, will place an extremely high value of "utility" on a cup of water: whereas the same man in urban Vienna or New York, with water plentiful around him, will place a very low valuation or "utility" on any given cup. Hence the *price* he will pay for a cup of water in the desert will be enormously greater than in New York City. In short, the acting individual is faced with, and chooses in terms of, specific units, or "margins"; and the Austrian finding was termed the "law of diminishing marginal utility." The reason that "bread" is so much cheaper than "diamonds" is that the number of loaves of bread available is enormously greater than the number of carats of diamonds: hence the value, and the price, of *each loaf* will be far less than the value and price of *each carat*. There is no contradiction between "use value" and "exchange value"; given the abundance of loaves available, each loaf is less "useful" than each carat of diamond to the individual.

The same concentration on the actions of the individual, and hence on "marginal analysis," also solved the problem of the "distribution" of income on the market. The Austrians demonstrated that each unit of a factor of production, whether of different types of labor, of land, or of capital equipment, is priced on the free market on the basis of its "marginal productivity": in short, on how much that unit actually contributes to the value of the final product purchased by the consumers. The greater the "supply," the quantity of units of any given factor, the less will its marginal productivity—and hence its price—tend to be; and the lower its supply, the higher will tend to be its price. Thus, the Austrians showed that there was no senseless and arbitrary class struggle or conflict between the different classes of factors; instead, each type of factor contributes harmoniously to the final product, directed to satisfying the most intense desires of the consumers in the most efficient manner (i.e., in the manner least costly

---

[3]See Eugen von Böhm-Bawerk, "The Ultimate Standard of Value" in *Shorter Classics of Böhm-Bawerk* (Grove City, Penn.: Libertarian Press, 1962).

of resources). Each unit of each factor then earns its marginal product, its own particular contribution to the productive result. In fact, if there was any conflict of interests, it was not between types of factors, between land, labor, and capital; it was between competing suppliers of the *same* factor. If, for example, someone found a new supply of copper ore, the increased supply would drive down the price of copper; this could only work to the benefit and the earnings of the consumers and of the cooperating labor and capital factors. The only unhappiness might be among existing copper mine owners who found the price declining for their own product.

The Austrians thus showed that on the free market there is no separation whatever between "production" and "distribution." The values and demands of consumers determine the final prices of the consumer goods, the goods purchased by consumers, which set the direction for productive activity, and in turn determine the prices of the cooperating units of factors: the individual wage rates, rents, and prices of capital equipment. The "distribution" of income was simply the consequence of the price of each factor. Hence, if the price of copper is 20 cents per pound, and a copper owner sells 100,000 pounds of copper, the owner will receive $20,000 in "distribution"; if someone's wage is $4 an hour, and he works forty hours a week, he will receive $160 per week, and so on.

What of profits and the problem of "frozen labor" (labor embodied in machinery)? Again working from analysis of the individual, Böhm-Bawerk saw that it was a basic law of human action that each person wishes to achieve his desires, his goals, as quickly as possible. Hence, each person will prefer goods and services in the present to waiting for these goods for a length of time in the future. A bird already in the hand will always be worth more to him than one bird in the bush. It is because of this basic primordial fact of "time preference" that people do not invest all their income in capital equipment so as to increase the amount of goods that will be produced in the future. For they must first attend to consuming goods now. But each person, in different conditions and cultures, has a different *rate* of time preference, of preferring goods now to goods later. The higher their rate of time preference, the greater the proportion of their income they will consume *now*; the lower the rate, the more they will save and invest in future production. It is the fact of time preference that results in interest and profit; and it is the degree and intensity of time preferences that will determine how high the rate of interest and profit will be.

Take, for example, the rate of interest on a loan. The scholastic philosophers of the Catholic Church, in the Middle Ages and in the early modern period, were in their way excellent economists and analyzers of the market; but one thing they could never explain or justify was the simple charging of interest on a loan. They could understand gaining profits for risky investments; but they had learned from Aristotle that money itself was barren and unproductive. Therefore, how could pure interest on a loan (assuming no risk of default) be justified? Not being able to find the answer, the church and the scholastics discredited their approach in the eyes of worldly men by condemning as sinful "usury" all interest on a loan. It was Böhm-Bawerk who finally found the answer in the concept of time preference. For when a creditor lends $100 to a debtor, in exchange for receiving $106 a year from now, the two men are not exchanging the same things. The creditor is giving the debtor $100 as a "present good," money that the debtor can use at any time in the present. But the debtor is giving the creditor in exchange, not money, but an IOU, the *prospect* of receiving money one year from now. In short, the creditor is giving the debtor a "present good," while the debtor is only giving the creditor a "future good," money which the creditor will have to wait a year before he can make use of. And since the universal fact of time preference makes present goods worth more than future goods, the creditor will have to charge, and the debtor will be willing to pay, a premium for the present good. That premium is the rate of interest. How large that premium will be will depend on the rates of time preference of everyone in the market.

This is not all for Böhm-Bawerk went on to show how time preference determined the rate of business profit in the same way: in fact that the "normal" rate of business profit *is* the rate of interest. For when labor or land is employed in the process of production, the crucial fact is that they do not have to wait, as they would in the absence of capitalist employers, for their money until the product is produced and sold to the consumers. If there were no capitalist employers, then laborers and landowners would have to toil for months and years without pay, until the final product—the automobile or bread or washing machine—is sold to the consumers. But capitalists perform the great service of saving up money from their income ahead of time and then paying laborers and landowners *now*, while they are working; the capitalists then perform the function of waiting until the final product is sold to the consumers and then receiving their money. It is for this vital service that the laborers and landowners are more than willing to "pay" the capitalists their profit or interest. The capitalists, in short, are in the position of "creditors" who save and pay out present money, and then wait for their eventual return; the laborers and landowners are, in a sense, "debtors" whose services will only bear fruit after a certain date in the future. Again, the normal rate of business profit will be determined by the height of the various rates of time preference.

Böhm-Bawerk also put this another way: capital goods are not simply "frozen labor"; they are *also* frozen *time* (and land); and it is in the crucial element of time and time preference that the explanation for profit and interest can be found. He also enormously advanced the economic analysis of capital; for in contrast not only to Ricardians but also to most economists of the present day, he saw that "capital" is not simply a homogeneous blob,[4] or a given quantity. Capital is an intricate latticework that has a time-dimension; and economic growth and increasing productivity comes from adding not simply to the quantity of capital but to its time-structure, to building "longer and longer processes of production." The lower people's rate of time preference, the more they are willing to sacrifice consumption now on behalf of saving and investing in these longer processes that will yield a significantly greater return of consumer goods at some date *in the future*.

---

[4]See Böhm-Bawerk, *Capital and Interest*, vol. II, *Positive Theory of Capital*, pp. 1–118.

CHAPTER 9

Exchange and the Division of Labor

I t is now time to bring other men into our Robinsonian idyll—to extend our analysis to interpersonal relations. The problem for our analysis is not simply more people: after all, we could simply postulate a world of a million Crusoes on a million isolated islands, and our analysis would not need to be expanded by one iota. The problem is to analyze the *interaction* of these people. Friday, for example, might land in another part of the island, and make contact with Crusoe, or he might land on a separate island, and then later construct a boat that could reach the other island.

Economics has revealed a great truth about the natural law of human interaction: that not only is *production* essential to man's prosperity and survival, but so also is exchange. In short, Crusoe, on his island or part thereof, might produce fish, while Friday, on his part, might grow wheat, instead of both trying to produce both commodities. By exchanging part of Crusoe's fish for some of Friday's wheat, the two men can greatly improve the amount of both fish and bread that both can enjoy.[1] This great gain for both men is made possible by two primordial facts of nature—natural

---

[1] On the economic analysis of all this, see Murray N. Rothbard, *Man, Economy, and State* (Princeton, N.J.: D. Van Nostrand, 1962), chap. 2.

Reprinted from chapter 7 "Interpersonal Relations: Voluntary Exchange," in *The Ethics of Liberty* (New York: New York University Press, 1998), pp. 35–41.

laws—on which all of economic theory is based: (a) the great variety of skills and interests among individual persons; and (b) the variety of natural resources in geographic land areas. If all people were equally skilled and equally interested in all matters, *and* if all areas of land were homogeneous with all others, there would be no room for exchanges. But, in the world as it is, the opportunity for specialization in the best uses for land and people enables exchanges to multiply vastly and immensely to raise the productivity and the standard of living (the satisfaction of wants) of *all* those participating in exchange.

If anyone wishes to grasp how much we owe to the processes of exchange, let him consider what would happen in the modern world if every man were suddenly prohibited from exchanging anything with anyone else. Each person would be forced to produce all of his own goods and services himself. The utter chaos, the total starvation of the great bulk of the human race, and the reversion to primitive subsistence by the remaining handful of people, can readily be imagined.

Another remarkable fact of human action is that A and B can specialize and exchange for their mutual benefit *even if* one of them is superior to the other in *both lines* of production. Thus, suppose that Crusoe is superior to Friday in fish and wheat production. It still benefits Crusoe to concentrate on what he is *relatively* best at. If, for example, he is a far better fisherman than Friday but only a moderately better farmer, he can gain more of both products by concentrating on fishing, and then exchanging his produce for Friday's wheat. Or, to use an example from an advanced exchange economy, it will pay a physician to hire a secretary for typing, filing, etc., *even* if he is better at the latter jobs, in order to free his time for far more productive work. This insight into the advantages of exchange, discovered by David Ricardo in his Law of Comparative Advantage, means that, in the free market of voluntary exchanges, the "strong" do not devour or crush the "weak," contrary to common assumptions about the nature of the free-market economy. On the contrary, it is precisely on the free market where the "weak" reap the advantages of productivity because it benefits the "strong" to exchange with them.

The process of exchange enables man to ascend from primitive isolation to civilization: it enormously widens his opportunities and the market for his wares; it enables him to invest in machines and other "high-order capital goods"; it forms a pattern of exchanges—the free market—which enables him to calculate economically the benefits and the costs of highly complex methods and aggregates of production.

But economists too often forget, in contemplating the critical importance and the glories of the free market, *what* precisely is being exchanged. For apples are *not* simply being exchanged for butter, or gold for horses. What is really being exchanged is not the commodities themselves, but the *rights to ownership* of them. When Smith exchanges a bag of apples for Jones's pound of butter, he is actually transferring his *ownership rights* in the apples in exchange for the ownership rights to the butter, and vice versa. Now that Smith rather than Jones is the absolute controller of the butter, it is Smith who may eat it or not at his will; Jones now has nothing to say in its disposition, and is instead absolute owner of the apples.

Returning now to Crusoe and Friday, suppose that more people, C, D, E ... join Crusoe and Friday on the island. Each specializes in different products; gradually one particular product emerges—because of such qualities as high value, steady demand, ready divisibility—*as a medium of exchange*. For it is discovered that the use of a medium enormously expands the scope of exchanges and the wants that can be satisfied on the market. Thus, a writer or an economics teacher would be hard put to exchange his teaching or writing services for loaves of bread, parts of a radio, a piece of a suit, etc. A generally acceptable medium is indispensable for any extensive network of exchange and hence for any civilized economy.

Such a generally acceptable medium of exchange is defined as a *money*. It has generally been found, on the free market, that the best commodities for use as a money have been the precious metals, gold and silver. The exchange sequence now appears as follows: A, owning his body and his labor, finds land, transforms it, produces fish which he then owns; B uses his labor similarly to produce wheat, which he then owns; C finds land containing gold, transforms it, produces the gold which he then owns. C then exchanges the gold for other services, say A's fish. A uses the gold to exchange for B's wheat, etc. In short, the gold "enters circulation," i.e., its ownership is transferred from person to person, as it is used as a general medium of exchange. In each case, the exchangers transfer ownership rights, and, in each case, ownership rights are acquired in two ways and two ways only: (a) by finding and transforming resources ("producing"), and (b) by exchanging one's produce for someone else's product—including the medium of exchange, or "money" commodity. And it is clear that method (b) *reduces* logically to (a), for the only way a person can obtain something in exchange is by giving up his own product. In short, there is only one route to ownership of goods: production-and-exchange. If Smith gives up a product in exchange for Jones's which Jones also acquired in a previous exchange, then *someone*, whether the person from whom Jones bought the product or someone else down the line, must have been the original finder—and—transformer of the resource.

A man then, can acquire "wealth"—a stock of useful capital or consumer goods—either by "producing" it himself, or by selling to its producer some other product in exchange. The exchange process reduces logically back to original production. Such production is a process by which a man "mixes his labor with the soil"—finding and transforming land resources *or*, in such cases as a teacher or writer, by producing and selling one's own labor services directly. Put another way: since all production of capital goods reduces ultimately back to the original factors of land and labor, all production reduces back either to labor services or to finding new and virgin land and putting it into production by means of labor energy.[2]

A man may also obtain wealth voluntarily in another way: through gifts. Thus Crusoe, upon stumbling on Friday at another end of the island, may give him some sustenance. In such a case, the giver receives, not another alienable good or service from the other party, but the psychic satisfaction of having done something for the receiver. In the case of a gift, also, the process of acquisition reduces back to production and exchange—and again ultimately to production itself, since a gift must be preceded by production, if not directly as in this case, then somewhere back down the line.

We have so far analyzed the exchange process for a multitude of exchanges of consumer goods. We must now complete our picture of the real world by analyzing exchanges along the structure of production. For exchanges in an advanced economy are not only "horizontal" (of consumer goods), but also "vertical": they proceed downward from the original transformation of land, down through the various types of capital goods, and finally to the ultimate state of consumption.

Let us consider a simple vertical pattern as it occurs in the exchange economy. Smith transforms land resources and constructs an axe; instead of using the axe to make another product, Smith, as a specialist in a vast exchange economy, sells his axe for gold (money). Smith, producer of the

---

[2]That capital goods reduce back to land and labor as original factors is a fundamental insight of the Austrian school of economics. In particular, see Eugen von Böhm-Bawerk, *The Positive Theory of Capital*, vol. 2 of *Capital and Interest* (South Holland, Ill.: Libertarian Press, 1959).

axe, transfers his right of ownership to Jones, in exchange for a certain amount of Jones's gold—the precise amount of gold being agreed upon voluntarily by the two parties. Jones now takes the axe and fells lumber, then sells the lumber to Johnson for gold; Johnson in turn sells the lumber to Robbins, a contractor, for gold, and Robbins in his turn constructs a house in exchange for the gold of his client/Benton. (It should be evident that this vertical network of exchange could not take place without the use of a monetary medium for the exchanges.)

To complete our picture of a market economy, let us suppose that Jones has cut down his lumber, but has to ship it down-river to transfer it to Johnson; Jones, then, sells the lumber to another intermediary, Polk, who *hires* the labor services of X, Y, and Z to transport the logs to Johnson. What has happened here, and why doesn't the use of X, Y, and Z's labor in transforming and transporting the logs to a more useful place give *them* rights to ownership of the logs?

What has happened is this: Polk transfers some gold to X and to Y, and to Z, in return for their selling to him their labor services of transporting the logs. Polk did *not* sell the logs to these men for money; instead, he "sold" them money in exchange for employing their labor services on his logs. In short, Polk may have bought the logs from Jones for 40 gold ounces, and then paid X, Y, and Z 20 gold ounces each to transport the logs, and *then* sold the logs to Johnson for 110 ounces of gold. Hence, Polk netted a gain of 10 gold ounces on the entire transaction. X, Y, and Z, if they had so desired, *could* have purchased the logs from Jones themselves for the 40 ounces, and then shipped the logs themselves, sold them to Johnson for 110 and pocketed the 10 extra ounces. Why didn't they? Because (a) they didn't have the *capital*; in short, they hadn't saved up the requisite money, by reducing their previous consumption sufficiently below their income to accumulate the 40 ounces; and/or (b) they wanted money payment *while they worked*, and were not willing to wait for the number of months it took for the logs to be shipped and sold; and/or (c) they were unwilling to be saddled with the risk that the logs might indeed not be saleable for 110 ounces. Thus, the indispensable and enormously important function of Polk, the *capitalist* in our example of the market economy, is to save the laborers from the necessity of restricting their consumption and thus saving up the capital themselves, and from waiting for their pay until the product would (hopefully) be sold at a profit further down the chain of production. Hence, the capitalist, far from somehow depriving the laborer of his rightful ownership of the product, makes possible a payment to the laborer considerably *in advance* of the sale of the product. Furthermore, the capitalist, in his capacity as forecaster or *entrepreneur*, saves the laborer from the risk that the product might not be sold at a profit, or that he might even suffer losses.

The capitalist, then, is a man who has labored, saved out of his labor (i.e., has restricted his consumption) and, in a series of voluntary contracts has (a) purchased ownership rights in capital goods, and (b) paid the laborers for their labor services in transforming those capital goods into goods nearer the final stage of being consumed. Note again that no one is preventing the laborers themselves from saving, purchasing capital goods from their owners and then working on their own capital goods, finally selling the product and reaping the profits. In fact, the capitalists are conferring a great benefit on these laborers, making possible the entire complex vertical network of exchanges in the modern economy. For they save the money needed to buy the capital goods and to pay the laborers in advance of sale for "producing" them further.[3]

At each step of the way, then, a man produces—by exerting his labor upon tangible goods. If this good was previously unused and unowned, then his labor automatically brings the good under his control, his "ownership." If the good was already owned by someone else, then the owner may either sell this (capital) good to our laborer for money, after which his labor is exerted on the good; *or* the previous owner may purchase the labor service for money in order to produce the good further and then sell it to the next buyer. This process, too, reduces back to the original production of unused resources and to labor, since the capitalist—the previous owner in our example—ultimately derived his own ownership from: original production; voluntary exchange; and the saving of money. Thus, all ownership on the free market reduces ultimately back to: (a) ownership by each man of his own person and his own labor; (b) ownership by each man of land which he finds unused and transforms by his own labor; and (c) the exchange of the products of this mixture of (a) and (b) with the similarly-produced output of other persons on the market.

---

[3]In technical economic terms, the laborers, by choosing to take their money in advance of sale, earn the "discounted marginal value product" of their labor—the discount being the value which the laborers achieve by getting their money *now* instead of *later*. The capitalists, by advancing money *now* and relieving the laborers of the burden of waiting until later, earn the discount for "time-preference"; the farsighted ones also earn the reward for being better at forecasting the future under conditions of uncertainty, in the form of "pure profits." The less farsighted entrepreneurs suffer losses for poor handling of decisions under uncertainty. See Rothbard, *Man, Economy, and State*, passim.

The same law holds true for all ownership, on the market, of the money commodity. As we have seen, money is either (1) produced by one's own labor transforming original resources (e.g., mining gold); or (2) obtained by selling one's own product—or selling goods previously purchased with the proceeds of one's own product—in exchange for gold owned by someone else. Again, just as (c) in the previous paragraph reduces logically back to (a) and (b), production coming before exchange—so here (2) ultimately reduces logically back to (1).

In the free society we have been describing, then, all ownership reduces ultimately back to each man's naturally given ownership over himself, *and* of the land resources that man transforms and brings into production. The *free market* is a society of voluntary and consequently mutually beneficial exchanges of ownership titles between specialized producers. It has often been charged that this market economy rests on the wicked doctrine that labor "is treated as a commodity." But the natural fact is that labor service is indeed a commodity, for, as in the case of tangible property, one's own labor service *can* be alienated and exchanged for other goods and services. A person's labor service is alienable, but his *will* is not. It is most fortunate, moreover, for mankind that this is so; for this alienability means (1) that a teacher or physician or whatever can sell his labor services for money; and (2) that workers can sell their labor services in transforming goods to capitalists for money. If this could not be done, the structure of capital required for civilization could not be developed, and no one's vital labor services could be purchased by his fellow men.

The distinction between a man's alienable labor service and his inalienable will may be further explained: a man can alienate his labor service, but he cannot *sell* the capitalized future value of that service. In short, he cannot, in nature, sell himself into slavery and have this sale enforced—for this would mean that his future will over his own person was being surrendered in advance. In short, a man can naturally expend his labor currently for someone else's benefit, but he cannot transfer himself, even if he wished, into another man's permanent capital good. For he cannot rid himself of his own will, which may change in future years and repudiate the current arrangement. The concept of "voluntary slavery" is indeed a contradictory one, for so long as a laborer remains totally subservient to his master's will voluntarily, he is not yet a slave since his submission is voluntary; whereas, if he later changed his mind and the master enforced his slavery by violence, the slavery would not then be voluntary. But more of coercion later on.

The society that we have been describing in this section—the society of free and voluntary exchanges—may be called the "free society" or the society of "pure liberty." The bulk of this work will be devoted to spelling out the implications of such a system. The term "free market," while properly signifying the critically important network of free and voluntary exchanges, is insufficient when going at all beyond the narrowly economic or praxeologic. For it is vital to realize that the free market is exchanges of titles to property, and that therefore the free market is necessarily embedded in a larger free society—with a certain pattern of property rights and ownership titles. We have been describing the free society as one where property titles are founded on the basic natural facts of man: each individual's ownership by his ego over his own person and his own labor, and his ownership over the land resources which he finds and transforms. The natural alienability of tangible property as well as man's labor service makes possible the network of free exchanges of ownership titles.

The regime of pure liberty—the libertarian society—may be described as a society where *no ownership titles are "distributed,"* where, in short, no man's property in his person or in tangibles is molested, violated, or interfered with by anyone else. But this means that *absolute freedom*, in the social sense, *can* be enjoyed, not only by an isolated Crusoe but by every man in any society, no matter how complex or advanced. For every man enjoys absolute freedom—pure liberty—if, like Crusoe, his "naturally" owned property (in his person and in tangibles) is free from invasion or molestation by other men. And, of course, being in a society of voluntary exchanges, each man can enjoy absolute liberty not in Crusoe-like isolation, but in a milieu of civilization, harmony, sociability, and enormously greater productivity through exchanges of property with his fellow men. Absolute freedom, then, need *not* be lost as the price we must pay for the advent of civilization; men *are* born free, and need *never* be in chains. Man may achieve liberty and abundance, freedom *and* civilization.

This truth will be obscured if we persist in confusing "freedom" or "liberty" with *power*. We have seen the absurdity of saying that man does not have free will because he has not the *power* to violate the laws of his nature-because he cannot leap oceans at a single bound. It is similarly absurd to say that a man is not "truly" free in the free society because, in that society, no man is "free" to aggress against another man or to invade his property. Here, again, the critic is not really dealing with freedom but with power; in a free society, no man would be permitted (or none would permit himself) to invade the property of another. This would mean that his *power* of action would be limited; as man's power is always limited by his nature; it would *not* mean any curtailment of his freedom. For if we define freedom, again, as the *absence of invasion* by another man of any man's person or property, the fatal confusion of freedom and power is at last laid to rest.[4] We then see clearly that a supposed "freedom to steal or assault"—in short, to aggress—would not be a state of freedom at all, because it would permit someone, the victim of an assault, to be deprived of his right to person and property—in short, to have his liberty violated.[5] Each man's power, then, is always necessarily limited by the facts of the human condition, by the nature of man and his world; but it is one of the glories of man's condition that each person *can* be absolutely free, even in a world of complex interaction and exchange. It is still true, moreover, that any man's power to act and do and consume is enormously greater in such a world of complex interaction than it could be in a primitive or Crusoe society.

A vital point: if we are trying to set up an ethic for man (in our case, the subset of ethics dealing with violence), then to be a valid ethic the theory must hold true for *all* men, whatever their location in time or place.[6] This is one of the notable attributes of natural law—its applicability to all men, regardless of time or place. Thus, ethical natural law takes its place alongside physical or "scientific" natural laws. But the society of liberty is the *only* society that can apply the same basic rule to every man, regardless of time or place. Here is one of the ways in which reason can select one theory of natural law over a rival theory—just as reason can choose between many economic or other competing theories. Thus, if someone claims that the Hohenzollern or Bourbon families have the "natural right" to rule everyone else, this kind of doctrine is easily refutable by simply pointing to the fact that there is here no uniform ethic for every person: one's rank in the ethical order being dependent on the accident of being,

---

[4]We shall see later that this definition of freedom or liberty must be clarified to read "absence of molestation of a man's *just* property," with justice implying, once again, ownership title to one's own self, to one's own transformed property, and to the fruits of voluntary exchanges built upon them.

[5]For a critique of the "freedom to steal or assault" argument against the libertarian position, see Murray N. Rothbard, *Power and Market*, 2nd ed. (Kansas City: Sheed Andrews and McMeel, 1977), p. 242.

[6]On the requirement that ethical laws be universally binding, see R.M. Hare, *The Language of Morals* (Oxford: Clarendon Press, 1952), p. 162; Marcus Singer, *Generalization in Ethics* (New York: Knopf, 1961), pp. 13–33.

or not being, a Hohenzollern. Similarly, if someone says that every man has a "natural right" to three square meals a day, it is glaringly obvious that this is a fallacious natural law or natural rights theory; for there are innumerable times and places where it is physically impossible to provide three square meals for all, or even for the majority, of the population. Hence this cannot be set forth as some kind of "natural right." On the other hand, consider the universal status of the ethic of liberty, and of the natural right of person and property that obtains under such an ethic. For every person, at any time or place, can be covered by the basic rules: ownership of one's own self, ownership of the previously unused resources which one has occupied and transformed; and ownership of all titles derived from that basic ownership-either through voluntary exchanges or voluntary gifts. These rules—which we might call the "rules of natural ownership"—can clearly be applied, and such ownership defended, regardless of the time or place, and regardless of the economic attainments of the society. It is impossible for any other social system to qualify as universal natural law; for if there is any coercive *rule* by one person or group over another (and *all* rule partakes of such hegemony), then it is impossible to apply the same rule for all; only a rulerless, purely libertarian world can fulfill the qualifications of natural rights and natural law, or, more important, can fulfill the conditions of a universal ethic for all mankind.

CHAPTER 10

The Division
of Labor Clarified

I have come to realize, since writing this essay, that I overweighted the contributions and importance of Adam Smith on the division of labor. And to my surprise, I did not sufficiently appreciate the contributions of Ludwig von Mises.

Despite the enormous emphasis on specialization and the division of labor in the *Wealth of Nations*, much of Smith's discussion was misplaced and misleading. In the first place, he placed undue importance on the division of labor *within* a factory (the famous pin-factory example), and scarcely considered the far more important division of labor among various industries and occupations. Second, there is the mischievous contradiction between the discussions in Book 1 and Book 5 in the *Wealth of Nations*. In Book 1, the division of labor is hailed as responsible for civilization as well as economic growth, and is also praised as expanding the alertness and intelligence of the population. But in Book 5 the division of labor is condemned as leading to the intellectual and moral degeneration of the same population, and to the loss of their "intellectual, social, and martial virtues." These complaints about the division of labor as well as

---

Excerpt from "Freedom, Inequality, Primitivism, and the Division of Labor," in *Egalitarianism as a Revolt Against Nature, and Other Essays* (Auburn, Ala.: Mises Institute, 2000), pp. 299–302.

similar themes in Smith's close friend Adam Ferguson, strongly influenced the griping about "alienation" in Marx and later socialist writers.[1]

But of greater fundamental importance was Smith's abandonment of the tradition, since Jean Buridan and the Scholastics, that emphasized that two parties always undertook an exchange because each expected to gain from the transaction. In contrast to this emphasis on specialization and exchange as a result of conscious human decision, Smith shifted the focus from mutual benefit to an alleged irrational and innate "propensity to truck, barter, and exchange," as if human beings were lemmings determined by forces external to their own chosen purposes. As Edwin Cannan pointed out long ago, Smith took this tack because he rejected the idea of innate differences in human talents and abilities, differences which would naturally lead people to seek out different specialized occupations.[2] Smith instead took an egalitarian-environmentalist position, still dominant today in neo-classical economics, holding that all men are uniform and equal, and therefore that differences in labor or occupations can only be the *result* rather than a cause of the system of division of labor. Moreover, Smith inaugurated the corollary tradition that differences in wage rates among this uniform population can only reflect differences in the cost of training.[3,4]

In contrast, the recent work of Professor Joseph Salerno has illuminated the profound contributions of Ludwig von Mises's emphasis on the division of labor as the "essence of society" and the "fundamental social

---

[1]On Ferguson's influence, see M.H. Abrams, *Natural Supernaturalism: Tradition and Revolution in Romantic Literature* (New York: Norton, 1971), pp. 220–21, 508.

[2]Edwin Cannan, *A History of the Theories of Production and Distribution in English Political Economy from 1776 to 1848* (3rd ed., London: Staples Press, 1917), p. 35.

[3]Contrast Smith's egalitarianism with the great early-fifteenth-century Italian Scholastic, San Bernardino of Siena (1380–1444). In his *On Contracts and Usury*, written in 1431–33, Bernardino pointed out that wage inequality on the market is a function of differences of ability and skill as well as training. An architect is paid more than a ditch digger, Bernardino explained, because the former's job requires more intelligence and ability as well as training, so that fewer men will qualify for the task. See Raymond de Roover, *San Bernardino of Siena and Sant' Antonio of Florence, The Two Great Economic Thinkers of the Middle Ages* (Boston: Baker Library, 1967), and Alejandro Chafuen, *Christians for Freedom: Late Scholastic Economics* (San Francisco: Ignatius Press, 1986), pp. 123–31.

[4]Modern neoclassical labor economics fits in this tradition by defining "discrimination" as any wage inequalities greater than differences in the cost of training. Thus, see the standard work by Gary Becker, *The Economics of Discrimination* (Chicago: University of Chicago Press, 1957).

phenomenon." For Mises, as I wrote in the essay, the division of labor stems from the diversity and inequality of human beings and of nature. Salerno, in addition, brings out with unparalleled clarity that for Mises the division of labor is a conscious choice of mutual gain and economic development. The process of social evolution therefore becomes "the development of the division of labor," and this allows Mises to refer to the worldwide division of labor as a vital "social organism" or "*oecumene.*" Mises also points out that division of labor is at the heart of biological organisms, and "the fundamental principle of all forms of life." The difference of the "social organism" is that, in contrast to biological organisms, "reason and will are the originating and sustaining form of the organic coalescence." Therefore, for Mises "human society is thus spiritual and teleological," the "product of thought and will." It therefore becomes of the utmost importance for people to understand the significance of maintaining and expanding the *oecumene* that consists of the free market and voluntary human exchanges, and to realize that breaching and crippling that market and *oecumene* can only have disastrous consequences for the human race.[5]

In the standard account, writers and social theorists are supposed to mellow and moderate their views as they get older. (Two glorious exceptions to this rule are such very different libertarian figures as Lysander Spooner and Lord Acton.) Looking back over the two decades since writing this essay, it is clear that my views, on the contrary, have radicalized and polarized even further. As unlikely as it would have seemed twenty years ago, I am even more hostile to socialism, egalitarianism, and Romanticism, far more critical of the British classical and modern neoclassical tradition, and even more appreciative of Mises's great insights than ever before. Indeed, for someone who thought that he had absorbed all of Mises's work many years ago, it is a constant source of surprise how rereading Mises continues to provide a source of fresh insights and of new ways of looking at seemingly trite situations. This phenomenon, in which many of us have experience, bears testimony to the remarkable

---

[5]Joseph T. Salerno, "Ludwig von Mises as Social Rationalist," *Review of Austrian Economics* 4 (1990): 26–54. See also Salerno's critique of Eamonn Butler's uncomprehending reaction to Mises's insights, charging Mises with the "organic fallacy," and "difficulty with English." Ibid., p. 29n. The implicit contrast of Mises's view with Hayek's emphasis on unconscious action and blind adherence to traditional rules is made explicit by Salerno in the latter part of this article dealing with the socialist calculation debate, and in Salerno, "Postscript," in Ludwig von Mises, *Economic Calculation in the Socialist Commonwealth* (Auburn, Ala.: Ludwig von Mises Institute, 1990), pp. 51–71.

quality and richness of Mises's thought. Although he died almost two decades ago, Ludwig von Mises remains more truly alive than most of our conventionally wise contemporaries.

CHAPTER 11

Monopoly and Competition

We're entering the wild, wonderful world of monopoly and competition. To sum up from the last lecture, what's happened is that the words "monopoly" and "competition" have been changed. In the seventeenth, eighteenth, and nineteenth centuries, and also in the mind of the ordinary person even today, what competition means is competing; in other words, rivalry, trying to offer a better product or a cheaper price than the other guy, the next guy in the industry. Competing means acts of competing and, as I say, it's what the average person thinks of, what businessmen think of, when hearing the word "competition."

Also, a very important point, competition can be potential as well as active. Even if you have one firm in an industry, it could still suffer or be subjected to the rigors of competition, because if it raises prices and cuts production, another firm might come in and outcompete it, and then it's stuck with the other firm forever. And what business firms hate more than anything else is to bring in other competitors. And if they cut production and raise prices when they enjoy a monopoly price, then their higher profits will attract more competitors. Other capitalists will come in with new equipment and new plants, more modern equipment than this firm has. So potential competition is just as powerful as actual competition in the

Lecture presented at New York Polytechnic University in 1986.

minds of the businessmen. We have competing, either actual or potential or both.

"Monopoly" meant, from the seventeenth century on, a grant of exclusive privilege by the government. It means exclusively either one person or one firm or several firms. So, for example, the king of England gave to John Smith the monopoly of production of all playing cards in the kingdom of England. Anybody else who produced cards was shot. Doing this put you in a state of illegality, in other words.

Why did the government do this? John Smith benefits and the consumers suffer and potential competitors suffer. Suppose a given price and quantity supplied for playing cards, decks of cards. You say that only John Smith can produce it. That means you're shifting the supply curve to the left and you're forcing consumers to pay more for a lower quantity supplied. You're keeping out all other competitors, people who would want to produce cards if they were allowed to do it.

You should ask yourself this in all cases of government interference, who benefits and who pays. Who? Whom?[1] In other words, who is screwing whom in any act of government whatsoever? The beneficiary is John Smith, the monopolist with playing cards. The losers are the consumers and the competitors, the people who would have competed; excluded competitors, in other words. Also benefiting is the king and his bureaucracy. In the old days, the king would simply sell the monopoly privilege to John Smith. John Smith gets a monopoly privilege producing playing cards for twenty years; the king gets paid for it. And also the king or the government builds up a bureaucracy and builds up political allies, in this case John Smith. This, of course, is happening all the time, not just with monopolies but also with cost-plus contracts, in fact with any government contract.

Take, for example, the New York City scandals right now, the famous parking violation scandal The City administration had a question, who should get the computer contract—it wanted to buy computerized machines that search for parking violators. Two companies competed for the contract, Motorola—it's an old distinguished computer company—and an obscure little outfit called CompuSource, one nobody ever heard of. CompuSource gets the contract. CompuSource has no money and no computers yet. Why did they get the contract? Because Stanley Friedman, the distinguished head of the Bronx Democracy—the Bronx Democratic Party—was the lobbyist of

---

[1] Editor's note: Rothbard is alluding to Lenin's slogan, formulated in 1921.

the contract. Stanley Friedman received no money but, in return for getting the contract, received a majority shareholdership of the company. In other words, he got $1.5 million in shares as his legal fee. He became the majority shareholder to a previously non-existent company, which was formed only for the purpose of getting the contract.

Who benefits? The recipient of the monopoly privilege or contract, and the government official. So whether it's the king who does it or some city official who does it, it really doesn't make much difference. The government is in a position of selling monopoly privileges and people are then buying them.

If roulette wheels are outlawed, for example, but if a police captain allows a certain roulette wheel establishment to operate in his district and he's on the take from the company that does it, then the police captain is selling monopoly privileges. The monopoly privilege is operating a roulette wheel in that district. This sort of thing is going on all the time. This is essentially known as the Government-Industrial Complex. In the defense area, it's called the Military-Industrial Complex, but it's wider than that. It's the Government-Industrial Complex, the Government-Business-Complex, also known as Government-Business Partnership. We'll see that examples of exclusive privilege are rife, for example in the taxi industry, the airlines before deregulation, etc., etc., etc.

Now, to continue with monopoly—the American Revolution was fought largely against monopoly. In other words, against the British government, which had given to the East India Company, a corporation which had a monopoly of all trade with the Far East, the exclusive privilege to import tea into America. And the Americans rose up against them and dumped the tea in Boston Harbor, in the so-called Boston Tea Party. This was an attack not only on the tax but also on the monopoly privilege. When the first American states were created, they put provisions in their constitutions outlawing monopoly. What they intended, of course, was not outlawing what is now meant by monopoly in the textbooks. They meant no grants of monopoly privilege by the government. Of course, this has become a dead letter basically; but at least it was there in the state constitutions to express the fact the American Revolution was an anti-monopoly revolution as well as an anti-tax one.

To simplify the situation, these were the definitions of "competition" and "monopoly" until the 1930s, basically. In the 1930s, a crazy new theory in microeconomics was coined slightly earlier than Keynesian macroeconomics. What we've had in the last thirty years is a process of roll-back by which Keynesianism is getting increasingly discredited in macroeconomics, and none too soon; and also increasingly discredited is this new monopolistic competition theory, which, however, is still in the textbooks. In other words, it's been rolled back quite a bit. It's not taken as seriously as it used to be, in the 1930s. But it's still there, the alleged ideal of perfect competition.

During the 1930s, competition and monopoly were redefined. But the old terms were retained and they kept the old value connotation they had with their customary meanings. In other words, everybody was in favor of competition and against monopoly. The American public, economists, intellectuals, and everybody else agreed that competition was good and monopoly was bad. Or if they wanted to speak in so-called scientific terms, competition was efficient and monopoly was inefficient; but basically, this was another way of saying good and bad. And for obvious reasons they redefined the words "competition" and "monopoly," and then applied the same old value judgments, the emotional baggage these terms had, to a new set of definitions.

Competition was defined as a state not of competing, but as a state of so-called perfection and purity. Monopoly was a state of imperfection—monopolistic meant imperfect and impure. Now, notice the terms here. They're supposed to be value-free scientific terms. But perfect—who does not prefer perfection to imperfection? I mean, the very terminology gets you to be in favor of perfect. Who doesn't prefer pure to impure? Who doesn't prefer perfect competition to monopolistic competition? So the term "monopolistic competition" is used to suggest a negative value judgment.

And the redefinition was as follows. Competition meant a situation where each firm, not the industry but the firm, faces a horizontal demand curve, an infinitely elastic demand curve. And monopoly—or monopolistic competition, or impure, imperfect competition—it's all the same, bad—is defined as a situation where each firm faces a falling demand curve. That's it. Now, this is really the definition. You cut through all the jargon and all the junk in many chapters of the textbooks and this is the heart of the matter. Fortunately, Miller has less of such junk than you'll find in most other textbooks.

In previous lectures, I've already proved—and it took me several weeks to demonstrate this—that all demand curves are falling. Where then do we get this horizontal demand curve from? We get it in this way: The model is the wheat industry. There are two million wheat farms in the world and you have Hiram Jones, who has 100 acres of wheat in Iowa. If Hiram Jones is a very, very tiny proportion of the total wheat industry, whatever he does on his wheat farm doesn't make any difference to the price. In other words, if he increases his production like 20 percent, it's not going to make a big dent in the total supply. We can therefore assume, according to the theory, that he's facing a horizontal demand curve. In other words, he can increase his supply by cutting the fat. He can sell it at the same price because it makes a very tiny dent on the total. In this model of the ideal, every firm is so tiny that it can't affect its price, relative to the total quantity supplied by the industry. Whether it goes out of business or triples its production will have no effect on price. This is supposed to be an ideal situation. Everything else is imperfect, impure, monopolistic.

And, of course, each one of us is a monopolist, by the way. Each one of us faces a falling demand curve, We're all monopolists, every one of us, if we're engineers or economists or whatever, If you go out in the engineering labor market and you insist on a higher wage rate, a very high wage rate, you're going to see a falling off of demand for your services. For example, you insist that you won't work for IBM for less than $500,000 a year, you'll probably get disemployed very fast. What kind of a crazy system is it where everybody is a monopolist? Everybody except possibly Hiram Jones and the wheat industry. It makes very little sense.

The next point is trying to figure out why it is that competition is better than so-called monopoly. Why is it? What's so great about a horizontal demand curve anyway? And by the way, the result of this was, all during the 1930s and 1940s, the Anti-Trust Division, which was influenced by the economists who have this view, was trying to break up big business into small parts so as to duplicate the small wheat-farm situation. In other words, it's like taking General Motors and Ford and breaking them up into two million teeny little blacksmith shop-sized automobile plants. Automobiles used to be made in blacksmith shops and bicycle shops when the auto industry first got started in the 1900s. Bicycle shops used the wheel and axle technology, so they were able to shift to producing cars. But these shops were very small. You're grinding out two cars a month. That's the ideal of the perfect competition supporters.

I'll now give you the whole shtick, the full argument about, why is this better, why a falling demand curve is supposed to be evil.[2] I'm going to set forth for you now a series of insane assumptions, none of which are

---

2Editor's note: "Shtick" is a Yiddish word, here meaning "gimmick."

realistic, and all of which are flawed, deeply flawed. Using these assumptions, we wind up with the conclusion that competition in the sense of a horizontal demand curve is better than monopoly in the sense of a falling demand curve.

First of all, we need to consider the concept of final or long-run equilibrium. Now, long-run equilibrium is different from what I've been talking about, supply and demand on a day-to-day basis. Long-run equilibrium is this: In the real business world, there are lots of changes taking place in values and resources and technology. Suppose that the angel Gabriel came to the earth and froze everything, all value scales, resources, supply, labor, land, and technology, etc. Then, in a few years, you would wind up with every corporation making the same long-run interest rate say, 6 percent. In other words, there would be no pure profit and no pure losses, because everything would be the same all the time. If you can foresee everything, you're not going to make any losses If a firm is now making heavy profits, for example one in a capital-poor industry, new firms will enter the industry, until you wind up with the usual 6 percent. If industries are making losses, firms will leave. You wind up after a kind of shuffling back and forth after a few years with everybody making 6 percent, no more, no less—or 4 percent, whatever the interest rate is.

But remember, final equilibrium does not exit; never can exist; never has existed and never will exist. You can't freeze the data. The data are always changing. Value scales are changing, fashions are changing; technology changes, investment changes and labor changes. A lot is changing all the time. So you never get to long-run equilibrium.

The important thing about long-run equilibrium is to show you how to analyze profits and interest. Equilibrium shows you that profits and losses are a matter of forecasting, and interest is a matter of time preference. It's really an analysis of where the economy is going. It should not be taken seriously as an existing situation because it never has existed and it never will.

But what has happened, unfortunately in microeconomics since the 1930s is that long-run equilibrium has been taken seriously as not only existing, but as something which should exist. But it shouldn't. If it did, we'd all be in miserable shape. We'd be in a state of stasis; where nothing ever improved and nothing ever changed. It would be pretty miserable, like an ant heap or a beehive. Anyway, this is supposed to be the ideal situation.

In this situation where all firms earn the same return, you wind up geometrically with total cost tangent to total revenue at whatever the production point is. In the average-cost diagram, you have your U-shaped average-cost curve and you have an average-revenue curve—they would have to be tangent in final equilibrium.

And given a U-shaped average cost curve, we can compare what happens when a firm faces a horizontal demand curve and a falling demand curve. The points of tangency will be different. With a firm facing a falling demand curve, the output will be smaller and the price will be higher than a firm with a horizontal demand curve. That's it. That's the whole shtick. The supporters of perfect competition compare this to a monopoly privilege where the government excludes firms. Here you have a smaller product at a higher price. The conclusion they draw is that consumers are being screwed by a monopoly whenever a firm faces a falling demand curve. Therefore, the Anti-Trust Division should come in and break every firm up into teeny parts so as to get to the bottom of the average cost curve.

Now, to say there are many problems with this is putting it kindly. In the first place, mean, just one question: How big is this difference in price and quantity anyway? You're going to the trouble of breaking up firms. Is this difference one half of 1 percent or is it really important? Nobody knows. Remember, all laws in economics are qualitative. You might be going through this entire headache for a very small fraction of return. As a matter of fact, some economists have tried to estimate what this percentage is. It's something like 2 percent. But that's the least of the problems here.

One problem is, who says we have a U-shaped cost curve? As we've already seen, it's not really U-shaped. In most cases, the cost curve goes down and it's flat. In a flat plateau, none of this works. This whole thing is out the window because, first of all, the intersection point is now a whole area, not just one point. You have a whole range at which marginal costs and average costs are equal. It's possible that a falling demand curve could intersect with the cost curve at its lowest point.

Don't forget, there's nothing that says that the falling demand curve has to be linear. Remember, the linear part is truly for simplification purposes. Nobody knows that it's a straight line. All we know is that it's falling. There could be a little gap in the line. And so you could easily twist it around a little bit so that a falling demand curve, like a horizontal demand curve, could hit the cost curve at the bottom. With a flat bottom, the intersection point is pretty extensive.

Second of all, the model only works in equilibrium. In other words, the rest of the time, in the real world when there is no equilibrium, none of this applies. There's no way you can say that output is smaller or priced higher in so-called monopolistic situations. You can only show that in long-run equilibrium. Since there never is long-run equilibrium, this whole thing is pointless. This situation, tangency at one point, never exists in real life. It never can exist. It never will exist. And we'd be in bad shape if it did exist. There's nothing great about long-run equilibrium.

Also, and finally, and probably the most important point here is, who says that the cost curve would remain the same if large firms were broken up? Where is it written? In fact, it's just the opposite. If we took General Motors or Ford and broke them up into 500,000 or whatever number of teeny plants, each the size of the blacksmith shop, you might hit the bottom of the cost curve, it's true. But the cost curve would be extremely high because each plant would be very inefficient. You wouldn't capture the advantage of large-scale production. So you might get a price of $5 million per car, which only a few millionaires could afford. This is, by the way, what happened in the early days of the automobile. It was a toy for the rich. Diamond Jim Brady and his like could ride around in them. And only when Henry Ford introduced mass production and interchangeable parts could the average person ride.

So in other words, we could have inefficient production in an industry, but the consumers would have the thrill of knowing that each firm would be at the bottom of the cost curve. You would have eliminated the so-called monopoly here. On the other hand, unfortunately, you would be paying $5 million a car because each cost curve would be enormously higher than the cost curve under large-scale production. So the fallacy of the perfect competition school is to assume the cost curves are equal after breaking up large firms. Cost curves are never equal. And the reason for large-scale production is precisely because the cost-curve is lower.

So all this, I think, is to demonstrate the egregious fallacy with this whole idea that somehow perfect or pure competition is better than so-called monopolistic competition, that there's something evil about a falling demand curve.

So how did this whole idea arise? And the answer is interesting. It was partly in the anti-business climate of the 1930s that this kind of doctrine became popular. So what's been happening over the years is that the economics profession has been slowly rolling backward from this commitment to this crazy perfect-competition doctrine. But it's still there as an idea. It's still listed as the ideal outcome. And it'll take quite a while before that gets blasted loose, I'm afraid.

What's happening now is the economists have essentially stopped endorsing the idea of breaking up all businesses into tiny little blacksmith-shop size. But they're still somehow intellectually committed to this alleged ideal, largely because you see the U tangency in equations in differential calculus. If everything is tangent and in equilibrium and the curves are smoothly arcing and so forth, you also have beautiful equations of tangency and the graphs are great. This produces the alleged hard science of economics. Of course, this hard science is only alleged; it's really a fabrication of hard science. But as soon as you drop tangency and equilibrium and bring in the real world, the graphs and equations have to be either modified or eliminated. The "science" has to be abandoned.

Another feature of the perfect competition doctrine is that goods are "given." This means that you can't have any improvement. Any improvement is "monopolistic," because only one firm will come out with a new product or invention.

So according to this doctrine, if Polaroid is the first firm that comes out with the Polaroid process, it becomes monopolistic right away. "Monopoly," taken in the way perfect competition people use the term, is good because without it, you wouldn't have any improvements at all. Under their ideal, every firm would be like a small wheat farm. No firm would be able to invent a new product or a new process. There wouldn't be any computers. There wouldn't be any Xerox. There wouldn't be any Polaroid. There would be nothing, no calculators. Everybody would be stuck in the old wheat-farm kind of situation, where no one firm could do anything. No firm could even be active as a competing force, much less do anything else. So what I'm saying here is that the whole alleged ideal is a lot of hocus pocus; it's mumbo jumbo based on a whole series of crazy assumptions.

In real life, again, the real problem of monopoly is not the falling demand curve. There's nothing wrong with a falling demand curve. There's nothing inefficient or unethical or anything of the sort. The problem of monopoly is once again the same problems we had in the seventeenth, eighteenth, and nineteenth centuries, namely government grants of exclusive privilege, either for one firm or for several firms. That's really the situation when monopoly comes in. Cost-plus or exclusive contracts, or keeping out different parts of the industry and, thereby, shifting the supply curve to the left, raising prices, keeping out competitors, that sort of thing, This always has existed and always has been the problem with monopoly. It still is.

Let's see how this works. For example, before the deregulation of airlines, from the 1930s to a couple of years ago, [before 1986] we had the Civil Aeronautics Board. It's a lovely institution. It served as a cartelizing device, in other words, a monopolizing device. The CAB was lobbied for by the big airlines. It was essentially staffed by people from the big airlines. The idea was to exclude competing airlines and to assign monopoly routes and also to regulate the rates so the rate would keep going up. For example, I think only Eastern Airlines could do the New York to Boston route in those days. If anybody else tried to fly from New York to Boston, they were shot. In other words, they were considered illegal. They were excluded by the CAB. The CAB gave Certificates of Convenience and Necessity, I think they were called, to any airline on the route. If the CAB said, no, you can't fly on that route, you couldn't do it. There was no free market, no free enterprise in the airline industry. I think at one point Pan Am had the entire Pacific locked up. All routes to the Pacific had to be flown by Pan Am. I think Pan Am was the Republican Airline and TWA was the Democratic. The Democrats came in and they allowed TWA to fly that route.

And there still [i.e., in 1986] is, by the way, a very powerful international airline cartel, the IATA, International Airline Transport Association, that has a lock up on all European flights. Now those of you who have never flown to Europe will see, to your horror, that it's more expensive to fly from London to Frankfurt than it is from New York to London, because the intra-European flights are locked up by a very powerful inter-governmental cartel.

In other words, you have a rationing situation. You assign routes. You exclude everybody except one or two airlines on each route. You lock up particularly the major routes, the most profitable routes, and jack up the price.

Now originally, I think until as late as the 1950s, there was no such thing as First Class and Coach. All classes were First Class. Everything was extremely expensive, at least relatively speaking. But one thing you have to realize, which we'll emphasize in this course, is that a big company doesn't necessarily outcompete a small one. Sometimes small competitors are more efficient. And so, in this case, the small airlines came in and started out competing the big ones by offering cheaper service and a no-frills service. What you had then were heroic little airlines. There had names like Transamerica and Continental and Transcontinental. They were named the poor-people express. And immediately, the CAB and the rest of the airlines came in and prohibited them from scheduling their flights.

There was no safety problem, by the way. Safety is handled by the FAA, the Federal Aviation Administration. The CAB was purely in charge of economic monopoly; it was part of the airline business. And these small airlines had very good safety records, much better than the big airlines per mile flown. But the CAB said, "You guys are unfair competitors; we won't allow you to schedule your flights." In other words, they couldn't have any timetable. They had to sit there on the runway until they filled up. So they could only say, "We're flying on Tuesday." They couldn't say, "We're flying Tuesday at 11:00 a.m." They were prohibited by the law and by the CAB from doing that. They were non-scheduled airlines, called the non-scheds.

Even as non-scheds, they were able to outcompete the big airlines. They were able to fly people from New York to LA, let's say, for half the price of United or American or TWA. It's true, there were no frills. Some of these outfits used to weigh you along with the luggage. It was the maximum weight of you plus the luggage. Those of us who are on the heavyset side thought of it as a kind of discrimination. Still, in all, it's a trade-off, the ignominy of getting weighed against the fact that it costs you a lot less.

I remember my wife flew from Los Angeles to New York on a non-sched. I think it was Transamerica. It was very cheap. It was kind of scary. At one point, they announced, "Please, everybody, go to the back of the plane." It didn't give you a feeling of great confidence. Also, at one point, it was raining, and there was a leak in the ceiling of the plane. The stewardess, with great aplomb, went up there and took a Band-Aid and put it on the leak.

They didn't give you great security. On the other hand, they had a very good safety record. They had no crashes that I remember. And the competition of Transamerica and Transcontinental forced the big five to create a Coach section in the rear of their planes, with a fare cut in half of the First Class price. That was in the 1950s.

Finally, the CAB, they simply forced them out of business, saying, from now on, you can't fly anymore. That was the end of that, the end of Transamerica and the end of Transcontinental and the rest of them.

And there was another plane that went to Europe a friend of mine used to go on. It would fly to Iceland and Luxemburg, and on the return trip would land somewhere in a field in New Hampshire. You would then make your way to New York by train or bus, Again, it was very cheap, much cheaper than the official fares in that period.

What, happened when minimum fares were set by the CAB at a very high rate? There are all sorts of ways to compete. If you can't compete on the basis of price, you can compete on the basis of quality of service, the frills.

And so you start giving better food or swankier portions, prettier steward-esses and so on. These became the methods of competition rather than price.

At one point, IATA cracked down and said, from now on, no more hot meals on Trans-Atlantic flights. You can only have sandwiches. And so what the individual airlines started to do in order to break the cartel was to have open-faced sandwiches. They took the whole Beef Bourguignon dinner and put it on a piece of bread and called it a sandwich, in this way, getting around the crazy cartel regulations. You see this pattern frequently in economic history: the government puts on crazy regulations and the market tries to get around them.

What finally began to happen on the airlines is characteristic of government granted monopolies. If you're a monopoly, you've got a very high profit; but in the long-run, the profit gets competed away and costs rise. In other words, you have a high demand curve, which generates high profits. That increases your demand for workers and raw materials and these prices start going up. You have very high salaries, for example, for pilots and stewardesses, much higher for these big airlines than for anybody else, such as the un-scheduled type. You have very high costs, plush offices and so forth; and an enormous amount of inefficiency. You wound up after about forty years of this with the airlines losing money, even though they're monopolistic. This, by the way, is what happened with the railroads. Rail-roads were overbuilt. They were then regulated. Their fares were kept up by the Interstate Commerce Commission.

Finally, when the move for deregulation came in the late years of the Carter administration, 1978, the airlines were almost ready for it. They had to try something new. So they more or less went along with it, even though reluctantly, because the monopoly just wasn't working. They were just losing money anyway. And they began to realize, maybe we would do better under deregulation. Their love for monopoly had more or less withered away after forty years.

And as a result of deregulation, you had tremendous changes in the airline industry. Some lines went bankrupt. Other lines have popped up as new and effective competitors, like People's Express, which offers much cheaper fares. On the other hand, you're not quite sure when they're going to take off because they might sit there, loading up. And you realize that you pay for the difference.

So various outfits have been involved, and there has been a lot of reshuffling in the airline industry. Another development was the invention of the hub and spoke plan, which came about when the market began to realize this plan was more efficient. There are hub cities, like Denver, let's say. Instead of having a lot of non-stop flights from New York to Los Angeles, you stop at Denver. You have a lot of airlines coming in from other cities into Denver and going out again. Nobody could have predicted it in advance, but this is what happened.

To keep you up on the news since the term has started, the current *Time* magazine, on the front cover, it says "Oil Price, Cheap Oil, Good News." And underneath, it has a headline, "Cheap Oil, Bad News." And then it has a typical *Time*-type discussion, which is very middle of the road, having quotes from both sides, saying "Cheap oil, good; Cheap oil bad." In the latest political flap, Vice President George H.W. Bush, who is, indeed, a Texas oil man came out in favor of raising the price of oil, "stabilizing it," thereby violating the current principles of the Reagan administration.

The price of oil has magnificently fallen from $30—$35 a barrel several years ago to about $10 a barrel now (1986). In real terms, since prices in general have tripled in the last twenty years, it's the equivalent of about $3 a barrel in 1967 or so. It's just a little bit higher than before the OPEC Arab oil explosion in the early 1970s.

So what happens with any price change? Hysteria hits. Whether the price is going up or down, most of the establishment and most of the media are attacking it. A terrible thing; it'll cause inflation or a depression, depending on the nature of the price change. The claims can't both be right. It couldn't have been a terrible thing to raise the price of oil from three bucks to $35 and also terrible to go down to $10. You can't have it both ways, unless you think that any change whatsoever is bad, which is an idiotic position.

So what's the real story here? If you're a Texas oil man, you love the $35 barrel crude oil price. You don't like it going down to $10. On the other hand, who cares about Texas oil men? Why should they set the standard for how we decide something?

You shouldn't judge these price changes by taking Gallup polls or asking a Texas congressman and a New England congressman. What you should do is figure out where the consumers stand on this thing. The whole point of production of an economy in general is for consumption. The whole point of producing oil is that it will eventually get to the consumer in the form of kerosene, gasoline, heating oil, or whatever it'll be used for. From the days of the caveman to the present, more and more consumer wants are being satisfied. The standard of living keeps going up. Everything gets cheaper and more abundant. The choices available to the consumer keep improving and increasing. New products come on the market and the old products get cheaper. That's what an increased standard of living means, that the consumers can get more and more goods and services.

So we know how to judge any price change up or down, namely, cheaper is better, Hold it in your heart. This of course, is what the average person's reaction is anyway. What you find in economics is that the average person's immediate reaction is usually correct. Unfortunately, this reaction is often misdirected by phony economics and bad advice people get from the media. Of course, if you have maximum price controls, you screw everything up. I'm talking about cheaper on the free market. A cheaper market is an expression of increased supply. Cheaper prices often result from breaking up cartels, and cartels are our next topic.

Notice some of the phony arguments you get about cheap prices. One is that the trouble with cheaper oil is that people use a lot of it and then it'll get more expensive. In response, we worry about it if and when it does get more expensive. You don't say that you have to jack up the price of oil now and re-establish the cartel, essentially what Bush wants to do, to avoid an increase in the price of oil ten years from now. The whole concept is nuts. That's an argument so ridiculous, nobody can really hold it. These arguments are advanced for sinister economic interests. By "sinister," I mean interests that want to re-establish the cartel, jack up the price of oil and lower the supply, against the public interest. Texas oil people want to do these things, of course.

The cartel is the situation where suppliers of any sort try to band together to restrict the supply and raise the price, taking advantage of an alleged inelastic demand curve. Let's assume the demand curve for the industry is inelastic. We know, of course, the demand curve of every firm is elastic. It's fairly flat. If, for example, Wonder Bread tried to raise the price to two bucks a loaf, nobody's going to buy it, except a couple of the very wealthy Wonder Bread fanatics. Everybody will shift to Pepperidge Farm or Tasty Bread. But if all the bread firms get together and try to raise the price, they're trying to go up their industry demand curve. This industry demand curve doesn't have to be inelastic; but if it is, firms are tempted to try to restrict production and raise the price, thereby benefiting each firm and screwing the consumer.

Most people think it's easy to have a cartel, but in this case, the average person has the wrong instincts. Let's say General Electric and Westinghouse are essentially a two-firm electrical industry. The vice presidents of each company get together over at the Union League Club and one says to the other, "Hey, Jim, why don't we increase our price by 20 percent? We'll both do it, and because we'll have an inelastic demand curve, we'll have increased profits." And Jim says, "That's a great idea, Joe." People think that's the end of it, but it isn't. It's very difficult to establish a cartel, even disregarding the anti-trust laws.

The reason is this. In order to have a viable rise in price, they have to cut production. But every businessman hates to cut production. Every businessman wants to expand his operations. So to form a cartel is a very difficult process, requiring months of negotiations.

Let's say that two or three firms in the industry each agree to cut production by 15 percent, using 1985 as the base year to determine the cuts. Well, they can do that. In a year or so, though, each one will say, "I've got new machines. I've got better equipment. I've got new products. Why should I be bound by the 1985 restrictions when I know that if I expand production, I can outcompete these other firms now? I can get a bigger share of the market." Each firm has to believe that, because to be an entrepreneur, you have to be an optimist. You're spending a lot of money, investing a lot of money. And pessimists don't last long in business. And so the cartel quotas tend to be busted. Each businessman tries to renegotiate the cartel agreement. They say, "I've got a better product. I want to increase my production this year." And the rival says, "No, you can't do that; you're violating the quota." And often, the whole agreement breaks up in mutual recriminations of hatred. So it's very difficult to maintain sustained quotas of this sort over time.

And, in addition to that, each firm has a tremendous temptation to cheat. They're restricted in production by 15 percent. They have a higher price and each is making higher profits. Each one says, "If I can cut my price secretly, I could pick up an enormous increase in sales. I'll go down the firm demand curve and make millions." So he goes to his customer, and says, "Look, Jim, I'll give you a secret discount, a rebate of 15 percent or 20 percent. Don't tell Westinghouse about it, because we have a cartel agreement to keep prices up and cut production." After about six months, everybody spies on everybody else. Each firm finds out that the others cheat and the whole cartel breaks up in mutual hatred.

When the railroads were the big business in the nineteenth century, a person who owned two railroads would form a pool or a cartel with another railroad. He couldn't get his own managers not to cheat. Each vice-president in charge of sales was devoted to increasing sales and hated to make cuts. Even though the one tycoon owned both railroads, the mangers still cheated.

Another reason cartels break up stems from the fact that there's a lot of loose capital around. Capitalists throughout the world, who have a lot of money they'd like to invest, are looking around for profitable investments. When they see a profitable cartel, they say, "Let's go in and put in a new plant, new equipment, and undercut the cartel." So a new capitalist comes in. They create a new railroad or a new plant. And the old firms are now confronted with this new plant with better equipment. Because it's starting from scratch, it's going to have new modern equipment. And then they're faced with a question: Either they have to cut the new firm into the cartel, which means they might have to cut their own production by 30 percent. Otherwise, the whole cartel gets busted, and you're back down again to square zero.

And when you have external pressure, when a new sugar refining plant comes in or a new shoe production plant or a new railroad, the new firm is there permanently. No industry likes the situation where a high-profit umbrella invites new, unwelcome competitors into the industry.

Every cartel in history, in the world, has broken up on the free market, very quickly broken up. It doesn't take very long either, a year or two. The cartel has to break up. The only thing which can sustain a cartel is government intervention, compulsory cartels to keep the price up, keep production limited, and keep new firms from coming in. This is a compulsory cartel, when the government comes in and forces the establishment of a cartel. It's the essence of what we're living under right now, whether you want to call it the warfare state, or the warfare-welfare state. Essentially, we have a cartelizing state where government intervenes to try to cartelize different industries.

CHAPTER 12

Are Diamonds Really Forever?

The international diamond cartel, the most successful cartel in history, far more successful than the demonized OPEC, is at last falling on hard times. For more than a century, the powerful DeBeers Consolidated Mines, a South African corporation controlled by the Rothschild Bank in London, has managed to organize the cartel, restricting the supply of diamonds on the market and raising the price far above what would have been market levels.

It is not simply that DeBeers mines much of the world's diamonds; DeBeers has persuaded the world's diamond miners to market virtually all their diamonds through DeBeer's Central Selling Organization (CSO), which then grades, distributes, and sells all the rough diamonds to cutters and dealers further down on the road toward the consumer.

Even an unchallenged cartel, of course, does not totally control its price or its market; even it is at the mercy of consumer demand. One of the reasons that diamond prices and profits are slumping is the current world recession. World demand, and particularly consumer demand in the US for diamonds, has fallen sharply, with consumers buying fewer diamonds and downgrading their purchases to cheaper gems, which of course particularly hits the market in the expensive stones.

Reprinted from *The Free Market* 10, no. 11 (November 1992).

But how could even this degree of cartel success occur in a free market? Economic theory and history both tell us that maintaining a cartel, for any length of time, is almost impossible on the free market, as the firms who restrict their supply are challenged by cartel members who secretly cut their prices in order to expand their share of the market as well as by new producers who enter the fray enticed by their higher profits attained by the cartelists. So, how could DeBeers maintain such a flourishing, century-long cartel on the free market?

The answer is simple: the market has not been really free. In particular, in South Africa, the major center of world diamond production, there has been no free enterprise in diamond mining.

The government long ago nationalized all diamond mines, and anyone who finds a diamond mine on his property discovers that the mine immediately becomes government property. The South African government then licenses mine operators who lease the mines from the government and, it so happened, that lo and behold!, the only licensees turned out to be either DeBeers itself or other firms who were willing to play ball with the DeBeers cartel. In short: the international diamond cartel was only maintained and has only prospered because it was enforced by the South African government.

And enforced to the hilt: for there were severe sanctions against any independent miners and merchants who tried to produce "illegal" diamonds, even though they were mined on what used to be private property. The South African government has invested considerable resources in vessels that constantly patrol the coast, firing on and apprehending the supposedly pernicious diamond "smugglers."

Back in the pre-Gorbachev era, it was announced that Russia had discovered considerable diamond resources. For a while, there was fear among DeBeers and the cartelists that the Russians would break the international diamond cartel by selling in the open market abroad. Never fear, however. The Soviet government, as a professional monopolist itself, was happy to cut a deal with DeBeers and receive an allocation of their own quota of diamonds to sell to the CSO.

But now the CSO and DeBeers are in trouble. The problem is not only the recession; the very structure of the cartel is at stake, with the problem centering on the African country of Angola.

Not that the communist government (or formerly communist, but now quasi-communist, government) refuses to cooperate with the cartel. It always has. The problem is threefold. First, even though the Angolan civil war is over, the results have left the government powerless to control most of the country. Second, the end of the war has given independent wildcatters access to the Cuango River in northern Angola, a territory rich in diamonds. And third, the African-drought has dried up the Cuango along with other rivers, leaving the rich alluvial diamond deposits in the beds and on the banks of the Cuango accessible to the eager prospectors.

With the diamond deposits available and free of war, and the central government unable to enforce the cartel, 50,000 prospectors have happily poured into the Cuango Valley of Angola. Furthermore, the prospectors are being protected by a private army of demobilized but armed Angolan soldiers. As one Johannesburg broker pointed out, "If you fly a patrol over the province you can get shot down by a missile. And it's a 100-mile river. You can't put a fence around it."

So far, DeBeers has been holding the line by buying up the "over-supply" caused by the influx of Angolan diamonds; this year, the cartel may be forced to buy no less than $500 million in "illegal" Angolan diamonds, twice as much as that country's official output. Consequently, DeBeers is taking heavy losses; as a result, Julian Ogilvie Thompson, the arrogant and aristocratic chairman of DeBeers, was forced to announce that the company was slashing its dividend, for only the second time since World War II. Immediately, DeBeers' shares plummeted by one-third, taking with it much of the Johannesburg Stock Exchange.

Overall, DeBeers's CSO had to purchase $4.8 billion of rough diamonds in 1992, while being able to sell only $3.5 billion. This huge pileup of inventory could break the cartel price; to stave off such a perceived disaster, DeBeers ordered cartel members to cut back 2.5 percent on the diamonds they had already contracted to market through the cartel. Such a large cutback sets the stage for individual firms to sneak supplies into the market and evade the cartel restrictions.

No wonder that Sir Harry Oppenheimer, the octogenarian head of DeBeers, decided to "vacation" in Russia at the end of August, presumably to persuade the Russians to resist any temptation to engage in free-market competition in the diamond market. With luck, however, the forces of free competition—as well as the world's consumers of diamonds—may triumph.

CHAPTER 13

The Infant-Industry Argument

The "infant-industry" argument has been considered as the only justifiable ground for a protective tariff by many "neoclassical" economists. The substance of the argument was clearly stated by one of its most noted exponents, Professor F.W. Taussig:

> The argument is that while the price of the protected article is temporarily raised by the duty, eventually it is lowered. Competition sets in ... and brings a lower price in the end. ... [T]his reduction in domestic price comes only with the lapse of time. At the outset the domestic producer has difficulties, and cannot meet foreign competition. In the end he learns how to produce to best advantage, and then can bring the article to market as cheaply as the foreigner, even more cheaply.[1]

---

[1]F.W. Taussig, *Principles of Economics*, 2nd ed. rev. (New York: Macmillan 1916), p. 527. Taussig went on to assert that "the theoretical validity of this argument has been admitted by almost all economists," and that the difficulties lay in the practical application of the policy.

Originally prepared for the William Volker Fund; date unknown. Reprinted in *Strictly Confidential: The Private Volker Fund Memos of Murray N. Rothbard*, David Gordon, ed. (Auburn, Ala.: Mises Institute,2010), pp. 249–53.

Thus, older competitors are alleged to have historically acquired skill and capital that enable them to outcompete any new "infant" rivals. Wise protection of the government for the new firms will, in the long run, promote, rather than hinder, competition.

The troublesome question arises; if long-run prospects in the new industry are so promising, why does private enterprise, ever on the lookout for profitable investment opportunities, persistently fail to enter the new field? Such unwillingness to invest signifies that such investment would be uneconomic, i.e., would waste capital and labor that might otherwise be invested in satisfying more urgent wants of consumers.

An infant industry will be established if the superiority of the new location outweighs the economic disadvantages of abandoning already-existing, nontransferable capital goods in the older plants. If that is the case, then the new industry will compete successfully with the old without benefit of special governmental protection. If the superiorities do not balance the disadvantages, then government protection constitutes a subsidy causing a wastage of scarce factors of production. Labor and capital (including land) is wastefully expended in building new plants, when an existing plant could have been used more economically. Consumers are forced to pay a subsidy for a wastage of goods needed to serve their wants. This does not imply that if, at one time, an infant industry is unprofitable on the free market, and hence uneconomic, that such will always be the case. In many instances, the new location becomes superior after a portion of the existing capital goods in the old plants has been allowed to wear away.

Protectionist economic historians are under pains to assert that no important infant industry can be established without substantial tariff protection against entrenched foreign competition. The high degree of tariff protection in the greater part of the history of the United States, has made this preeminent industrial country a favorite "proof" of the infant-industry argument.

Ironically, it is the United States that provides the most striking illustrations of the fallaciousness of the infant-industry doctrine. Within its vast borders, the United States offers an example of one of the world's largest free-trade areas. The frequent regional shifts in American industries provide numerous examples of birth and growth of infant industries, and decline of old, established industries. One of the most striking examples is that of the cotton textile industry.

One of America's important industries, cotton textiles were manufactured almost exclusively in New England from 1812 to 1880. During that period, there were practically no textile plants in the cotton-growing areas of the South. In 1880, the cotton textile industry began to grow rapidly in the South, rising at a far greater rate than the industry in the "entrenched" New England area, despite absence of special protection. By 1925, half of the country's cotton textile production occurred in the South. In the early 1920s, moreover, cotton textile production in New England began a sharp absolute decline as well, so that, at present, the South produces approximately three-fourths of the country's cotton textiles, and the New England area less than one-fourth.[2]

Another striking example of a regional shift is the clothing industry, which was highly concentrated in New York City and Chicago (close to the retail markets) until the 1921 depression. At that time, under the pressure of union-maintained wage rates and work rules in the face of falling prices, the clothing industry moved with great rapidity to disperse in rural areas. Other important shifts have been the relative dispersal of steelmaking from the Pittsburgh area, the growth of coal mining in West Virginia, airplane manufacturing in California, etc.

Logically, the "infant-industry" argument must apply to interlocal and regional as well as national trade, and failure to apply it to those areas is one of the reasons for the persistence of this point of view. Logically extended, the argument would imply that it is difficult or impossible for any firm to exist and grow against the competition of existing firms in the industry, wherever located. Illustrations of this growth, and of decay of old firms, however, are innumerable, particularly in the United States. That, in many instances, a firm with almost no capital can successfully outcompete a firm with existing "entrenched" capital need only be demonstrated by

---

[2]Cf. Jules Backman and Martin Gainsbrugh, *Economics of the Cotton Textile Industry* (New York: National Industrial Conference Board, 1946). Some of the reasons for the shift in capital from North to South were (1) lower wage rates for comparable labor in the South—about half in 1900; (2) development of power in the South; (3) more rapid unionization in the North, and hence, shorter hours, and great work restrictions, raising the unit labor cost; (4) earlier wage and hour legislation in the North; (5) higher taxes in the North. These factors took on greater importance after World War I, when immigration restrictions sharply reduced the supply of mill labor in the North, while the labor supply of the poor Ozark Southerners continued to be plentiful, and when unions and social legislation became more powerful.

the case of the lowly peddler, who is legally banned or restricted at the instance of his rivals throughout the world.

HISTORICAL APPENDIX

It is ironic that the American cotton textile industry provides a major example of the growth of an unprotected infant industry, for the infant-industry argument first came into prominence precisely in connection with this industry. Although the infant-industry argument has been traced back to mid-seventeenth-century England,[3] it was first widely used after the War of 1812 in America. During the war, when foreign trade had practically ceased, American capital turned to investment in domestic manufactures, particularly cotton textiles in New England and the Mid-Atlantic states. After 1815, these new firms had to compete with established English and East Indian competition. The protectionists first appeared in force upon the American scene, urging that the new industry must be protected in its infant stages. Mathew Carey, Philadelphia printer, brought the argument into prominence, and he exerted great influence on young Friedrich List, who was later to become the infant-industry argument's best-known advocate.[4]

---

[3]Cf. Jacob Viner, *Studies in the Theory of International Trade* (New York: Harper and Brothers, 1937), pp. 71–72.

[4]Cf. Mathew Carey, *Essays in Political Economy* (Philadelphia: H.C. Carey & I. Lea, 1822); Joseph Dorfman, *Economic Mind in American Civilization*, vols. 1 and 2 (New York: Viking Press, 1946).

CHAPTER 14

Airport Congestion: A Case of Market Failure?

The press touted it as yet another chapter in the unending success story of "government-business cooperation." The traditional tale is that a glaring problem arises, caused by the unchecked and selfish actions of capitalist greed. And that then a wise and farsighted government agency, seeing deeply and having only the public interest at heart, steps in and corrects the failure, its sage regulations gently but firmly bending private actions to the common good.

The latest chapter began in the summer of 1984, when it came to light that the public was suffering under a 73 percent increase in the number of delayed flights compared to the previous year. To the Federal Aviation Agency (FAA) and other agencies of government, the villain of the piece was clear. Its own imposed quotas on the number of flights at the nation's airports had been lifted at the beginning of the year, and, in response to this deregulation, the shortsighted airlines, each pursuing its own profits, over-scheduled their flights in the highly remunerative peak hours of the day. The congestion and delays occurred at these hours, largely at the biggest and most used airports. The FAA soon made it clear that it was prepared to impose detailed, minute-by-minute maximum limits on takeoffs and landings at each airport, and threatened to do so if the airlines themselves did

Reprinted from *The Free Market* 3, no. 1 (January 1986).

not come up with an acceptable plan. Under this bludgeoning, the airlines came up with a "voluntary" plan that was duly approved at the end of October, a plan that imposed maximum quotas of flights at the peak hours. Government-business cooperation had supposedly triumphed once more.

The real saga, however, is considerably less cheering. From the beginning of the airline industry until 1978, the Civil Aeronautics Board (CAB) imposed a coerced cartelization on the industry, parceling out routes to favored airlines, and severely limiting competition, and keeping fares far over the free-market price. Largely due to the efforts of CAB chairman and economist Alfred E. Kahn, the Airline Deregulation Act was passed in 1978, deregulating routes, flights, and prices, and abolishing the CAB at the end of 1984.

What has really happened is that the FAA, previously limited to safety regulation and the nationalization of air traffic control services, has since then moved in to take up the torch of cartelization lost by the CAB. When President Reagan fired the air-controllers during the PATCO strike in 1981, a little-heralded consequence was that the FAA stepped in to impose coerced maxima of flights at the various airports, all in the name of rationing scarce air-control services. An end of the air-controller crisis led the FAA to remove the controls in early 1984, but now here they are more than back again as a result of the congestion.

Furthermore, the quotas are now in force at the six top airports. Leading the parade in calling for the controls was Eastern Airlines, whose services using Kennedy and LaGuardia airports have, in recent years, been outcompeted by scrappy new People's Express, whose operations have vaulted Newark Airport from a virtual ghost airport to one of the top six (along with LaGuardia, Kennedy, Denver, Atlanta, and O'Hare at Chicago.) In imposing the "voluntary" quotas, it does not seem accidental that the peak hour flights at Newark Airport were drastically reduced (from 100 to 68), while the LaGuardia and Kennedy peak hour flights were actually increased.

But, in any case, was the peak hour congestion a case of market failure? Whenever economists see a shortage, they are trained to look immediately for the maximum price control below the free market. And sure enough, this is what has happened. We must realize that all commercial airports in this country are government-owned and operated—all by local governments except Dulles and National, owned by the federal government. And governments are not interested, as is private enterprise, in rational pricing, that is, in a pricing that achieves the greatest profits.

Other political considerations invariably take over. And so every airport charges fees for its "slots" (landing and takeoff spots on its runways) far below the market-clearing price that would be achieved under private ownership. Hence congestion occurs at valuable peak hours, with private corporate jets taking up space from which they would obviously be out-competed by the large commercial airliners. The only genuine solution to airport congestion is to impose market-clearing pricing, with far higher slot fees at peak than at non-peak hours. And this would accomplish the task while encouraging rather than crippling competition by the compulsory rating of underpriced slots imposed by the FAA. But such rational pricing will only be achieved when airports are privatized—taken out of the inefficient and political control of government.

There is also another important area to be privatized. Air control services are a compulsory monopoly of the federal government, under the aegis of the FAA. Even though the FAA promised to be back to pre-strike air control capacity by 1983, it still employs 19 percent fewer air controllers than before the strike, all trying to handle 6 percent greater traffic.

Once again, the genuine solution is to privatize air-traffic control. There is no real reason why pilots, aircraft companies, and all other aspects of the airline industry can be private, but that somehow air control must always remain a nationalized service. Upon the privatization of air control, it will be possible to send the FAA to join the CAB in the forgotten scrap heap of history.

CHAPTER 15

The Union Problem

L abor unions are flexing their muscles again. Last year, a strike against the *New York Daily News* succeeded in inflicting such losses upon the company that it was forced to sell cheap to British tycoon Robert Maxwell, who was willing to accept union terms. Earlier, the bus drivers' union struck Greyhound and managed to win a long and bloody strike. How were the unions able to win these strikes, even though unions have been declining in numbers and popularity since the end of World War II? The answer is simple: in both cases, management hired replacement workers and tried to keep producing. In both cases, systematic violence was employed against the product and against the replacement workers.

In the *Daily News* strike, the *Chicago Tribune* Company, which owned the *News*, apparently did not realize that the New York drivers' union had traditionally been in the hands of thugs and goons; what the union apparently did was commit continuing violence against the newsstands—injuring the newsdealers and destroying their stands, until none would carry the *News*. The police, as is typical almost everywhere outside the South, were instructed to remain "neutral" in labor disputes, that is, look the other way when unions employ gangster tactics against employers and non-striking workers. In fact, the only copies of the News

---

Reprinted from *The Free Market* (December 1991); reprinted in *Making Economic Sense* (1995, 2006).

visible during the long strike were those sold directly to the homeless, who peddled them in subways. Apparently, the union felt that beating up or killing the homeless would not do much for its public relations image. In the Greyhound strike, snipers repeatedly shot at the buses, injuring drivers and passengers. In short, the use of violence is the key to the winning of strikes.

Union history in America is filled with romanticized and overblown stories about violent strikes: the Pullman strike, the Homestead strike, and so on. Since labor historians have almost all been biased in favor of unions, they strongly imply that almost all the violence was committed by the employer's guards, wantonly beating up strikers or union organizers. The facts are quite the opposite. Almost all the violence was committed by union goon squads against the property of the employer, and in particular, against the replacement workers, invariably smeared and dehumanized with the ugly word "scabs." (Talk about demeaning language!)

The reason unions are to blame is inherent in the situation. Employers don't want violence; all they want is peace and quiet, the unhampered and peaceful production and shipment of goods. Violence is disruptive, and is bound to injure the profits of the company. But the victory of unions depends on making it impossible for the company to continue in production, and therefore they must zero in on their direct competitors, the workers who are replacing them.

Pro-union apologists often insist that workers have a "right to strike." No one denies that. Few people—except for panicky instances where, for example, President Truman threatened to draft striking steel workers into the army and force them back into the factories—advocate forced labor. Everyone surely has the right to quit. But that's not the issue. The issue is whether the employer has the right to hire replacement workers and continue in production.

Unions are now flexing their muscle politically as well, to pass legislation in Congress to prohibit employers from hiring permanent replacement workers, that is, from telling the strikers, in effect: "OK, you quit, so long!" Right now, employers are already severely restricted in this right: they cannot hire permanent replacement workers, that is, fire the strikers, in any strikes over "unfair labor" practices. What Congress should do is extend the right to fire to these "unfair labor" cases as well.

In addition to their habitual use of violence, the entire theory of labor unions is deeply flawed. Their view is that the worker somehow "owns" his job, and that therefore it should be illegal for an employer to bid permanent farewell to striking workers. The "ownership of jobs" is of course a clear violation of the property right of the employer to fire or not hire anyone he wants. No one has a "right to a job" in the future; one only has the right to be paid for work contracted and already performed. No one should have the "right" to have his hand in the pocket of his employer forever; that is not a "right" but a systematic theft of other people's property.

Even when the union does not commit violence directly, it should be clear that the much revered picket line, sanctified in song and story, is nothing but a thuggish attempt to intimidate workers or customers from crossing the line. The idea that picketing is simply a method of "free expression" is ludicrous: if you want to inform a town that there's a strike, you can have just one picket, or still less invasively, take out ads in the local media. But even if there is only one picket, the question then arises: on whose property does one have the right to picket, or to convey information? Right now, the courts are confused or inconsistent on the question: do strikers have the right to picket on the property of the targeted employer? This is clearly an invasion of the property right of the employer, who is forced to accept a trespasser whose express purpose is to denounce him and injure his business.

What of the question: does the union have the right to picket on the sidewalk in front of a plant or of a struck firm? So far, that right has been accepted readily by the courts. But the sidewalk is usually the responsibility of the owner of the building abutting it, who must maintain it, keep it unclogged, etc. In a sense, then, the building owner also "owns" the sidewalk, and therefore the general ban on picketing on private property should also apply here.

The union problem in the United States boils down to two conditions in crying need of reform. One is the systematic violence used by striking unions. That can be remedied, on the local level, by instructing the cops to defend private property, including that of employers; and, on the federal level by repealing the infamous Norris-LaGuardia Act of 1932, which prohibits the federal courts from issuing injunctions against the use of violence in labor disputes.

Before 1932, these injunctions were highly effective in blocking union violence. The act was passed on the basis of much-esteemed but phony research by Felix Frankfurter, who falsely claimed that the injunctions had been issued not against violence but against strikes *per se*.[1]

The second vital step is to repeal the sainted "Wagner Act" (National Labor Relations Act) of 1935, which still remains, despite modifications, the fundamental law of labor unions in the United States, and in those states that have patterned themselves after federal law. The Wagner Act is misleadingly referred to in economics texts as the bill that "guarantees labor the right to bargain collectively." Bunk. Labor unions have always had that right. What the Wagner Act did was to force employers to bargain collectively "in good faith" with any union which the federal National Labor Relations Board decides has been chosen in an NLRB election by a majority of the "bargaining unit"—a unit which is defined arbitrarily by the NLRB.

Workers in the unit who voted for another union, or for no union at all, are forced by the law to be "represented" by that union. To establish this compulsory collective bargaining, employers are prevented from firing union organizers, are forced to supply unions with organizing space, and are forbidden to "discriminate" against union organizers.

In other words, we have been suffering from compulsory collective bargaining since 1935. Unions will never meet on a "fair playing field" and we will never have a free economy until the Wagner and Norris-LaGuardia Acts are scrapped as a crucial part of the statism that began to grip this country in the New Deal, and has never been removed.

---

[1]For a masterful and definitive refutation of Frankfurter, which unfortunately came a half-century too late, see Sylvester Petro, "Unions and the Southern Courts—The Conspiracy and Tort Foundations of Labor Injunction," *The North Carolina Law Review* (March 1982): 544–629.

CHAPTER 16

Outlawing Jobs:
The Minimum Wage,
Once More

There is no clearer demonstration of the essential identity of the two political parties than their position on the minimum wage. The Democrats proposed to raise the legal minimum wage from $3.35 an hour, to which it had been raised by the Reagan administration during its allegedly free-market salad days in 1981. The Republican counter was to allow a "sub-minimum" wage for teenagers, who, as marginal workers, are the ones who are indeed hardest hit by any legal minimum.

This stand was quickly modified by the Republicans in Congress, who proceeded to argue for a teenage subminimum that would last only a piddling ninety days, after which the rate would rise to the higher Democratic minimum (of $4.55 an hour). It was left, ironically enough, for Senator Edward Kennedy to point out the ludicrous economic effect of this proposal: to induce employers to hire teenagers and then fire them after eighty-nine days, to rehire others the day after.

Finally, and characteristically, George Bush got the Republicans out of this hole by throwing in the towel altogether, and plumping for a Democratic plan, period. We were left with the Democrats forthrightly proposing a big increase in the minimum wage, and the Republicans, after a series of illogical waffles, finally going along with the program.

Reprinted from *The Free Market* (December 1998); reprinted in *Making Economic Sense* (Auburn, Ala.: Mises Institute, 1995, 2006).

In truth, there is only one way to regard a minimum wage law: it is *compulsory unemployment*, period. The law says: it is illegal, and therefore criminal, for anyone to hire anyone else below the level of X dollars an hour. This means, plainly and simply, that a large number of free and voluntary wage contracts are now outlawed and hence that there will be a large amount of unemployment. Remember that the minimum wage law provides no jobs; it only outlaws them; and outlawed jobs are the inevitable result.

All demand curves are falling, and the demand for hiring labor is no exception. Hence, laws that prohibit employment at any wage that is relevant to the market (a minimum wage of 10 cents an hour would have little or no impact) must result in outlawing employment and hence causing unemployment.

If the minimum wage is, in short, raised from $3.35 to $4.55 an hour, the consequence is to disemploy, permanently, those who would have been hired at rates in between these two rates. Since the demand curve for any sort of labor (as for any factor of production) is set by the perceived marginal productivity of that labor, this means that the people who will be disemployed and devastated by this prohibition will be precisely the "marginal" (lowest wage) workers, e.g., blacks and teenagers, the very workers whom the advocates of the minimum wage are claiming to foster and protect.

The advocates of the minimum wage and its periodic boosting reply that all this is scare talk and that minimum wage rates do not and never have caused any unemployment. The proper riposte is to raise them one better; all right, if the minimum wage is such a wonderful anti-poverty measure, and can have no unemployment-raising effects, why are you such pikers? Why you are helping the working poor by such piddling amounts? Why stop at $4.55 an hour? Why not $10 an hour? $100? $1,000?

It is obvious that the minimum wage advocates do not pursue their own logic, because if they push it to such heights, virtually the entire labor force will be disemployed. In short, *you can have as much unemployment as you want*, simply by pushing the legally minimum wage high enough.

It is conventional among economists to be polite, to assume that economic fallacy is solely the result of intellectual error. But there are times when decorousness is seriously misleading, or, as Oscar Wilde once wrote, "when speaking one's mind becomes more than a duty; it becomes a positive pleasure." For if proponents of the higher minimum wage were simply wrong-headed people of good will, they would not stop at $3 or $4 an hour, but indeed would pursue their dimwit logic into the stratosphere.

The fact is that they have always been shrewd enough to stop their minimum wage demands at the point where only marginal workers are affected, and where there is no danger of disemploying, for example, white adult male workers with union seniority. When we see that the most ardent advocates of the minimum wage law have been the AFL-CIO, and that the concrete effect of the minimum wage laws has been to cripple the low-wage competition of the marginal workers as against higher-wage workers with union seniority, the true motivation of the agitation for the minimum wage becomes apparent.

This is only one of a large number of cases where a seemingly purblind persistence in economic fallacy only serves as a mask for special privilege at the expense of those who are supposedly to be "helped."

In the current agitation, inflation—supposedly brought to a halt by the Reagan administration—has eroded the impact of the last minimum wage hike in 1981, reducing the real impact of the minimum wage by 23 percent. Partially as a result, the unemployment rate has fallen from 11 percent in 1982 to under 6 percent in 1988. Possibly chagrined by this drop, the AFL-CIO and its allies are pushing to rectify this condition, and to boost the minimum wage rate by 34 percent.

Once in a while, AFL-CIO economists and other knowledgeable liberals will drop their mask of economic fallacy and candidly admit that their actions will cause unemployment; they then proceed to justify themselves by claiming that it is more "dignified" for a worker to be on welfare than to work at a low wage. This of course, is the doctrine of many people on welfare themselves. It is truly a strange concept of "dignity" that has been fostered by the interlocking minimum wage-welfare system.

Unfortunately, this system does not give those numerous workers who still prefer to be producers rather than parasites the privilege of making their own free choice.

CHAPTER 17

The Myth of Tax "Reform"

Everyone will agree that the American tax system is a mess. Taxes are far too high, and the patchwork system is so complicated that even IRS officials don't understand it. Hence the evident need for some sort of dramatic, even drastic, reform. As often happens, a group of dedicated and determined reformers has arisen to satisfy that need. But before we embrace this new gospel, we should heed the old maxim about jumping from the frying pan into the fire, and also remember the warning of the great H.L. Mencken, who defined "reform" as "Mainly a conspiracy of prehensile charlatans to mulct the American taxpayer." And we should also bear in mind that all acts of government, however worthy they may seem, have a way of winding up solving no problems and only making matters worse.

Working within current tax realities, the reformers' plans are varied and change nearly daily, as they meet conflicting political pressures. But whether they be Kemp-Kasten, Bradley-Gephardt, the Treasury plan of fall, 1984 (Regan, or Reagan I), or the final Reagan plan of spring, 1985 (Reagan II), there is one common and seemingly simple goal: that every person or group should pay the same proportional tax on their net income,

Reprinted from *World Market Perspective* 18, no. 11 (November 1985); *The Logic of Action Two* (Auburn, Ala.: Mises Institute and Cheltenham, UK: Edward Elgar, 1997).

and that all deductions, exemptions, and shelters be abolished in the name of this uniform proportional tax (a "flat tax with no exemptions").

The flat tax reformers have much in common with militant ideologues that we have become all too familiar with in the twentieth century. In the first place, they are egalitarians in this case, assuming it to be sinful or at least grossly "unfair" for any person or group to escape the scythe of the great uniform tax. Second, and along with this egalitarianism, they assume in brusque and lordly fashion that they alone represent and embody the "general interest," and that all objections to a uniform flat tax may be quickly dismissed as the self-interested croakings of the "special interests." It doesn't seem to matter if the "special interests" encompass most of the American populace; they must be unceremoniously swept aside to achieve the flat tax paradise. The fact that most of the impetus for this and other reforms comes from academic economists puts the icing on the flat tax cake. Academic idealists have always been accustomed to sweeping aside everyone else's interests and concerns as petty and "special," while they speak automatically for the larger interests of mankind. At best, the reformers cavalierly overlook the enormous amount of harm and pain they will inflict in the course of their grandiose reform.

One example: the flat tax would impose an enormous amount of harm and damage on every American homeowner. In their wisdom, the flat taxers have decided that deduction of interest payments on your mortgage is a "subsidy" granted by the tax system, and that your true net income would permit no such deduction. They have also concluded that the unwitting homeowner also enjoys another "subsidy" from the government: failure to tax his "imputed rent"; that is, the amount that he would have had to pay in rent if he had been renting the house instead of owning it. One of the many problems with the latter proposal is that the poor homeowner is never able to pay his "imputed" taxes; no, his taxes would have to be paid in cold cash, even though his income is "psychic" and not earned in money. But we press on. A third body blow to the homeowner would be the flat taxer's insistence on eliminating federal tax deductions for state and local taxes, most of which are property taxes on one's home. Thus, we have a three-fold tax increase inflicted on the homeowner, and the effect of this one-two-three punch would be a permanent lowering of the market value of one's home, which consists of the present value of expected future returns from the house.

These are but a few of the many grave consequences and damages that would flow from the reformers' measures. But the reformers literally do not care; no pains (almost invariably suffered by others) must be permitted to block or delay the speedy achievement of their Utopia. Any alterations are only grudging concessions to the fierce resistance of the "special interests" to the advent of the flat taxers' New Jerusalem. Thus, the Regan plan of fall, 1984 (Reagan I), proposed to increase drastically the capital gains tax, toward the ideal of raising it to the precise level of the income tax, and also suggested a sharp lowering of oil depletion allowances. Great resistance was offered to the plan by risky venture capitalists, who would be particularly crushed by a high capital gains tax, and by the similarly damaged oil interests, always considered sinister in the popular imagination. As a result, the reformers were forced to abandon these two aspects of their Grand Plan in Reagan II. But in the long run, these forced retreats are not important; their goal—a uniform across-the-board flat tax—always remains the same.

But why is this plan so grand? So vitally important that our pain and hardships should be treated as nothing? Here the reformers offer little argument. Basically, their reasons boil down to two: their tax system would be simple (you could calculate your tax on a postcard), and above all, it would be fair.

THE ARGUMENT FOR SIMPLICITY

Making out your taxes, the reformers claim, would be simplicity itself. No more back-breaking work trying to figure out what's going on, no more hiring tax lawyers or accountants. But the sweet simplicity of the argument can be disposed of very quickly. In the first place, anyone who wants simplicity can have it now, by using the short E-Z form, and two-thirds of Americans do so at the present time. So then the question to ask is: why do one-third of us choose complexity by spending many painful hours over the complex form, and why do we hire expensive lawyers and accountants to aid us? Surely, not because we love complexity and expense for their own sakes, but because we believe that there are things in life worse than complexity, and one of them is paying more taxes! We are willing to suffer some complexity in order to lower some of our monstrous tax burden. And by eliminating our deductions, exemptions, shelters, and so on, the reformers are imposing compulsory simplicity against our wishes. They are truly what the great nineteenth century Swiss historian Jacob Burckhardt said of the statist intellectuals of his day, "terrible simplifiers."

But the joke is on us, for the reformers' system would really in no way be simple. We would still have to go through a complex and murky maze. For the key to the flat taxers is that the uniform proportionate tax is to be levied on all net income. But what is net income? The answers are far from simple, and good arguments can be found on either side. The interesting and crucial fact is that, on each of these arguments, the flat taxers invariably come down against the harried taxpayer, and in favor of bringing ever more of our income and assets into the greedy maw of the taxing Leviathan State.

Thus, are "capital gains" income? The reformers say yes, and call for taxing it to the same extent as ordinary income. Western Europe has not gone down the economic drain partly because its capital gains taxes have always been far lower than its income taxes, but this fact does not and cannot count in the harsh calculus of our reformers. Should capital gains be taxed as they accrue on our books or only as they are realized in cash? Once again, the reformers opt for accrual, grabbing our assets at an earlier date, and heedless of our problem of paying taxes in money while our "gains" have only accrued in our psyche or on paper. Are the losses in our tax shelters phony, or should they be treated as real losses to write off our income? The reformers insist that they are phony, and that therefore they must be disregarded when our taxes are estimated. But who is to say so? Who is to say that if I buy a horse farm in Virginia, and suffer losses, that these are losses I welcome in order to reduce my taxes? Who is equipped to look into my heart and mind and find out if these losses are "genuine" or not? And since when has the IRS acquired occult powers, along with the rest of its totalitarian armamentarium?

And what about the cherished American institution of the three-martini lunch? Reformers from Carter to Reagan have tried to crush that lunch, and to claim that these are not genuine or worthy business expenses. Net income is arrived at by deducting costs from gross income. But is the three-martini lunch a "genuine" cost of business, or is it a sneaky way of earning income that is not subject to tax? Who knows? Who knows how much genuine business, if any, is conducted at such lunches? Once again, the reformers know! And they know that such deductions can be swept away.

And there is the problem of the corporation. Corporations are entities. Should their income be taxed at the same rate as personal income? Economists have come to recognize that there is no living thing called a corporation. A corporate income tax is a double tax upon stockholders, first as a "corporation," and next upon their personal income. But while economists have been increasingly calling for abolition of the corporate tax, the reformers have in their wisdom decided that since all entities' income must be taxed uniformly, the corporate income tax must be included and even raised if necessary to be taxed at the same rate.

None of these arguments is simple, but it's instructive that in each and every case, the reformers have come down fiercely on the side of including all these incomes or assets in the taxation category. Their bias in favor of tax, tax, and more tax should be clear by now.

THE ARGUMENT FOR FAIRNESS

The major argument of the flat taxers is that it is "fairness" that demands a swift forced march toward their ideal. "Fairness" is worth almost any cost. But it is strange that this ethical argument comes from a profession (academic economists) who have made a career of loudly proclaiming that all of their doctrines are "value-free science" that have nothing to do with ethics. So when did they become expert ethicists? Indeed, the fairness argument is generally and blithely assumed to be true, after which the reformers can gleefully denounce every resister to higher or broader taxes as embodiments of sinister "special" interests.

One argument holds that fairness demands that everyone pay his or her equal share of the "services" of government. Let us set aside for a moment the surely important point that these "services" are often dubious, are inordinately expensive, and sometimes mean that the taxpayer is forced to pay for his own surveillance and oppression. Since when does "fairness" demand that everyone pay the same proportion of his income for a good or service? Mixed in with the argument for fairness is the view that government should do nothing to penalize one industry or occupation, or subsidize another. This neutral-to-the-market argument puts the flat taxers in the guise of militant adherents of free enterprise. This sounds admirable, but why does it imply that everyone should pay the same proportion of his income? When David Rockefeller and I buy a loaf of Wonder Bread at the supermarket, each of us pays the same price; no one is there to inspect our annual incomes and levy a proportionate fine. No one forces Rockefeller to pay $1,000 for a loaf of Wonder Bread, just because his income is a thousand times that of the next man. The free market tends toward uniform and equal pricing for each product; one price for everyone, whatever that person's race, creed, class, color, or income. Why should it suddenly be different for taxes? In short, a quiet but highly important change has here been made in the concept of "equal," from equal and uniform price for all on the free market, to equal proportion to income in the hands of the flat taxers.

"Subsidy" True and False

At the heart of the fairness and neutral-to-the-market assumptions of the flat taxers is their express desire to eliminate subsidies, which are assumed to be both evil and non-neutral to the free market. The problem here is an equivocation on the term "subsidy." It's certainly true that our tax and budget system is riddled with subsidies, properly defined as taxing one group of people to line the pockets of another, or robbing Peter to pay Paul. If you or I are taxed to subsidize tobacco growers, or highway builders, or contractors, or welfare recipients, then these are indeed subsidies, cases where productive people are being robbed by the government to support groups who function, in effect, as parasites upon the producers. These are subsidies that should be eliminated forthwith. But what about, say, deductions for payment of interest on mortgages, tax credits for investment, or deductions for payment of state and local taxes? In what sense are they "subsidies"? Instead, what is really happening here is that some people—homeowners, investors, or state and local taxpayers—are graciously allowed by the government to keep more of their own money than they would have otherwise. I submit that being allowed to keep more of your hard-earned money is not a subsidy in any true sense; it simply means that you are being fleeced less intensely than you would have been. If a robber assaults you on the highway, and is about to run off with all of your funds, and you persuade him to let you keep some bus fare, is he "subsidizing" you? Surely not. Being allowed to keep your own money can scarcely be called a subsidy.

We are now able to see through two very different senses of the concept of "special interest." It is all too true that the tobacco planter or the highway contractor who eagerly demands government funds are special interests aggressively dedicated to fleecing the taxpayer. But the investor, or the homeowner, or the venture capitalist, or whatever, who lobbies to be able to keep 'more of his own money is a "special interest" in a very different sense. They are resisters properly dedicated to defending their own rights and assets against government assault. "Special" they might be, but they are, whether they know it or not, engaged in the noble effort of defending the rights and the freedoms of all of us against assault and depredation.

By focusing on defenders of their property and rights as alleged subsidy-seekers, the flat taxers are engaging in a strategy of "divide and conquer." The reformers have taken a growing movement of rebellion, resentment, and call for lower taxes and split the taxpayer forces by encouraging one set of us to seek out and persecute the other set. The flat taxers have managed to shift the focus of discussion from "lower taxes for all" to the proposition: "If you want your taxes to be lower, seek out and confiscate the assets of those bad people whose taxes are 'unfairly' low." The focus becomes raising the other guy's taxes instead of lowering yours and everyone else's. This clever ploy of the high taxers unfortunately seems to be working.

The flat taxers like to proclaim their plan to be "revenue-neutral," that is, the overall tax burden will not change. The lowering of some taxes on upper income groups, then, must be offset by "broadening the base," or by extending the tax burden to more people and sources of income. But who is to guarantee that once the base is broadened, and more income sources are brought under government's sway, it will not follow its natural proclivities and once again raise taxes for everyone?

What Is a Loophole?

It is ironic that the slogan "close the loopholes," which used to be a hallmark of left-liberalism, has now been adopted by the Reagan administration and by the flat taxers. The great free-market economist Ludwig von Mises once rose up in a conference on taxation that devoted much energy to the closing of tax loopholes, and asked the crucial question: "What is a loophole?" He answered that the assumption of the loophole theorists seemed to be that all of everyone's income really belongs to the government, and that if the government fails to tax all of it away, it is thereby leaving a "loophole" that must be closed. The same charge applies to the deductions, exemptions, credits, and all the other loopholes out of a flat tax so condemned by our tax reformers.

Let us now consider the vexed question of ending deductibility of state and local taxes—a vital point to our reformers—because ending deductibility will provide a huge bonanza for our federal tax collectors. The flat taxers argue that by allowing deductions, the citizens of low-tax cities and states are "subsidizing" the citizens of high-tax states, and that an end to deductions will put all regions on a plane of fairness and uniformity. Governor Mario Cuomo, on behalf of the notoriously tax-oppressed citizens of New York, accepted the charge of subsidy, and then eloquently threw it back to the critics of New York, asking, in effect, "What's wrong with a subsidy? Are you against the citizens of New York subsidizing tobacco farmers in North Carolina, or subsidizing highway contractors in Iowa?" As a rare consistent supporter of left-liberalism, Cuomo was able to reveal the hypocrisy of those whose attacks on subsidies habitually suffer from a convenient double (or triple) standard. Being a left-liberal, Cuomo was not equipped to go one step further—to step outside the mammoth subsidy system and ask the crucial question: Are Iowans really subsidizing New Yorkers under deductibility? Or are the oppressed and cruelly taxed New Yorkers being spared from being doubly taxed on their own income? The average New Yorker is not responsible for his high taxation; he suffers unwillingly under the highest sales, income, and property taxes in the country. Why should he suffer more than the average Iowan? What is so "fair" about that?

The Reagan administration supporters of ending deductibility offer a pragmatic or strategic argument in reply. If you tax New Yorkers higher up by eliminating deductions, then they will rise up and roll back New York state and city taxes to the lower Iowan level. This is the old the-worse-the-better argument that unfortunately, in addition to being strategic rather than moral, never seems to work. One of the main arguments for bringing in the income tax in the early twentieth century was that now, in contrast to the indirect tariff, everyone would directly feel such a tax, and therefore the public would rise up to keep taxes low. Obviously it didn't work that way. Instead, we kept and increased tariffs, and we exploited a new tax source and raised it to gigantic and crippling proportions.

"Fairness": Equal Slavery

One dramatic way of looking at our tax system in relation to the question of subsidy or fairness is to assume for a moment that this is 1850, and that the question arises in the North as to what should be done with slaves who had managed to escape from the South. Let us assume that both sides of a growing debate are ardently in favor of freedom and are opposed to slavery. Group A hails the slaves' escape and advocates setting them free. But Group B argues as follows:

We are, of course, just as ardent a champion of slave freedom as the people of Group A. But we believe it is unfair
for one group of slaves to escape, while the remainder of
their brothers and sisters remain in slavery. Therefore, we
hold that these escapees should be shipped back into slavery until such time as all the slaves can be freed together
and simultaneously.

What would we think of such an argument? To call it specious would
be a kindly understatement. But I submit that believers in the free market
are arguing in precisely the same way when they say that all taxes must
be uniform, and that all specific tax deductions or exemptions must be
canceled until such time as everyone's taxes can be reduced uniformly.
In both cases, the egalitarians are arguing not for equal freedom but for
equal slavery or equal robbery in the name of "fairness." In both cases, the
rebuttal holds that the enslavement or plunder of one group can in no way
justify the enslavement or plunder of another, be it in the name of fairness,
equity, or whatever.

THE ARGUMENT FOR MISALLOCATION OF RESOURCES

The most sophisticated argument of the flat tax reformers is that
deductions, exemptions, and loopholes distort the allocation of resources
from what it would be on the free market, and therefore should be abolished. This is an integral part of the neutrality-to-the-market argument,
and is particularly insidious, because it makes the reformers appear to be
knowledgeable and dedicated adherents of the free market. Let us take,
for example, two credits or deductions: an investment tax credit, and an
energy credit. The reformers argue that the result of the "subsidy" of tax
credits is that more resources are now going into investment or energy,
and less are going into other areas, than would on the free market, and that
therefore these credits should be eliminated.

It is true that more resources are now going into investment, energy,
and a slew of other areas, than would have in a purely free market system. But the reformers leave out a crucial point: what is the alternative? If
investment, energy, or other credits or deductions are abolished, resources
will not automatically go into more productive areas; instead, they go into
government, via higher taxes. In short, the alternatives to energy credits
are not merely Energy or All Other Consumption and Investment. They
are threefold: Energy, Other Forms of Expenditure, and Government. And

a higher tax will simply be wasted, thrown down the rathole of unproductive and profligate government spending. In short, there is no waste—no misallocation—like government; anything else would be an improvement.

THE WAY OUT OF THE MESS

The policy conclusions that flow from our analysis are diametrically opposed to those of the flat taxers. In looking at the history of reform and at the arguments of the flat taxers, one can almost sympathize with Richard L. Doernberg, professor of law at Emory University, who throws up his hands and concludes that "We have a lousy system; let's leave it alone or it will get worse." Doernberg urges that the current tax code, as bad as it is, should remain precisely the way it is forever, so that at least people will know the score and be able to plan around its provisions.

But we can do better than that. We have to look differently at taxation. We have to stop looking at taxes as a mighty system for achieving social goals, which merely needs to be made "fair" and rational in order to usher in Utopia. We have to start looking at taxation as a vast system of robbery and oppression, by which some people are enabled to live coercively and parasitically at the expense of others. We must realize that from the point of view of justice or of economic prosperity, the less people are taxed, the better. That is why we should rejoice at every new loophole, new credit, new manifestation of the "underground" economy. The Soviet Union can produce or work only to the extent that individuals are able to avoid the myriad of controls, taxes, and regulations. The same is true of most Third World countries, and the same is increasingly true of us. Every economic activity that escapes taxes and controls is not only a blow for freedom and property rights; it is also one more instance of a free flow of productive energy getting out from under parasitic repression.

That is why we should welcome every new loophole, shelter, credit, or exemption, and work, not to shut them down but to expand them to include everyone else, including ourselves.

If, then, the standard for proper reform is to lower any and all taxes as much as possible, how might government services be supplied? To answer we must take a very hard look at government services. Are they "services," or are they embodiments of repression? Or are they "services," at best, that no one really wants? And if they are genuine services, wouldn't they be supplied more efficiently, as well as voluntarily, by private enterprise? And if our friends the tax reformers are so all-fired concerned about the free market, shouldn't they answer this question: Why not put your emphasis on privatizing and thereby drastically lowering/eliminating government services? Wouldn't that be really neutral to, and consistent with, the free market? How do we explain the fact that if we go back to the earlier years of our nation, the level of government spending and taxation—even adjusted for inflation and population growth—was enormously less, on every level of jurisdiction, than it is today? And yet the Republic survived, and even flourished.

We must, in short, get past the tax reformers' favorite ploy of revenue neutrality. Why must total revenue remain the same? Instead, it should be lowered drastically, and as much as possible.

We now return to the old question of "fairness": if there are any taxes or government spending left after our drastic cuts, how should the remaining taxes be levied? Here we reopen the point that fairness is the closest possible approximation to neutrality toward the free market. One method would be user fees, so that only direct users would pay for a service and there would be no extra coercion on non-users. For the rest, we should look at the free-market system of one price for a good or service. We might then suggest a system not of equal proportional income tax, but of equal tax, period. This is the age-old system of the "head tax," in which every citizen pays an equal amount each year to the government, in payment for whatever services may have been conferred upon him from governments' existence during that year. The abolition of the income tax would mean the end of snooping and surveillance by the IRS as well as the elimination of vast economic distortions and oppression caused by the system; the end of sales and property taxes would also be a great boon to the freedom and prosperity of Americans.

We would then and only then have a tax system that truly, and at long last, fulfilled the proclaimed goals of our flat tax reformers. For here would be a system that would be truly simple, truly fair, and genuinely neutral to the free market. Short of that goal, we could settle temporarily for former Congressman Ron Paul's (R-TX) interesting variant of the flat tax proposal: reducing all income tax rates to 10 percent, while at the same time keeping all existing deductions, credits, and exemptions. The principle should be clear: to support all reductions in taxes, whether they be by lower rates or widening of exemption and deductions; and to oppose all rate increases or exemption decreases. In short, to seek in every instance to remove the blight of taxation as much as possible. Here is one reform, at least, that could not fall under Mencken's definition of a plot to injure the American taxpayer.

Section IV

Money, Banking,
and the Business Cycle

CHAPTER 18

Essentials
of Money and Inflation

Money is a crucial command post of any economy, and therefore of any society. Society rests upon a network of voluntary exchanges, also known as the "free-market economy"; these exchanges imply a division of labor in society, in which producers of eggs, nails, horses, lumber, and immaterial services such as teaching, medical care, and concerts, exchange their goods for the goods of others. At each step of the way, every participant in exchange benefits immeasurably, for if everyone were forced to be self-sufficient, those few who managed to survive would be reduced to a pitiful standard of living.

Direct exchange of goods and services, also known as "barter," is hopelessly unproductive beyond the most primitive level, and indeed every "primitive" tribe soon found its way to the discovery of the tremendous benefits of arriving, on the market, at one particularly marketable commodity, one in general demand, to use as a "medium" of "indirect exchange." If a particular commodity is in widespread use as a medium in a society, then that general medium of exchange is called "money."

The money-commodity becomes one term in every single one of the innumerable exchanges in the market economy. I sell my services as a teacher for money; I use that money to buy groceries, typewriters, or travel

---

Originally appeared as "Taking Money Back," *The Freeman* (October 1995), part 1.

accommodations; and these producers in turn use the money to pay their workers, to buy equipment and inventory, and pay rent for their buildings. Hence the ever-present temptation for one or more groups to seize control of the vital money-supply function.

Many useful goods have been chosen as moneys in human societies. Salt in Africa, sugar in the Caribbean, fish in colonial New England, tobacco in the colonial Chesapeake Bay region, cowrie shells, iron hoes, and many other commodities have been used as moneys. Not only do these moneys serve as media of exchange; they enable individuals and business firms to engage in the "calculation" necessary to any advanced economy. Moneys are traded and reckoned in terms of a currency unit, almost always units of weight. Tobacco, for example, was reckoned in pound weights. Prices of other goods and services could be figured in terms of pounds of tobacco; a certain horse might be worth eighty pounds on the market. A business firm could then calculate its profit or loss for the previous month; it could figure that its income for the past month was 1,000 pounds and its expenditures 800 pounds, netting it a 200 pound profit.

GOLD OR GOVERNMENT PAPER

Throughout history, two commodities have been able to outcompete all other goods and be chosen on the market as money—two precious metals, gold and silver (with copper coming in when one of the other precious metals was not available). Gold and silver abounded in what we can call "moneyable" qualities, qualities that rendered them superior to all other commodities. They are in rare enough supply that their value will be stable, and of high value per unit weight; hence pieces of gold or silver will be easily portable, and usable in day-to-day transactions; they are rare enough too, so that there is little likelihood of sudden discoveries or increases in supply. They are durable so that they can last virtually forever, and so they provide a safe "store of value" for the future. And gold and silver are divisible, so that they can be divided into small pieces without losing their value; unlike diamonds, for example, they are homogeneous, so that one ounce of gold will be of equal value to any other.

The universal and ancient use of gold and silver as moneys was pointed out by the first great monetary theorist, the eminent fourteenth-century French scholastic Jean Buridan, and then in all discussions of money down to money and banking textbooks until the Western governments abolished the gold standard in the early 1930s. Franklin D. Roosevelt joined in this deed by taking the United States off gold in 1933.

There is no aspect of the free-market economy that has suffered more scorn and contempt from "modern" economists, whether frankly statist Keynesians or allegedly "free market" Chicagoites, than has gold. Gold, not long ago hailed as the basic staple and groundwork of any sound monetary system, is now regularly denounced as a "fetish" or, as in the case of Keynes, as a "barbarous relic." Well, gold is indeed a "relic" of barbarism in one sense; no "barbarian" worth his salt would ever have accepted the phony paper and bank credit that we modern sophisticates have been bamboozled into using as money.

But "gold bugs" are not fetishists; we don't fit the standard image of misers running their fingers through their hoard of gold coins while cackling in sinister fashion. The great thing about gold is that it, and only it, is money supplied by the free market, by the people at work. For the stark choice before us always is: gold (or silver), or government. Gold is market money, a commodity which must be supplied by being dug out of the ground and then processed; but government, on the contrary, supplies virtually costless paper money or bank checks out of thin air.

We know, in the first place, that all government operation is wasteful, inefficient, and serves the bureaucrat rather than the consumer. Would we prefer to have shoes produced by competitive private firms on the free market, or by a giant monopoly of the federal government? The function of supplying money could be handled no better by government. But the situation in money is far worse than for shoes or any other commodity. If the government produces shoes, at least they might be worn, even though they might be high-priced, fit badly, and not satisfy consumer wants.

Money is different from all other commodities: other things being equal, more shoes, or more discoveries of oil or copper benefit society, since they help alleviate natural scarcity. But once a commodity is established as a money on the market, no more money at all is needed. Since the only use of money is for exchange and reckoning, more dollars or pounds or marks in circulation cannot confer a social benefit: they will simply dilute the exchange value of every existing dollar or pound or mark. So it is a great boon that gold or silver are scarce and are costly to increase in supply.

But if government manages to establish paper tickets or bank credit as money, as equivalent to gold grams or ounces, then the government, as dominant money-supplier, becomes free to create money costlessly and at will. As a result, this "inflation" of the money supply destroys the value of the dollar or pound, drives up prices, cripples economic calculation, and hobbles and seriously damages the workings of the market economy.

The natural tendency of government, once in charge of money, is to inflate and to destroy the value of the currency. To understand this truth, we must examine the nature of government and of the creation of money. Throughout history, governments have been chronically short of revenue. The reason should be clear: unlike you and me, governments do not produce useful goods and services that they can sell on the market; governments, rather than producing and selling services, live parasitically off the market and off society. Unlike every other person and institution in society, government obtains its revenue from coercion, from taxation. In older and saner times, indeed, the king was able to obtain sufficient revenue from the products of his own private lands and forests, as well as through highway tolls. For the State to achieve regularized, peacetime taxation was a struggle of centuries. And even after taxation was established, the kings realized that they could not easily impose new taxes or higher rates on old levies; if they did so, revolution was very apt to break out.

Controlling the Money Supply

If taxation is permanently short of the style of expenditures desired by the State, how can it make up the difference? By getting control of the money supply, or, to put it bluntly, by counterfeiting. On the market economy, we can only obtain good money by selling a good or service in exchange for gold, or by receiving a gift; the only other way to get money is to engage in the costly process of digging gold out of the ground. The counterfeiter, on the other hand, is a thief who attempts to profit by forgery, e.g., by painting a piece of brass to look like a gold coin. If his counterfeit is detected immediately, he does no real harm, but to the extent his counterfeit goes undetected, the counterfeiter is able to steal not only from the producers whose goods he buys. For the counterfeiter, by introducing fake money into the economy, is able to steal from everyone by robbing every person of the value of his currency. By diluting the value of each ounce or dollar of genuine money, the counterfeiter's theft is more sinister and more truly subversive than that of the highwayman; for he robs everyone in society, and the robbery is stealthy and hidden, so that the cause-and-effect relation is camouflaged.

Recently, we saw the scare headline: "Iranian Government Tries to Destroy U.S. Economy by Counterfeiting $100 Bills." Whether the ayatollahs had such grandiose goals in mind is dubious; counterfeiters don't need a grand rationale for grabbing resources by printing money. But all counterfeiting is indeed subversive and destructive, as well as inflationary.

But in that case, what are we to say when the government seizes control of the money supply, abolishes gold as money, and establishes its own printed tickets as the only money? In other words, what are we to say when the government becomes the legalized, monopoly counterfeiter?

Not only has the counterfeit been detected, but the Grand Counterfeiter, in the United States the Federal Reserve System, instead of being reviled as a massive thief and destroyer, is hailed and celebrated as the wise manipulator and governor of our "macroeconomy," the agency on which we rely for keeping us out of recessions and inflations, and which we count on to determine interest rates, capital prices, and employment. Instead of being habitually pelted with tomatoes and rotten eggs, the chairman of the Federal Reserve Board, whoever he may be, whether the imposing Paul Volcker or the owlish Alan Greenspan, is universally hailed as Mr. Indispensable to the economic and financial system.

Indeed, the best way to penetrate the mysteries of the modern monetary and banking system is to realize that the government and its central bank act precisely as would a Grand Counterfeiter, with very similar social and economic effects. Many years ago, the *New Yorker* magazine, in the days when its cartoons were still funny, published a cartoon of a group of counterfeiters looking eagerly at their printing press as the first $10 bill came rolling off the press. "Boy," said one of the team, "retail spending in the neighborhood is sure in for a shot in the arm."

And it was. As the counterfeiters print new money, spending goes up on whatever the counterfeiters wish to purchase: personal retail goods for themselves, as well as loans and other "general welfare" purposes in the case of the government. But the resulting "prosperity" is phony; all that happens is that more money bids away existing resources, so that prices rise. Furthermore, the counterfeiters and the early recipients of the new money bid away resources from the poor suckers who are down at the end of the line to receive the new money, or who never even receive it at all.

New money injected into the economy has an inevitable ripple effect; early receivers of the new money spend more and bid up prices, while later receivers or those on fixed incomes find the prices of the goods they must buy unaccountably rising, while their own incomes lag behind or remain the same. Monetary inflation, in other words, not only raises prices and destroys the value of the currency unit; it also acts as a giant system of expropriation of the late receivers by the counterfeiters themselves and by the other early receivers. Monetary expansion is a massive scheme of hidden redistribution.

When the government is the counterfeiter, the counterfeiting process not only can be "detected"; it proclaims itself openly as monetary statesmanship for the public weal. Monetary expansion then becomes a giant scheme of hidden taxation, the tax falling on fixed income groups, on those groups remote from government spending and subsidy, and on thrifty savers who are naive enough and trusting enough to hold on to their money, to have faith in the value of the currency.

Spending and going into debt are encouraged; thrift and hard work discouraged and penalized. Not only that: the groups that benefit are the special interest groups who are politically close to the government and can exert pressure to have the new money spent on them so that their incomes can rise faster than the price inflation. Government contractors, politically connected businesses, unions, and other pressure groups will benefit at the expense of the unaware and unorganized public.

CHAPTER 19

On the Definition
of the Money Supply

The concept of the supply of money plays a vitally important role, in differing ways, in both the Austrian and the Chicago schools of economics. Yet, neither school has defined the concept in a full or satisfactory manner; as a result, we are never sure to which of the numerous alternative definitions of the money supply either school is referring.

The Chicago school definition is hopeless from the start. For, in a question-begging attempt to reach the conclusion that the money supply is the major determinant of national income, and to reach it by statistical rather than theoretical means, the Chicago school *defines* the money supply as that entity which correlates most closely with national income. This is one of the most flagrant examples of the Chicagoite desire to avoid essentialist concepts, and to "test" theory by statistical correlation; with the result that the supply of money is not really defined at all. Furthermore, the approach overlooks the fact that statistical correlation cannot establish causal connections; this can only be done by a genuine theory that works with definable and defined concepts.[1]

---

[1]In a critique of the Chicago approach, Leland Yeager writes:

Originally appeared as a chapter in *New Directions in Austrian Economics*, Louis M. Spadaro, ed. (Kansas City: Sheed Andrews, and McMeel, 1978); reprinted in *Economic Controversies* (Auburn, Ala.: Mises Institute, 2011).

In Austrian economics, Ludwig von Mises set forth the essentials of the concept of the money supply in his *Theory of Money and Credit*, but no Austrian has developed the concept since then, and unsettled questions remain (e.g., are savings deposits properly to be included in the money supply?).[2] And since the concept of the supply of money is vital both for the theory and for applied historical analysis of such consequences as inflation and business cycles, it becomes vitally important to try to settle these questions, and to demarcate the supply of money in the modern world. In *The Theory of Money and Credit*, Mises set down the correct guidelines: money is the general medium of exchange, the thing that all other goods and services are traded for, the final payment for such goods on the market.

In contemporary economics, definitions of the money supply range widely from cash + demand deposits (M_1) up to the inclusion of virtually all liquid assets (a stratospherically high M). No contemporary economist excludes demand deposits from his definition of money. But it is useful to consider exactly why this should be so. When Mises wrote *The Theory of Money and Credit* in 1912, the inclusion of demand deposits in the money supply was not yet a settled question in economic thought. Indeed, a controversy over the precise role of demand deposits had raged throughout

---

But it would be awkward if the definition of money accordingly had to change from time to time and country to country. Furthermore, even if money defined to include certain near-moneys does correlate somewhat more closely with income than money narrowly defined, that fact does not necessarily impose the broad definition. Perhaps the amount of these near-moneys depends on the level of money-income and in turn on the amount of medium of exchange. ... More generally, it is not obvious why the magnitude with which some other magnitude correlates most closely deserves overriding attention. ... The number of bathers at a beach may correlate more closely with the number of cars parked there than with either the temperature or the price of admission, yet the former correlation may be less interesting or useful than either of the latter. (Leland B. Yeager, "Essential Properties of the Medium of Exchange," *Kyklos* [1968], reprinted in *Monetary Theory*, ed. R.W. Clower [London: Penguin Books, 1969], p. 38)

Also see, Murray N. Rothbard, "The Austrian Theory of Money," in Edwin Dolan, ed., *The Foundations of Modern Austrian Economics* (Kansas City, Kansas: Sheed and Ward, 1976), pp. 179–82.

[2]Ludwig von Mises, *The Theory of Money and Credit*, 3rd ed. (New Haven, Conn.: Yale University Press, 1953).

the nineteenth century. And when Irving Fisher wrote his *Purchasing Power of Money* in 1913, he still felt it necessary to distinguish between M (the supply of standard cash) and M_1, the total of demand deposits.[3] Why then did Mises, the developer of the Austrian theory of money, argue for including demand deposits as part of the money supply "in the broader sense"? Because, as he pointed out, bank demand deposits were *not* other goods and services, other assets exchangeable for cash; they were, instead, redeemable for cash at par on demand. Since they were so redeemable, they functioned, not as a good or service exchanging for cash, but rather as a warehouse receipt for cash, redeemable on demand at par as in the case of any other warehouse. Demand deposits were therefore "money-substitutes" and functioned as equivalent to money in the market. Instead of exchanging cash for a good, the owner of a demand deposit and the seller of the good would both treat the deposit *as if* it were cash, a surrogate for money. Hence, receipt of the demand deposit was accepted by the seller as final payment for his product. And *so long* as demand deposits *are* accepted as equivalent to standard money, they will function as part of the money supply.

It is important to recognize that demand deposits are not automatically part of the money supply by virtue of their very existence; they continue as equivalent to money only so long as the subjective estimates of the sellers of goods on the market *think* that they are so equivalent and accept them as such in exchange. Let us hark back, for example, to the good old days before federal deposit insurance, when banks were liable to bank runs at any time. Suppose that the Jonesville Bank has outstanding demand deposits of $1 million; that million dollars is then its contribution to the aggregate money supply of the country. But suppose that suddenly the soundness of the Jonesville Bank is severely called into question; and Jonesville demand deposits are accepted only at a discount, or even not at all. In that case, as a run on the bank develops, its demand deposits no longer function as part of the money supply, certainly not at par. So that a bank's demand deposit only functions as part of the money supply so long as it is treated as an equivalent substitute for cash.[4]

---

[3]Irving Fisher, *The Purchasing Power of Money* (New York: Macmillan, 1913).

[4]Even now, in the golden days of federal deposit insurance, a demand deposit is not always equivalent to cash, as anyone who is told that it will take 15 banking days to clear a check from California to New York can attest.

It might well be objected that since, in the era of fractional reserve banking, demand deposits are not *really* redeemable at par on demand, that then only standard cash (whether gold or fiat paper, depending upon the standard) can be considered part of the money supply. This contrasts with 100 percent reserve banking, when demand deposits are *genuinely* redeemable in cash, and function as genuine, rather than pseudo, warehouse receipts to money. Such an objection would be plausible, but would overlook the Austrian emphasis on the central importance in the market of *subjective* estimates of importance and value. Deposits are not *in fact* all redeemable in cash in a system of fractional reserve banking; but so long as individuals on the market *think* that they are so redeemable, they continue to function as part of the money supply. Indeed, it is precisely the expansion of bank demand deposits beyond their reserves that accounts for the phenomena of inflation and business cycles. As noted above, demand deposits must be included in the concept of the money supply so long as the market *treats* them as equivalent; that is, so long as individuals *think* that they are redeemable in cash. In the current era of federal deposit insurance, added to the existence of a central bank that prints standard money and functions as a lender of last resort, it is doubtful that this confidence in redeemability can ever be shaken.

All economists, of course, include standard money in their concept of the money supply. The justification for including demand deposits, as we have seen, is that people believe that these deposits are redeemable in standard money on demand, and therefore treat them as equivalent, accepting the payment of demand deposits as a surrogate for the payment of cash. But if demand deposits are to be included in the money supply for this reason, then it follows that any other entities that follow the same rules must also be included in the supply of money.

Let us consider the case of savings deposits. There are several common arguments for *not* including savings deposits in the money supply: (1) they are not redeemable on demand, the bank being legally able to force the depositors to wait a certain amount of time (usually thirty days) before paying cash; (2) they cannot be used directly for payment. Checks can be drawn on demand deposits, but savings deposits must first be redeemed in cash upon presentation of a passbook; (3) demand deposits are pyramided upon a base of total reserves as a multiple of reserves, whereas savings deposits (at least in savings banks and savings and loan associations) can only pyramid on a one-to-one basis on top of demand deposits (since such deposits will rapidly "leak out" of savings and into demand deposits).

Objection (1), however, fails from focusing on the legalities rather than on the economic realities of the situation; in particular, the objection fails to focus on the *subjective* estimates of the situation on the part of the depositors. In reality, the power to enforce a thirty-day notice on savings depositors is never enforced; hence, the depositor invariably thinks of his savings account as redeemable in cash on demand. Indeed, when, in the 1929 depression, banks tried to enforce this forgotten provision in their savings deposits, bank runs promptly ensued.[5]

Objection (2) fails as well, when we consider that, even within the stock of standard money, some part of one's cash will be traded more actively or directly than others. Thus, suppose someone holds part of his supply of cash in his wallet, and another part buried under the floorboards. The cash in the wallet will be exchanged and turned over rapidly; the floorboard money might not be used for decades. But surely no one would deny that the person's floorboard hoard is just as much part of his money stock as the cash in his wallet. So that mere lack of activity of part of the money stock in no way negates its inclusion as part of his supply of money. Similarly, the fact that passbooks must be presented before a savings deposit can be used in exchange should not negate its inclusion in the money supply. As I have written elsewhere, suppose that for some cultural quirk—say widespread revulsion against the number "five"—no seller will accept a five-dollar bill in exchange, but only ones or tens. In order to use five-dollar bills, then, their owner would first have to go to a bank to exchange them for ones or tens, and then use those ones or tens in exchange. But surely, such a necessity would not mean that someone's stock of five-dollar bills was not part of his money supply.[6]

Neither is Objection (3) persuasive. For while it is true that demand deposits are a multiple pyramid on reserves, whereas savings bank deposits are only a one-to-one pyramid on demand deposits, this distinguishes the sources or volatility of different forms of money, but should not exclude savings deposits from the supply of money. For demand deposits, in turn, pyramid on top of cash, and yet, while each of these forms of money is

---

[5]On the equivalence of demand and savings deposits during the Great Depression, and on the bank runs resulting from attempts to enforce the 30-day wait for redemption, see Murray N. Rothbard, *America's Great Depression*, 3rd ed. (Kansas City, Kansas: Sheed and Ward, 1975), pp. 84, 316. Also see Lin Lin, "Are Time Deposits Money?" *American Economic Review* (March 1937): 76–86.

[6]Rothbard, "The Austrian Theory of Money," p. 181.

generated quite differently, so long as they exist each forms part of the total supply of money in the country. The same should then be true of savings deposits, whether they be deposits in commercial or in savings banks.

A fourth objection, based on the third, holds that savings deposits should not be considered as part of the money supply because they are efficiently if indirectly controllable by the Federal Reserve through its control of commercial bank total reserves and reserve requirements for demand deposits. Such control is indeed a fact, but the argument proves far too much; for, after all, demand deposits are themselves and in turn indirectly but efficiently controllable by the Fed through its control of total reserves and reserve requirements. In fact, control of savings deposits is not nearly as efficient as of demand deposits; if, for example, savings depositors would keep their money and active payments in the savings banks, instead of invariably "leaking" back to checking accounts, savings banks *would* be able to pyramid new savings deposits on top of commercial bank demand deposits by a large multiple.[7]

Not only, then, should savings deposits be included as part of the money supply, but our argument leads to the conclusion that no valid distinction can be made between savings deposits in commercial banks (included in M_2) and in savings banks or savings and loan associations (also included in M_3).[8] Once savings deposits are conceded to be part of the money supply, there is no sound reason for balking at the inclusion of deposits of the latter banks.

On the other hand, a *genuine* time deposit—a bank deposit that would indeed only be redeemable at a certain point of time in the future, would merit very different treatment. Such a time deposit, not being redeemable on demand, would instead be a credit instrument rather than a form of warehouse receipt. It would be the result of a credit transaction rather than a warehouse claim on cash; it would therefore not function in the market as a surrogate for cash.

Ludwig von Mises distinguished carefully between a *credit* and a *claim* transaction: a credit transaction is an exchange of a present good (e.g.,

---

[7]In the United States, the latter is beginning to be the case, as savings banks are increasingly being allowed to issue checks on their savings deposits. If that became the rule, moreover, Objection (2) would then fall on this ground alone.

[8]Regardless of the legal form, the "shares" of formal ownership in savings and loan associations are economically precisely equivalent to the new deposits in savings banks, an equivalence that is universally acknowledged by economists.

money which can be used in exchange at any present moment) for a future good (e.g., an IOU for money that will only be available in the future). In this sense, a demand deposit, while legally designated as credit, is actually a present good—a warehouse claim to a present good that is similar to a bailment transaction, in which the warehouse pledges to redeem the ticket at any time on demand.

Thus, Mises wrote:

> It is usual to reckon the acceptance of a deposit which can be drawn upon at any time by means of notes or cheques as a type of credit transaction and juristically this view is, of course, justified; but economically, the case is not one of a credit transaction. If *credit* in the economic sense means the exchange of a present good or a present service against a future good or a future service, then it is hardly possible to include the transactions in question under the conception of credit. A depositor of a sum of money who acquires in exchange for it a claim convertible into money at any time which will perform exactly the same service for him as the sum it refers to has exchanged no present good for a future good. The claim that he has acquired by his deposit is also a present good for him. The depositing of the money in no way means that he has renounced immediate disposal over the utility it commands.[9]

It might be, and has been, objected that credit instruments, such as bills of exchange or Treasury bills, can often be sold easily on credit markets—either by the rediscounting of bills or in selling old bonds on the bond market; and that therefore they should be considered as money. But many assets are "liquid," i.e., can easily be sold for money. Blue-chip stocks, for example, can be easily sold for money, yet no one would include such stocks as part of the money supply. The operative difference, then, is not whether an asset is liquid or not (since stocks are no more part of the money supply than, say, real estate) but whether the asset is redeemable at a fixed rate, at par, in money. Credit instruments, similarly to the case of shares of stock, are sold for money on the market at fluctuating rates. The current tendency of some economists to include assets as money purely because of their liquidity must be rejected; after all, in some cases, inventories of retail goods might be as

---

[9]Mises, *Theory of Money and Credit*, p. 268.

liquid as stocks or bonds, and yet surely no one would list these inventories as part of the money supply. They are *other* goods sold for money on the market.[10]

One of the most noninflationary developments in recent American banking has been the emergence of *certificates of deposit* (CDs), which are genuine time and credit transactions. The purchaser of the CD, or at least the large-denomination CD, knows that he has loaned money to the bank which the bank is only bound to repay at a specific date in the future; hence, large-scale CDs are properly not included in the M_2 and M_3 definitions of the supply of money. The same might be said to be true of various programs of time deposits which savings banks and commercial banks have been developing in recent years: in which the depositor agrees to retain his money in the bank for a specified period of years in exchange for a higher interest return.

There are worrisome problems, however, that are attached to the latter programs, as well as to *small-denomination* CDs; for in these cases, the deposits *are* redeemable before the date of redemption at fixed rates, but at penalty discounts rather than at par. Let us assume a hypothetical time deposit, due in five years' time at $10,000, but redeemable at present at a penalty discount of $9,000. We have seen that such a time deposit should certainly not be included in the money supply in the amount of $10,000. But should it be included at the fixed, though penalty rate of $9,000, or not be included at all? Unfortunately, there is no guidance on this problem in the Austrian literature. Our inclination is to include these instruments in the money supply at the penalty level (e.g., $9,000), since the operative distinction, in our view, is not so much the par redemption as the ever-ready possibility of redemption at some fixed rate. If this is true, then we must also include in the concept of the money supply federal savings bonds, which are redeemable at fixed, though penalty rates, until the date of official maturation.

Another entity which should be included in the total money supply on our definition is *cash surrender values* of life insurance policies; these values represent the investment rather than the insurance part of life insurance and are redeemable in cash (or rather in bank demand deposits) at any time on demand. (There are, of course, no possibilities of cash surrender in other forms of insurance, such as term life, fire, accident, or medical.)

---

[10]For Mises's critique of the view that endorsed bills of exchange in early nineteenth-century Europe were really part of the money supply, see ibid., pp. 284–86.

Statistically, cash surrender values may be gauged by the total of policy reserves less policy loans outstanding, since policies on which money has been borrowed from the insurance company by the policyholder are not subject to immediate withdrawal. Again, the objection that policyholders are reluctant to cash in their surrender values does not negate their inclusion in the supply of money; such reluctance simply means that this part of an individual's money stock is relatively inactive.[11]

One caveat on the inclusion of noncommercial bank deposits and other fixed liabilities into the money supply: just as the cash and other reserves of the commercial banks are not included in the money supply, since that would be double counting once demand deposits are included; in the same way, the demand deposits owned by these noncommercial bank creators of the money supply (savings banks, savings and loan companies, life insurance companies, etc.) should be deducted from the total demand deposits that are included in the supply of money. In short, if a commercial bank has demand deposit liabilities of $1 million, of which $100,000 are owned by a savings bank as a reserve for its outstanding savings deposits of $2 million, then the total money supply to be attributed to these two banks would be $2.9 million, deducting the savings bank reserve that is the base for its own liabilities.

One anomaly in American monetary statistics should also be cleared up: for a reason that remains obscure, demand deposits in commercial banks or in the Federal Reserve Banks owned by the Treasury are excluded from the total money supply. If, for example, the Treasury taxes citizens by $1 billion, and their demand deposits are shifted from public accounts to the Treasury account, the total supply of money is considered to have fallen by $1 billion, when what has really happened is that $1 billion worth of money has (temporarily) shifted from private to governmental hands. Clearly, Treasury deposits should be included in the national total of the money supply.

Thus, we propose that the money supply should be defined as all entities which are redeemable on demand in standard cash at a fixed rate, and that, in the United States at the present time, this criterion translates into:

---

[11]For hints on the possible inclusion of life insurance cash surrender values in the supply of money, see Gordon W. McKinley, "Effects of Federal Reserve Policy on Nonmonetary Financial Institutions," in Herbert V. Prochnow, ed., *The Federal Reserve System* (New York: Harper and Bros., 1960), p. 217n; and Arthur F. Burns, *Prosperity without Inflation* (Buffalo: Economica Books, 1958), p. 50.

M_a (a = Austrian) = total supply of cash-cash held in the banks + total demand deposits + total savings deposits in commercial and savings banks + total shares in savings and loan associations + time deposits and small CDs at current redemption rates + total policy reserves of life insurance companies—policy loans outstanding—demand deposits owned by savings banks, saving and loan associations, and life insurance companies + savings bonds, at current rates of redemption.

M_a hews to the Austrian theory of money, and, in so doing, broadens the definition of the money supply far beyond the narrow M_1, and yet avoids the path of those who would broaden the definition to the virtual inclusion of all liquid assets, and who thus would obliterate the uniqueness of the money phenomenon as the final means of payment for all other goods and services.

CHAPTER 20

Deflation Reconsidered

This is an aspect of thinking which has been called "thinking the unthinkable," deflation having had an extremely bad press everywhere. I want to reconsider the concept of deflation even though it is now unthinkable. After all, five to ten years ago the concept of default in New York was also unthinkable, and yet it has at least partially happened and hopefully will continue to intensify in the future.

If default was previously unthinkable and is now thinkable, not only for New York City but for cities and states across the country, then perhaps deflation is also thinkable. I am going to define deflation for the purposes of discussion in the normal manner as falling prices and, despite Professor Mundell's talk today, falling prices in dollar terms even though I probably have at least as little regard for dollars as he has, maybe even less. But we are sort of stuck with dollars right now so I am going to continue to be dollar-centric even though I don't like it. In the first place, of all the various facets of deflation, we can consider one of its aspects as that of a secular long-term trend. Now there used to be, back in the good old days of the 1910s and 1920s, intense discussion between economists as to whether or not the price level should be falling or whether it should be constant over

Originally appeared as "Deflation Reconsidered," in *Georgraphical Aspects of Inflationary Processes*, Peter Corbin and Murray Sabrin, eds. (Pleasantville, N.Y.: Redgrave Publishing, 1976), vol. 1.

time. And even though the falling price level economists won out in theory, of course in practice they didn't. But I would like to return to that discussion for a moment, and say that as far as I am concerned the trend of an unhampered free market economy will usually be a falling price level. In other words, as productivity increases, as capital investment increases, as technology improves, prices will tend to fall, thereby spreading increasing real income to all consumers. Indeed, over the nineteenth century, generally prices fell and money wages remained approximately constant so that real wages kept going up. We can see even now, in many specific cases, the glorious effects of falling prices in those particular situations where productivity and the mass market has zoomed into the picture, permitting falling prices even in the face of our general inflationary trend.

For example, TV sets on which in 1948 it was almost impossible to see the image, then cost something like $2,000. And now they are infinitely better in quality and cost about $100.00. So that if you look at the price per unit quality of TV sets and think of that in contrast to the general price level, there is a tremendous and magnificent deflation—if you want to use that term for TV sets. I think this deflation is a great thing. This is the way real income increases and should increase. The same thing happened to penicillin, which started out when first discovered with its price so high that it was only available to extremely wealthy people. Now, of course, it is used for almost every nosebleed. And the same is true for electronic calculators, pocket calculators, which are now down to $20.00. So this is the sort of economy I would like to see across the board, not just for TV sets and pocket calculators. This is what would happen if we had a sound monetary system.

In contrast to the Fisher-Chicago idea of a stable price level somehow being divinely providential and being the goal which should be sought, as far as I am concerned, a falling price level should be the desideratum. As far as I can see, the original idea of the Fisher-Friedman view (the original idea of Fisher), of why there should be a constant price level is because he believed that money is supposed to be a measure of values. Since we now know, or at least should know, that values are subjective and unmeasurable, I think that the philosophical groundwork for the idea of the stable price level is no longer valid. And yet it still carries on, trailing clouds of glory behind it without anyone really reconsidering why a stable price level should be particularly desirable. Of course a stable price level is better than the rising price level we have now, but still we are talking about what goal we should set for ourselves. So as far as the secular trend goes, I think we should advocate the falling price level which would occur without monetary inflation.

How about other aspects of deflation? How about the shorter-run aspects? For example, there is the concept of hoarding. The idea being that a short-run fall in prices is brought about because people's desire for hoarding increases. Hoarding, of course, is a smear term. It is a loaded, value-laden term conjuring up the image of a miserly hoarder rifling through his gold coins or his paper money in the closet, cackling as the world falls around him. I do not think that is a fair image. I think the so-called hoarder is the person who wants to increase the real value of his cash balances for one reason or another. And, I see nothing wrong with that aspiration. I see no reason why the market should not fulfill it as it fulfills most aspirations if let alone. The usual way in which the aspiration for an increase in real cash balances is fulfilled, given a constant money supply, is that prices fall. Of course, as prices fall the real value of one's cash balances increases. That however, has fallen in to disfavor among the authorities, pundits, and the establishment in general so that now the alternative way of fulfilling increasing real cash balances is to inflate the money supply. This, of course, is the method we are using now. Inflating the money supply, in addition to causing all sorts of other ill-effects, brings about redistribution of wealth, destruction of the rational calculation system of prices, the confiscation of wealth and income of one set of producers for another set of nonproducers, and so on. In addition to the usual bad effects of inflation which most people acknowledge, there is the Austrian insight of generating the business cycle and causing the eventual breakdown of the currency through hyperinflation.

Finally, there is another problem related to the idea of fulfilling the desire to increase real cash balances by increasing the money supply, namely, that in the long run it does not work. In other words, as new money is pumped into the system people's desire for cash begins to fall as they anticipate rising prices. We then begin the spiral upward to accelerating hyperinflation. In other words, after a certain period of time as inflation continues and the public anticipates further inflation, they begin to lower their demand for cash balances. Then prices go up faster than the money supply, and then when the government monetary authorities try to raise real cash balances by expanding the money supply, prices continue to go up faster than the money supply, and real cash balances fall. When they try to raise real cash balances by pumping in more money, there begins the spiral upward toward disaster. Now there is the famous statement by the head of the German Reichsbank in 1923 when the German hyper-inflation was accelerating, namely, to put it into folksy terms, "Don't worry folks. There is a shortage of money, we realize that (a shortage of money in the sense of a drop in real cash balances). We will offset this shortage, we will compensate for this by turning on the printing presses twenty-four hours a day."

This alleviates the money shortage, in other words, raising real cash balances back up to the preinflation level. Of course that did not work and one would think that looking back on 1923 with our superior wisdom, that the monetary authorities and pundits would not make the same mistake again. However, they are in the process of doing so, because in 1973, I forget exactly what months, when inflation was rapidly accelerating in contrast to the money supply, Walter Heller wrote an article saying, in effect, "It is not true that the increase in money supply is causing the inflation. On the contrary, there is a fall in real cash balances because prices are going up faster than the money supply. Therefore, it is the job of the monetary authorities to pump in more money so that real cash balances will go back up to the preinflation level." So even though we may think we have learned something since Rudolph Havenstein of the German Reichsbank in 1923, it looks like we have not done so.

What I advocate then is allowing the desire for increasing real cash balances to be satisfied through a fall in the price level, not through the disastrous and finally self-defeating process of inflationary monetary expansion.

Another point about deflation which I think is admirable, and which very few people talk about, is that if there is deflation, it is inevitably a postinflationary deflation. As a matter of fact, it is almost impossible to have deflation without a previous inflation. Under a pure gold standard of course, it would be impossible—period. After our long process of inflation, a deflation would mean that the fixed-income groups or the relatively fixed-income groups—academics for one, the traditional widows and orphans, people on pensions, creditors—would finally get a little bit of their own back. I see nothing wrong with that. It seems to me that after decades of the compulsory redistribution of wealth from the fixed-income groups to the other groups, there is nothing wrong with a little bit of restitution. A little bit of "reparations" on behalf of those of us on more of a fixed-income level. So I think that there is a good in itself too—the prospect of a little bit of compensatory deflation.

There is another point which I cannot demonstrate here because it involves the Austrian theory of the business cycle which has been talked about this morning—a view of mine which is heretical even within the Austrian camp, which is small enough. Namely, that a deflation coming in the form of a credit contraction would speed up the necessary process of readjustment toward a healthy economic situation. It would speed up the liquidation of unsound investments and thereby spur the recovery process. Since we have had inflationary credit expansion over many years and since the current recession or depression has not succeeded in finishing the entire cleansing work of readjustment, this would facilitate the recovery process. So that is another argument for deflation. In other words, the business cycle argument that deflation would speed up the recovery in liquidating the unsound investments of the boom period.

Another thing about deflation which is extremely important has been generally overlooked—namely, that deflation sugarcoats the pill of recession. From the ordinary person's point of view, the average consumer's point of view, there is only one really good thing about a depression, even the depression of 1929 and the 1930s—namely, that at least the cost of living went down. Therefore, if you were employed in the 1930s, you were in pretty good shape. Many people overlook that. It's true that there was a severe unemployment rate in the 1930s of about 25 percent, but that still meant that 75 percent of the labor force was employed. Those people who were employed were, after all, in pretty good shape since the prices of furniture, food and other consumer goods fell to a nice low level so that their real income increased. My family, for example, bought all their furniture during the depression. My father was among the 75 percent of those who were employed. They never had it so good before or since. As a result of fine tuning and the Keynesian policies or Keynesian-Friedmanite policies which we have been pursuing for a long time, after forty years of being promised full employment and prosperity, we have now wound up with both inflation and recession at the same time. This is the great achievement of the Nixon-Democratic program. What I am saying is that by doing this we have at last eliminated the fall in the cost of living which used to sugarcoat the recession pill. So that now we have the recession adjustments, we have the liquidation of inventory and all the rest that goes along with an Austrian recession adjustment. But along with that we now have inflation and a rise in the cost of living. So the consumer doesn't even get that consolation from the fact of recession. What I am saying is that consolation was a good thing; it is a good thing to have the cost of living fall and therefore there should be deflation from that point of view too.

Another great thing about deflation and this, of course, I cannot demonstrate today, but can only indicate my present position,—is that without the interference of the Federal Deposit Insurance Corporation, deflation could finally and at long last smash the fractional reserve banking system. It has deserved this fate for many decades. Once the public recognized the fraudulence and innate bankruptcy of the fractional reserve banking system, because it is bankrupt, let's face it—they have not got the money they say they have to pay on demand. When the public cottoned onto this in 1931, 1932, and 1933 and the banking system was in the process of being smashed in every state of the Union, that was a great and glorious day for those of us who are hard-money people (and in favor of the cause of truth and honesty). We were in the process of smashing the banking system, and then the various governors, and Hoover and Roosevelt came in with the bank holidays and the Federal Deposit Insurance Corporation which bailed the banks out. If not for that bail-out, there was a golden opportunity to eliminate fractional reserve banking forevermore. There wouldn't even have been the problem of a transition period because we were in a transition, it was just a matter of leaving the thing alone for a few more months and the deed would have been done. Deflation would have helped in this process of smashing the fractional reserve banking system. Why it should have been smashed is that that system has been a constant threat and source of inflation and special privilege, the business cycle, and a whole raft of other evils.

The one problem which emerges from such deflation is the objection that wage rates are rigid downward and that there would be severe unemployment. Well, it's true that wage rates are rigid downward, and again the Keynesian way of solving that, a tricky end run around rigid wage rates, was of course to cure the situation by lowering real-wage rates through inflationary monetary expansion and price increases. Being fairly sure that wages are going to lag behind prices, you can make an end run around unions and minimum wage laws, and unemployment insurance, and all the other rigid wage producing measures, and lower real wages and reduce unemployment through that kind of tricky, deceptive method. Well, it worked for a while, but now I think everyone has got onto the game. Unions have economists too and they understand about the cost of living index and all of that. As a result, I think this policy has become less and less viable; this idea of fooling the working class through lowering real wages through inflation.

Therefore, finally and at long last we will have to tackle the problem of rigid wage rates downward, honestly and directly. Tackling it directly would be politically difficult, there is no question about that, but so is hyperinflation politically difficult. I think the choice is basically that between run-away hyperinflation on the one hand, and smashing rigid wage rates downward on the other. And the way you smash rigid wage rates downward is fairly simple, conceptually simple, although politically difficult—namely, by repealing minimum wage laws, repealing special privileges to unions (notably the Wagner Act and the Norris-LaGuardia Act), and removing unemployment insurance and welfare payments, etc., so that wage rates would at long last be flexible downward. I think if you are going to have any kind of free price system at all this will have to he tackled sooner or later and therefore the sooner the better, because once again accelerated inflation is on the horizon now, and it's not just a theoretical problem.

Finally, I was moved by Professor Lerner's statement today about trusting human beings. We have in this country a Bill of Rights. The First Amendment is a notable achievement, it seems to me, which very simply does not trust human beings, in other words it does not trust human beings in the government, in charge of the state apparatus. It doesn't trust them one bit, because the general tendency on the part of the state apparatus throughout history is to censor, to oppress, to put people in jail without due process of law.

The First Amendment and the Bill of Rights in general were designed to check government and to show that we do not really trust the government and are putting in these severe limitations on government action. Now perhaps Professor Lerner wants to repeal the Bill of Rights, which is his privilege, but if he does he should say so. It seems to me we also cannot trust government in the monetary sphere. There are good reasons for this too. And I think one particularly good reason is that the state is inherently an inflationary instrument. The reason is that the state has acquired over the centuries a legal monopoly on the business or the function of counterfeiting. In other words, the state has arrogated to itself a compulsory monopoly of the counterfeiting business; a business of printing money, creating new money. I submit that any group of people, if handed the power of compulsory monopoly of the money supply, of the counterfeiting business, will use it. I don't care how "good" they are. I do not consider the state as being particularly good even in general. Even I, handed the legal monopoly of the money supply, might be tempted strongly to start using it. First you pay off some debts, then you buy yourself a new house, etc., and pretty soon the temptation feeds upon itself and you're off to the races.

What I want to do then, the reason why I want to go back to gold or forward to gold, is to eliminate the state's compulsory monopoly of the printing press; to eliminate the counterfeiting power altogether, which I consider antisocial, parasitic, antiproductive, destructive, etc. And I recognize again that to do this, to have a free price system in the first place, and secondly to induce the state to give up its compulsory monopoly power, is not an easy task. It requires a political movement, a mass movement from below, if you will, to do it. But again, I think this has to be done.

CHAPTER 21

Anatomy of a Bank Run

I t was a scene familiar to any nostalgia buff: all-night lines waiting for the banks (first in Ohio, then in Maryland) to open; pompous but mendacious assurances by the bankers that all is well and that the people should go home; a stubborn insistence by depositors to get their money out; and the consequent closing of the banks by government, while at the same time the banks were permitted to stay in existence and collect the debts due them by their borrowers.

In other words, instead of government protecting private property and enforcing voluntary contracts, it deliberately violated the property of the depositors by barring them from retrieving their own money from the banks.

All this was, of course, a replay of the early 1930s: the last era of massive runs on banks. On the surface the weakness was the fact that the failed banks were insured by private or state deposit insurance agencies, whereas the banks that easily withstood the storm were insured by the federal government (FDIC for commercial banks; FSLIC for savings and loan banks).

Reprinted from *The Free Market* (September 1985); reprinted in *Making Economic Sense* (Auburn, Ala.: Mises Institute, 1995, 2006).

But why? What is the magic elixir possessed by the federal government that neither private firms nor states can muster? The defenders of the private insurance agencies noted that they were technically in better financial shape than FSLIC or FDIC, since they had greater reserves per deposit dollar insured. How is it that private firms, so far superior to government in all other operations, should be so defective in this one area? Is there something unique about money that requires federal control?

The answer to this puzzle lies in the anguished statements of the savings and loan banks in Ohio and in Maryland, after the first of their number went under because of spectacularly unsound loans. "What a pity," they in effect complained, "that the failure of this one unsound bank should drag the sound banks down with them!"

But in what sense is a bank "sound" when one whisper of doom, one faltering of public confidence, should quickly bring the bank down? In what other industry does a mere rumor or hint of doubt swiftly bring down a mighty and seemingly solid firm? What is there about banking that public confidence should play such a decisive and overwhelmingly important role?

The answer lies in the nature of our banking system, in the fact that both commercial banks and thrift banks (mutual-savings and savings-and-loan) have been systematically engaging in fractional-reserve banking: that is, they have far less cash on hand than there are demand claims to cash outstanding. For commercial banks, the reserve fraction is now about 10 percent; for the thrifts it is far less.

This means that the depositor who thinks he has $10,000 in a bank is misled; in a proportionate sense, there is only, say, $1,000 or less there. And yet, both the checking depositor and the savings depositor think that they can withdraw their money at any time on demand. Obviously, such a system, which is considered fraud when practiced by other businesses, rests on a confidence trick: that is, it can only work so long as the bulk of depositors do not catch on to the scare and try to get their money out. The confidence is essential, and also misguided. That is why once the public catches on, and bank runs begin, they are irresistible and cannot be stopped.

We now see why private enterprise works so badly in the deposit insurance business. For private enterprise only works in a business that is legitimate and useful, where needs are being fulfilled. It is impossible to "insure" a firm, even less so an industry, that is inherently insolvent. Fractional reserve banks, being inherently insolvent, are uninsurable.

What, then, is the magic potion of the federal government? Why does everyone trust the FDIC and FSLIC even though their reserve ratios are lower than private agencies, and though they too have only a very small fraction of total insured deposits in cash to stem any bank run? The answer is really quite simple: because everyone realizes, and realizes correctly, that only the federal government—and not the states or private firms—can print legal tender dollars. Everyone knows that, in case of a bank run, the US Treasury would simply order the Fed to print enough cash to bail out any depositors who want it. The Fed has the unlimited power to print dollars, and it is this unlimited power to inflate that stands behind the current fractional reserve banking system.

Yes, the FDIC and FSLIC "work," but only because the unlimited monopoly power to print money can "work" to bail out any firm or person on earth. For it was precisely bank runs, as severe as they were that, before 1933, kept the banking system under check, and prevented any substantial amount of inflation.

But now bank runs—at least for the overwhelming majority of banks under federal deposit insurance—are over, and we have been paying and will continue to pay the horrendous price of saving the banks: chronic and unlimited inflation.

Putting an end to inflation requires not only the abolition of the Fed but also the abolition of the FDIC and FSLIC. At long last, banks would be treated like any firm in any other industry. In short, if they can't meet their contractual obligations they will be required to go under and liquidate. It would be instructive to see how many banks would survive if the massive governmental props were finally taken away.

CHAPTER 22

Lessons of the Recession

I t's official! Long after everyone in America knew that we were in a severe recession, the private but semi-official and incredibly venerated National Bureau of Economic Research has finally made its long-awaited pronouncement: we've been in a recession ever since last summer. Well! Here is an instructive example of the reason why the economics profession, once revered as a seer and scientific guide to wealth and prosperity, has been sinking rapidly in the esteem of the American public. It couldn't have happened to a more deserving group. The current recession, indeed, has already brought us several valuable lessons:

Lesson #1: You don't need an economist. One of the favorite slogans of the 1960s New Left was: "You don't need a weatherman to tell you how the wind is blowing." Similarly, it is all too clear that you don't need an economist to tell you whether you've been in a recession. So how is it that the macro-mavens not only can't forecast what will happen next, they can't even tell us where we are, and can barely tell us where we've been? To give them their due, I am pretty sure that Professors Hall, Zarnowitz, and the other distinguished solons of the famed Dating Committee of the National Bureau have known we've been in a recession for quite a while, maybe even since the knowledge percolated to the general public.

Reprinted from *The Free Market* (July 1991).

The problem is that the Bureau is trapped in its own methodology, the very methodology of Baconian empiricism, meticulous data-gathering and pseudo-science that has brought it inordinate prestige from the economics profession.

For the Bureau's entire approach to business cycles for the past five decades has depended on dating the precise month of each cyclical turning point, peak and trough. It was therefore not enough to say, last fall, that "we entered a recession this summer." That would have been enough for common-sense, or for Austrians, but even one month off the precise date would have done irreparable damage to the plethora of statistical manipulations—the averages, reference points, leads, lags, and indicators—that constitute the analytic machinery, and hence the "science," of the National Bureau. If you want to know whether we're in a recession, the last people to approach is the organized economics profession.

Of course, the general public might be good at spotting where we are at, but they are considerably poorer at causal analysis, or at figuring out how to get out of economic trouble. But then again, the economics profession is not so great at that either.

Lesson #2: There ain't no such thing as a "new era." Every time there is a long boom, by the final years of that boom, the press, the economics profession, and financial writers are rife with the pronouncement that recessions are a thing of the past, and that deep structural changes in the economy, or in knowledge among economists, have brought about a "new era." The bad old days of recessions are over. We heard that first in the 1920s, and the culmination of that first new era was 1929; we heard it again in the 1960s, which led to the first major inflationary recession of the early 1970s; and we heard it most recently in the later 1980s. In fact, the best leading indicator of imminent deep recession is not the indices of the National Bureau; it is the burgeoning of the idea that recessions are a thing of the past.

More precisely, recessions will be around to plague us so long as there are bouts of inflationary credit expansion which bring them into being.

Lesson #3: You don't need an inventory boom to have a recession. For months into the current recession, numerous pundits proclaimed that we couldn't be in a recession because business had not piled up excessive inventories. Sorry. It made no difference, since malinvestments brought about by inflationary bank credit don't necessarily have to take place in inventory form. As often happens in economic theory, a contingent symptom was mislabeled as an essential cause.

Unlike the above, other lessons of the current recession are not nearly as obvious. One is:

Lesson #4: Debt is not the crucial problem. Heavy private debt was a conspicuous feature of the boom of the 1980s, with much of the publicity focused on the floating of high-yield ("junk") bonds for buyouts and take-overs. Debt *per se*, however, is not a grave economic problem.

When I purchase a corporate bond I am channeling savings into investment much the same way as when I purchase stock equity. Neither way is particularly unsound. If a firm or corporation floats too much debt as compared to equity, that is a miscalculation of its existing owners or managers, and not a problem for the economy at large. The worst that can happen is that, if indebtedness is too great, the creditors will take over from existing management and install a more efficient set of managers. Creditors, as well as stockholders, in short, are entrepreneurs.

The problem, therefore, is not debt but credit, and not all credit but bank credit financed by inflationary expansion of bank money rather than by the genuine savings of either shareholders or creditors. The problem in other words, is not debt but loans generated by fractional-reserve banking.

Lesson #5: Don't worry about the Fed "pushing on a string." Hard money adherents are a tiny fraction in the economics profession; but there are a large number of them in the investment newsletter business. For decades, these writers have been split into two warring camps: the "inflationists" versus the "deflationists." These terms are used not in the sense of advocating policy, but in predicting future events.

"Inflationists," of whom the present writer is one, have been maintaining that the Fed, having been freed of all restraints of the gold standard and committed to not allowing the supposed horrors of deflation, will pump enough money into the banking system to prevent money and price deflation from ever taking place.

"Deflationists," on the other hand, claim that because of excessive credit and debt, the Fed has reached the point where it cannot control the money supply, where Fed additions to bank reserves cannot lead to banks expanding credit and the money supply. In common financial parlance, the Fed would be "pushing on a string." Therefore, say the deflationists, we are in for an imminent, massive, and inevitable deflation of debt, money, and prices.

One would think that three decades of making such predictions that have never come true would faze the deflationists somewhat, but no, at the first sign of trouble, especially of a recession, the deflationists are invariably back, predicting imminent deflationary doom. For the last part of 1990, the money supply was flat, and the deflationists were sure that their day had come at last. Credit had been so excessive, they claimed, that businesses could no longer be induced to borrow, no matter how low the interest rate is pushed.

What deflationists always overlook is that, even in the unlikely event that banks could not stimulate further loans, they can always use their reserves to purchase securities, and thereby push money out into the economy. The key is whether or not the banks pile up excess reserves, failing to expand credit up to the limit allowed by legal reserves. The crucial point is that never have the banks done so, in 1990 or at any other time, apart from the single exception of the 1930s. (The difference was that not only were we in a severe depression in the 1930s, but that interest rates had been driven down to near zero, so that the banks were virtually losing nothing by not expanding credit up to their maximum limit.) The conclusion must be that the Fed pushes with a stick, not a string.

Early this year, moreover, the money supply began to spurt upward once again, putting an end, at least for the time being, to deflationist warnings and speculations.

Lesson #6: The banks might collapse. Oddly enough there is a possible deflation scenario, but not one in which the deflationists have ever expressed interest. There has been, in the last few years, a vital, and necessarily permanent, sea-change in American opinion. It is permanent because it entails a loss of American innocence. The American public, ever since 1933, had bought, hook, line and sinker, the propaganda of all Establishment economists, from Keynesians to Friedmanites, that the banking system is safe, SAFE, because of federal deposit insurance.

The collapse and destruction of the savings and loan banks, despite their "deposit insurance" by the federal government, has ended the insurance myth forevermore, and called into question the soundness of the last refuge of deposit insurance, the FDIC. It is now widely known that the FDIC simply doesn't have the money to insure all those deposits, and that in fact it is heading rapidly toward bankruptcy.

Conventional wisdom now holds that the FDIC will be shored up by taxpayer bailout, and that it will be saved. But no matter: the knowledge that the commercial banks might fail has been tucked away by every American for future reference. Even if the public can be babied along, and the FDIC patched up for this recession, they can always remember this fact at some future crisis, and then the whole fractional-reserve house of cards will come tumbling down in a giant, cleansing bank run. To offset such a run, no taxpayer bailout would suffice.

But wouldn't that be deflationary? Almost, but not quite. Because the banks could still be saved by a massive, hyper-inflationary printing of money by the Fed, and who would bet against such emergency rescue?

Lesson #7: There is no "Kondratieff cycle," no way, no how. There is among many people, even including some of the better hard-money investment newsletter writers, an inexplicable devotion to the idea of an inevitable fifty-four-year "Kondratieff cycle" of expansion and contraction. It is universally agreed that the last Kondratieff trough was in 1940. Since fifty-one years have elapsed since that trough, and we are still waiting for the peak, it should be starkly clear that such a cycle does not exist.

Most Kondratieffists confidently predicted that the peak would occur in 1974, precisely fifty-four years after the previous peak, generally accepted as being in 1920. Their joy at the 1974 recession, however, turned sour at the quick recovery. Then they tried to salvage the theory by analogy to the alleged "plateau" of the 1920s, so that the visible peak, or contraction, would occur nine or ten years after the peak, as 1929 succeeded 1920.

The Kondratieffists there fell back on 1984 as the preferred date of the beginning of the deep contraction. Nothing happened, of course; and, now, seven years later, we are in the last gasp of the Kondratieff doctrine. If the current recession does not, as we have maintained, turn into a deep deflationary spiral, and the recession ends, there will simply be no time left for any plausible cycle of anything approaching fifty-four years. The Kondratieffist practitioners will, of course, never give up, any more than other seers and crystal-ball gazers; but presumably, their market will at last be over.

Section V

History of Economic Thought

CHAPTER 23

Mercantilism

MERCANTILISM AS THE ECONOMIC ASPECT OF ABSOLUTISM

By the beginning of the seventeenth century, royal absolutism had emerged victorious all over Europe. But a king (or, in the case of the Italian city-states, some lesser prince or ruler) cannot rule all by himself. He must rule through a hierarchical bureaucracy. And so the rule of absolutism was created through a series of alliances between the king, his nobles (who were mainly large feudal or post-feudal landlords), and various segments of large-scale merchants or traders. "Mercantilism" is the name given by late-nineteenth-century historians to the politico-economic system of the absolute state from approximately the sixteenth to the eighteenth centuries. Mercantilism has been called by various historians or observers a "system of Power or State-building" (Eli Heckscher), a system of systematic state privilege, particularly in restricting imports or subsidizing exports (Adam Smith), or a faulty set of economic theories, including protectionism and the alleged necessity for piling up bullion in a country. In fact, mercantilism was all of these things; it was a comprehensive system of statebuilding, state privilege, and what might be called "state monopoly capitalism."

Reprinted from "Mercantilism: Serving the Absolute State," in *Economic Thought Before Adam Smith: An Austrian Perspective on the History of Economic Thought*, vol. 1 (Cheltenham, U.K.: Edward Elgar, 1995), chap. 7.

As the economic aspect of state absolutism, mercantilism was of necessity a system of state-building, of Big Government, of heavy royal expenditure, of high taxes, of (especially after the late seventeenth century) inflation and deficit finance, of war, imperialism, and the aggrandizing of the nation-state. In short, a politico-economic system very like that of the present day, with the unimportant exception that now large-scale industry rather than mercantile commerce is the main focus of the economy. But state absolutism means that the state must purchase and maintain allies among powerful groups in the economy, and it also provides a cockpit for lobbying for special privilege among such groups.

Jacob Viner put the case well:

> The laws and proclamations were not all, as some modern admirers of the virtues of mercantilism would have us believe, the outcome of a noble zeal for a strong and glorious nation, directed against the selfishness of the profit-seeking merchant but were the product of conflicting interests of varying degrees of respectability. Each group, economic, social, or religious, pressed constantly for legislation in conformity with its special interest. The fiscal needs of the crown were always an important and generally a determining influence on the course of trade legislation. Diplomatic considerations also played their part in influencing legislation, as did the desire of the crown to award special privileges, *con amore*, to its favorites, or to sell them, or to be bribed into giving them, to the highest bidders.[1]

In the area of state absolutism, grants of special privilege included the creation by grant or sale of privileged "monopolies," i.e., the exclusive right granted by the Crown to produce or sell a given product or trade in a certain area. These "patents of monopoly" were either sold or granted to allies of the Crown, or to those groups of merchants who would assist the king in the collection of taxes. The grants were either for trade in a certain region, such as the various East India companies, which acquired the monopoly right in each country to trade with the Far East, or were internal—such as the grant of a monopoly to one person to manufacture playing cards in

---

[1]Jacob Viner, *Studies in the Theory of International Trade* (New York: Harper & Bros., 1937), pp. 58–59.

England. The result was to privilege one set of businessmen at the expense of their potential competitors and of the mass of English consumers. Or, the state would cartelize craft production and industry and cement alliances by compelling all producers to join and obey the orders of privileged urban guilds.

It should be noted that the most prominent aspects of mercantilist policy—taxing or prohibiting imports or subsidizing exports—were part and parcel of this system of state monopoly privilege. Imports were subject to prohibition or protective tariffs in order to confer privilege on domestic merchants or craftsmen; exports were subsidized for similar reasons. The focus in examining mercantilist thinkers and writers should not be the fallacies of their alleged economic "theories." Theory was the last consideration in their minds. They were, as Schumpeter called them, "consultant administrators and pamphleteers"—to which should be added lobbyists. Their "theories" were any propaganda arguments, however faulty or contradictory, that could win them a slice of boodle from the state apparatus.

As Viner wrote:

> The mercantilist literature ... consisted in the main of writings by or on behalf of "merchants" or businessmen, who had the usual capacity for identifying their own with the national welfare. ... The great bulk of the mercantilist literature consisted of tracts which were partly or wholly, frankly or disguisedly, special pleas for special economic interests. Freedom for themselves, restrictions for others, such was the essence of the usual program of legislation of the mercantilist tracts of merchant authorship.[2]

---

[2]Ibid., p. 59.

CHAPTER 24

Frédéric Bastiat: Champion of Laissez-faire

Particularly suffering from historical neglect is the most famous of the French *laissez-faire* economists, Claude Frédéric Bastiat (1801–50), to whom the two-volume *Dictionnaire d'Économie Politique* (1852) was respectfully and affectionately dedicated. Bastiat was indeed a lucid and superb writer, whose brilliant and witty essays and fables to this day are remarkable and devastating demolitions of protectionism and of all forms of government subsidy and control. He was a truly scintillating advocate of an untrammelled free market. Frédéric Bastiat's justly famous "Petition of the Candlemakers" is still anthologized in books of economic readings; in this satiric petition to the French parliament, the candlemakers' trade association petitions the government to protect their industry, which employs many thousands of men, from the unfair, unjust, invasive competition of a foreign light source: the sun. Bastiat's candlemakers petition the government to shut out the sunlight all over France—a protective device that would give employment to many millions of worthy French candlemakers.

Bastiat's fable of the broken window also brilliantly refuted Keynesianism nearly a century before its birth. Here, he outlines three levels of economic analysis. A mischievous boy hurls a rock at a plate glass store

Reprinted from *Classical Economics: An Austrian Perspective on the History of Economic Thought* (Cheltenham, U.K.: Edward Elgar, 1995), vol. 2.

window, and breaks the glass. As a crowd gathers round, the first-level analysis, common sense, comments on the event. Common sense deplores the destruction of property in breaking the window, and sympathizes with the storekeeper for having to spend his money repairing the window. But then, says Bastiat, comes the second-level, sophisticated analyst or what we might call a proto-Keynesian. The Keynesian says: oh, but you people don't realize that the breaking of the window is *really* an economic blessing. For, in having to repair the window, the storekeeper invigorates the economy by his spending, and gives welcome employment to glaziers and their workers. Destruction of property, by compelling spending, therefore stimulates the economy and has an invigorating "multiplier effect" on production and employment.

But then in steps Bastiat, the third-level analyst, and points out the grievous fallacy in the destructionist proto-Keynesian position. The alleged sophisticated critic, says Bastiat, concentrates on "what is seen" and neglects "what is not seen." The sophisticate sees that the storekeeper must give employment to glaziers by spending money to repair his window. But what he doesn't see is the storekeepers's opportunity foregone. If he did not have to spend the money on repairing the window, he could had *added* to his capital, and to everyone's standard of living, and thereby employed people in the act of advancing, rather than merely trying to sustain, the current stock of capital. Or, the storekeeper might have spent the money on his own consumption, employing people in *that* form of production.

In this way, the "economist," Bastiat's third-level observer, vindicates common sense and refutes the apologia for destruction of the pseudo-sophisticate. He considers what is not seen as well as what is seen. Bastiat, the economist, is the *truly* sophisticated analyst.[1]

Frédéric Bastiat was also a perceptive political, or politico-economic, theorist. Attacking statism as a growing parasitic burden upon producers in the market, he defined the state as "the great fiction by which everyone tries to live off everyone else." And in his work on *The Law* (1850), Bastiat insisted that law and government must be strictly limited to defending the persons, the liberty, and the property of people against violence; any going beyond that role would be destructive of liberty and prosperity.

---

[1] A century later, Bastiat's broken window fallacy served as the inspiration and centerpiece of Henry Hazlitt's excellent and best-selling economic primer, *Economics in One Lesson* (New York: Harper & Bros., 1946).

While often praised as a gifted popularizer, Bastiat has been systematically derided and undervalued as a theorist. Criticizing the classical Smithian distinction between "productive" labor (on material goods) and "unproductive" labor (in producing immaterial services), Bastiat made an important contribution to economic theory by pointing out that *all* goods, including material ones, are productive and are valued precisely because they produce immaterial services. Exchange, he pointed out, consists of the mutually beneficial trade of such services. In emphasizing the centrality of immaterial services in production and consumption, Bastiat built on J.B. Say's insistence that all market resources were 'productive', and that income to productive factors were payments for that productivity. Bastiat also built upon Charles Dunoyer's thesis in his *Nouveau traité d'économie social* (New Treatise on Social Economy) (1830) that "value is measured by services rendered, and that products exchange according to the quality of services stored in them."[2]

Perhaps most important, in stark contrast to the Smith-Ricardo classical school's exclusive emphasis on production, and neglect of the goal of economic endeavours—consumption, Bastiat proclaimed once again the continental emphasis on consumption as the goal and hence the determinant of economic activity. Bastiat's own oft-repeated triad: "Wants, Efforts, Satisfactions" summed it up: wants are the goal of economic activity, giving rise to efforts, and eventually yielding satisfactions. Furthermore, Bastiat noted that human wants are unlimited, and hierarchically ordered by individuals in their scales of value.[3]

Bastiat's concentration on *exchange*, and on analysis of exchange, was also a highly important contribution, especially in contrast to the British classicists' focus on production of material wealth. It was the emphasis on exchange that led Bastiat and the French school to stress the ways in which the free market leads to a smooth and harmonious organization of the economy. Hence the importance of *laissez-faire*.[4]

Frédéric Bastiat was born in 1801 in Bayonne, in southwestern France, the son of a landowner and prominent merchant in the Spanish trade.

---

[2]Dean Russell, *Frédéric Bastiat: Ideas and Influence* (Irvington-on-Hudson, N.Y.: Foundation for Economic Education, 1965), p. 20.

[3]See Joseph T. Salerno, "The Neglect of the French Liberal School in Anglo-American Economics: A Critique of Received Explanations," *Review of Austrian Economics* 2 (1988): 127.

[4]See the sensitive appreciation of this aspect of Bastiat's contribution in Israel M. Kirzner, *The Economic Point of View* (Princeton, N.J.: D. Van Nostrand, 1960), pp. 82–84.

Orphaned at the age of nine, Bastiat entered his uncle's business firm in 1818; when, seven years later, he inherited his grandfather's landed estate, Bastiat left the firm and became a gentleman farmer. But his interests were neither in trade nor in agriculture, but in the study of political economy. Fluent in English, Italian and Spanish, Bastiat steeped himself in all the extant economic literature in these languages. Apart from an unsuccessful attempt to establish an insurance firm in Portugal in the early 1840s, as well as being a member of the district council and his undemanding service as a country judge, Bastiat spent two decades in quiet study and reflection on economic problems. He was most heavily influenced by J.B. Say, partially by Adam Smith, by Destutt de Tracy, and particularly by the great four-volume *laissez-faire* libertarian work of Charles Comte, *A Treatise on Legislation* (1827). Indeed, as a teenager, Bastiat had been a subscriber to Comte and Dunoyer's journal, *Le Censeur*, and he was to become a friend and colleague of Dunoyer's in the struggle for free trade.

Bastiat entered the economic literature with a sparkling attack on protectionism in France and England in the *Journal des Économistes* in late 1844, an article which created a sensational impact. Bastiat followed this up with another article in the *Journal*, in early 1845, denouncing socialism and the concept of a "right to labor." During the few years he had left on earth, Bastiat poured forth a stream of lucid and influential writings. His two-volume *Economic Sophisms* (1845), a collection of witty essays on protectionism and government controls, sold out quickly, going into several editions, and was swiftly translated into English, Spanish, Italian and German. During the same year, Bastiat published *Cobden et la Ligue*, his tribute to Cobden and the Anti-Corn Law League: a history of the League that included the principal speeches and articles by Cobden, Bright, and other stalwarts of the League.

After setting up a free trade association in Bordeaux in 1846, Bastiat moved to Paris, where he stepped up his literary efforts and organized a national association for free trade. He became the secretary-general of the national association, as well as editor-in-chief of *Le Libre-Échange* (Free Trade), the periodical of the French free trade association. Even though in frail health, Bastiat also participated in the revolution of 1848, being elected to the constituent and then the legislative assembly, where he served from 1848 until his death.

Bastiat's final political service has been undervalued by most historians. While generally voting in the minority in the assembly as a stalwart of individual liberty and *laissez-faire*, Bastiat was highly influential as vice-president (and often acting president) of the assembly's finance committee. There he fought tirelessly for lower government spending, lower taxes, sound money, and free trade. While he fought ardently in opposition to socialist and communist schemes, Bastiat elected to sit on the Left, as a proponent of *laissez-faire* and the republic, and as an opponent of protectionism, absolute monarchy, and a warlike foreign policy. As a consistent civil libertarian, Bastiat also fought against the jailing of socialists, the outlawry of peaceful trade unionism, or the declaration of martial law. Bastiat also made his mark by at least partially converting the man who would become the president of the provisional republic in 1848, the eminent poet and orator Alphonse Marie Louis Lamartine (1790–1869) from his previous socialism to (an admittedly inconsistent) *laissez-faire* position.[5]

Bastiat died young in 1850, leaving his two-volume theoretical *magnum opus*, *Economic Harmonies*, only partially published; the remainder was published posthumously. It was a fitting memorial to Bastiat that his friend Michel Chevalier, the man whom he had converted to free trade and *laissez-faire*, should have been the one to conclude, with Richard Cobden, the great free trade Anglo-French treaty of 1860.

Bastiat met Cobden on his first trip to England in the summer of 1845, and for the remainder of Bastiat's life the two men were close friends and frequent correspondents, visiting each other frequently. The two influenced each other greatly, Bastiat providing Cobden with broader theoretical insights in his devotion to free trade, and the latter inspiring Bastiat to organize a movement in France similar to the Anti-Corn Law League. In particular, Cobden took from Bastiat a devotion to natural law and natural rights; an emphasis on the harmony of individuals, groups, and nations through the mutual benefits of the free market; and a staunch opposition to war and an interventionist foreign policy, and a devotion to international peace. The two also shared a consistent devotion to *laissez-faire* devoid of the numerous hesitancies and qualifications imposed by the classical economists, or of the gloomy Ricardian hostility to landlords or to land rent.[6]

---

[5]On the trials and tribulations which the *laissez-faire* liberals had with the Revolution of 1848, which generally had an unfavorable effect on the *laissez-faire* movement, see David M. Hart, "Gustave de Molinari and the Anti-Statist Liberal Tradition, Part I," *The Journal of Libertarian Studies* 5 (Summer 1981): 273–76.

[6]For Cobden's encomiums to Bastiat, see Russell, *Frédéric Bastiat*, pp. 73–74, note 3.

CHAPTER 25

Keynes's Political Economy

In *The General Theory*, Keynes set forth a unique politico-economic sociology, dividing the population of each country into several rigidly separated economic classes, each with its own behavioral laws and characteristics, each carrying its own implicit moral evaluation. First, there is the mass of consumers: dumb, robotic, their behavior fixed and totally determined by external forces. In Keynes's assertion, the main force is a rigid proportion of their total income, namely, their determined "consumption function."

Second, there is a subset of consumers, an eternal problem for mankind: the insufferably bourgeois savers, those who practice the solid puritan virtues of thrift and farsightedness, those whom Keynes, the would-be aristocrat, despised all of his life. All previous economists, certainly including Keynes's forbears Smith, Ricardo, and Marshall, had lauded thrifty savers as building up long-term capital and therefore as responsible for enormous long-term improvements in consumers' standard of living. But Keynes, in a feat of prestidigitation, severed the evident link between savings and investment, claiming instead that the two are unrelated.

Reprinted from *Dissent on Keynes: A Critical Appraisal of Keynesian Economics*, Mark Skousen, ed. (New York: Praeger, 1992), chap. 11; reprinted as *Keynes, the Man* (Auburn, Ala.: Mises Institute, 2010), pp. 47–52.

In fact, he wrote, savings are a drag on the system; they "leak out" of the spending stream, thereby causing recession and unemployment. Hence Keynes, like Mandeville in the early eighteenth century, was able to condemn thrift and savings; he had finally gotten his revenge on the bourgeoisie.

By also severing interest returns from the price of time or from the real economy and by making it only a monetary phenomenon, Keynes was able to advocate, as a linchpin of his basic political program, the "euthanasia of the rentier" class: that is, the state's expanding the quantity of money enough so as to drive down the rate of interest to zero, thereby at last wiping out the hated creditors. It should be noted that Keynes did not want to wipe out investment: on the contrary, he maintained that savings and investment were separate phenomena. Thus, he could advocate driving down the rate of the interest to zero as a means of maximizing investment while minimizing (if not eradicating) savings.

Since he claimed that interest was purely a monetary phenomenon, Keynes could then also sever the existence of an interest rate from the scarcity of capital. Indeed, he believed that capital is not *really* scarce at all. Thus, Keynes stated that his preferred society "would mean the euthanasia of the rentier, and consequently, the euthanasia of the cumulative oppressive power of the capitalist to exploit the scarcity-value of capital."

But capital is not *really* scarce: "Interest today rewards no genuine sacrifice, any more than does the rent of land. The owner of capital can obtain interest because capital is scarce, just as the owner of land can obtain rent because land is scarce. But whilst there may be intrinsic reasons for the scarcity of land, there are no intrinsic reasons for the scarcity of capital." Therefore, "we might aim in practice ... at an increase in the volume of capital until it ceases to be scarce, so that the functionless investor [the rentier] will no longer receive a bonus." Keynes made it clear that he looked forward to a gradual annihilation of the "functionless" rentier, rather than to any sort of sudden upheaval.[1]

Keynes then came to the third economic class, to whom he was somewhat better disposed: the investors. In contrast to the passive and robotic

---

[1]John Maynard Keynes, *The General Theory of Employment, Interest and Money* (London: Macmillan, 1936), pp. 375–76, and Henry Hazlitt, *The Failure of the "New Economics,"* 2nd ed. (New Rochelle, N.Y.: Arlington House, [1959] 1973), pp. 379–84. See also the illuminating article by Andrew Rutten (1989). I am indebted to Dr. Rutten for calling this article to my attention.

consumers, investors are *not* determined by an external mathematical function. On the contrary, they are brimful of free will and active dynamism. They are also not an evil drag on the economic machinery, as are the savers. They are important contributors to everyone's welfare.

But, alas, there is a hitch. Even though dynamic and full of free will, investors are erratic creatures of their own moods and whims. They are, in short, productive but irrational. They are driven by psychological moods and "animal spirits." When investors are feeling their oats and their animal spirits are high, they invest heavily, but too much; overly optimistic, they spend too much and bring about inflation. But Keynes, especially in *The General Theory*, was not really interested in inflation; he was concerned about unemployment and recession, caused, in his starkly superficial view, by pessimistic moods, loss of animal spirits, and hence underinvestment.

The capitalist system is, accordingly, in a state of inherent macroinstability. Perhaps the market economy does well enough on the micro-, supply-and-demand level. But in the macro world, it is afloat with no rudder; there is no internal mechanism to keep its aggregate spending from being either too low or too high, hence causing recession and unemployment or inflation.

Interestingly enough, Keynes came to this interpretation of the business cycle as a good Marshallian. Ricardo and his followers of the Currency school correctly believed that business cycles are generated by expansions and contractions of bank credit and the money supply, as generated by a central bank, whereas their opponents in the Banking school believed that expansions of bank money and credit were merely passive effects of booms and busts and that the real cause of business cycles was fluctuation in business speculation and expectations of profit—an explanation very close to Pigou's later theory of psychological mood swings and to Keynes's focus on animal spirits.

John Stuart Mill had been a faithful Ricardian except in this one crucial area. Following his father, Mill had adopted the Banking school's causal theory of business cycles, which was then adopted by Marshall.[2]

To develop a way out, Keynes presented a fourth class of society. Unlike the robotic and ignorant consumers, this group is described as full of free will, activism, and knowledge of economic affairs. And unlike the hapless

[2]Paul Trescott, "J.M. Keynes as a Marshallian: Comment," *Journal of Economic Issues* 21 (1987): 452–57.

investors, they are not irrational folk, subject to mood swings and animal spirits; on the contrary, they are supremely rational as well as knowledgeable, able to plan best for society in the present as well as in the future.

This class, this *deus ex machina* external to the market, is of course the state apparatus, as headed by its natural ruling elite and guided by the modern, scientific version of Platonic philosopher kings. In short, government leaders, guided firmly and wisely by Keynesian economists and social scientists (naturally headed by the great man himself), would save the day. In the politics and sociology of *The General Theory*, all the threads of Keynes's life and thought are neatly tied up.

And so the state, led by its Keynesian mentors, is to run the economy, to control the consumers by adjusting taxes and lowering the rate of interest toward zero, and, in particular, to engage in "a somewhat comprehensive socialisation of investment." Keynes contended that this would not mean total state Socialism, pointing out that

> it is not the ownership of the instruments of production which it is important for the State to assume. If the State is able to determine the aggregate amount of resources devoted to augmenting the instruments and the basic rate of reward to those who own them, it will have accomplished all that is necessary.[3]

Yes, let the state control investment completely, its amount and rate of return in addition to the rate of interest; then Keynes would allow private individuals to retain formal ownership so that, within the overall matrix of state control and dominion, they could still retain "a wide field for the exercise of private initiative and responsibility." As Hazlitt puts it,

> Investment is a key decision in the operation of any economic system. And government investment is a form of socialism. Only confusion of thought, or deliberate duplicity, would deny this. For socialism, as any dictionary would tell the Keynesians, means the ownership and control of the means of production by government. Under the system proposed by Keynes, the government would *control* all investment in the means of production and would *own* the part it had itself directly invested. It is at best mere muddleheadedness, therefore, to present the

---

[3]Keynes, *The General Theory*, p. 378.

Keynesian nostrums as a free enterprise or "individualistic" *alternative* to socialism.[4]

There was a system that had become prominent and fashionable in Europe during the 1920s and 1930s that was precisely marked by this desired Keynesian feature: private *ownership*, subject to comprehensive government *control* and planning. This was, of course, fascism.

Where did Keynes stand on overt fascism? From the scattered information now available, it should come as no surprise that Keynes was an enthusiastic advocate of the "enterprising spirit" of Sir Oswald Mosley, the founder and leader of British fascism, in calling for a comprehensive "national economic plan" in late 1930. By 1933, Virginia Woolf was writing to a close friend that she feared Keynes was in the process of converting her to "a form of fascism." In the same year, in calling for national self-sufficiency through state control, Keynes opined that "Mussolini, perhaps, is acquiring wisdom teeth."[5] But the most convincing evidence of Keynes's strong fascist bent was the special foreword he prepared for the German edition of *The General Theory*. This German translation, published in late 1936, included a special introduction for the benefit of Keynes's German readers and for the Nazi regime under which it was published. Not surprisingly, Harrod's idolatrous *Life of Keynes* makes no mention of this introduction, although it was included two decades later in volume seven of the *Collected Writings* along with forewords to the Japanese and French editions.

The German introduction, which has scarcely received the benefit of extensive commentary by Keynesian exegetes, includes the following statements by Keynes:

> Nevertheless the theory of output as a whole, which is what the following book purports to provide, is much

---

[4]Hazlitt, *Failure of the "New Economics,"* p. 388, and Karl Brunner "The Sociopolitical Vision of Keynes," in *The Legacy of Keynes*, David A. Reese, ed. (San Francisco: Harper and Row, 1987), pp. 30, 38.

[5]John Maynard Keynes, "Sir Oswald Mosely's Manifesto," *National and Atheneum* 13 (December 1930): 766; and Elizabeth Johnson and Harry G. Johnson, *The Shadow of Keynes* (Oxford: Basil Blackwell, 1978), p. 22. On the relationship between Keynes and Mosely, see Robert Skidelsky, *Oswald Mosely* (New York: Holt, Rinehart and Winston, 1975), pp. 241, 305–06; Oswald Mosely, *My Life* (New Rochelle, N.Y.: Arlington House, 1968), pp. 178, 207, 237–38, 253; Colin Cross, *The Fascists in Britain* (New York: St. Martin's Press, 1963), pp. 35–36.

more easily adapted to the conditions of a totalitarian state, than is the theory of production and distribution of a given output produced under conditions of free competition and a large measure of laissez-faire.[6]

[6]John Maynard Keynes, *The General Theory of Employment, Interest and Money. The Collected Writings of John Maynard Keynes* (London: Macmillan and Cambridge University Press, 1973), vol. 7, p. xxvi; Hazlitt, *Failure of the "New Economics,"* p. 277; Brunner, "The Sociopolitical Vision of Keynes," pp. 38ff.; F.A. Hayek, *Studies in Philosophy, Politics and Economics* (Chicago: University Chicago Press, 1967), p. 346.

CHAPTER 26

The Chicago School

I must say that the more I read the general, all-around works of the "Chicago school" of economics, the less I am impressed.

A good example of the approach of this school is Clark Lee Allen, James M. Buchanan, and Marshall R. Colberg, *Prices, Income, and Public Policy.*[1] As you will see, I was impressed neither by the technical economic analysis nor by the more politico-economic sections.

Let us take the broader or more "political" sections first. First it must be said that on the two great foci of attack on the free-market economy by left-wingers—the Keynesian problem of "cyclical instability" and unemployment, and the alleged problems of "monopoly,"—Allen, Buchanan, and Colberg take up the hue and cry against the market with the rest of the "pack." Oh, very gently and very moderately, compared to most other textbooks, it is true; but still the essence of the charges is there, and the case has been given away.

In the "national income" field, the authors enlist themselves wholeheartedly as what we may call "moderate Keynesians." The crucial thing

---

[1] Second edition (New York: McGraw-Hill, 1959).

Letter to Ivan R. Bierly, Volker Fund, February 3, 1960. Reprinted in *Strictly Confidential: The Private Volker Fund Memos of Murray N. Rothbard*, David Gordon, ed. (Auburn, Ala.: Mises Institute, 2010), pp. 295–301.

here is that they accept the fundamental Keynesian point and accept it blithely as above discussion: that the free market, left to itself, has no mechanism for keeping its aggregate self in balance, for avoiding business cycles, depressions, unemployment, etc. Government, then, must step in to regulate the system: to keep the price level stable, to pump in money in depressions in order to cure unemployment, to tighten up money in booms. Government is considered the natural and indispensable regulator. The free market has no way of keeping national income high enough or savings and investment in balance. Thus, the fundamental Keynesian point has been conceded.

It is true that surrounding this hard core, the authors put in "conservative" modifiers: they prefer the government to use monetary policy in its contracyclical efforts rather than fiscal policy, and they even hint the latest Friedman line that they might prefer automatic monetary rules to managed, discretionary monetary policy. But while an improvement over most textbooks, this is not good enough. The authors, in the usual Chicago tradition, show themselves completely ignorant of the Misesian theory of the business cycle, and loftily dismiss the gold standard as hardly worthy of note—never even considering that they might find the monetary automaticity they are seeking in the gold-coin standard. But the most important flaw is their conceding the fundamental Keynesian point.

The authors worry a lot, also, about monopoly. Of course, they think that monopoly can abound on the free market—we cannot expect any economist to take the revolutionary step of denying *that* proposition. But they can be condemned for not even getting as realistic about the market as Chamberlin or, from another direction, Lawrence Abbott, whose seminal book is ignored by these authors as well as everyone else. In fact, the authors cling to the absurd and dangerous Chicago model of "perfect" or "pure" competition, which they persist in considering the normative ideal.

Of course, empirically, they overlaid this terrible flaw with some good remarks: indicating that they believe that the most important empirical instances of monopoly power are caused by government intervention, attacking the fair-trade laws, etc. But these good qualifiers are hardly enough to save the day. On the contrary, what the authors do is to say: "*Well yes, we admit that the whole market is interlarded with 'monopoly power,' and this is unfortunate but really unimportant, except that. ...*" And here, the authors feel free to engage in sudden hit-and-run attacks on cases which *they*, for some reason, feel are important instances of monopoly power that should be busted or regulated by government. Thus, the authors are strong for the antitrust laws, and want to see them strengthened further and enforced more stringently. They have the gall to call the decision outlawing basing-point pricing a great "victory for society," and they endorse the FTC's desire to get the power to enjoin any mergers in advance. Using the "perfect competition" model, the authors also show great hostility toward the alleged great "wastes" of advertising.

The authors are pretty good in criticizing the "monopoly power" of unions, but here again their case is greatly weakened by their conceding validity to the absurd and fallacious "problem of monopsony," which somehow makes out employers to be as inherently monopolistic as unions. They also concede that "natural monopolies," such as public utilities, have to be regulated by government, even though they point out, very well, many of the pitfalls and inconsistencies inherent in public utility regulation. But the force of the latter are, once again, vitiated by their concession to the opponents of freedom of their fundamental point: that public utilities simply *have* to be regulated by government.

The authors also endorse all the fallacious arguments for government action such as the "collective goods" argument and the free-rider, or external-benefits, argument. Thus, they endorse public education because of the alleged long-run benefits to everyone, which people are too short-sighted to pay for voluntarily. On the theory of exchange rates, they are good as far as they go in pointing to the functions of the free exchange market and the perils of exchange control, but they seem to be completely ignorant of the purchasing-power-parity explanation of the determinants, on the free market, of what makes the exchange rates what they are.

On foreign aid and underdeveloped countries, they are surprisingly poor and weak, their section on underdeveloped countries saying very little and including none of the Bauer insights, and actually endorsing both the economics and politics of foreign aid to these countries.

Rather than multiply examples of flaws further, I think it important to emphasize that this book brings home as few have done to me how much can go wrong if one's philosophical approach—one's epistemology—is all wrong. At the root of almost all the troubles of the book lies the weak, confused, and inconsistent *positivism*: the willingness to use false assumptions if their "predictive value" seems to be of some use. It is this crippling positivist willingness to let anything slip by, to *not* be rigorous about one's theory because "the assumptions don't have to be true or realistic anyway," that permeates and ruins this book.

For example, the authors are keen enough, in the monopoly sections, to sense that there in something very wrong with the whole current theory of monopoly, that it is even impossible to *define* monopoly cogently, or define monopoly of a commodity. But while they see these things, they never do anything about it, or start from there to construct an economics that will stand up—because they are thoroughly misled by their positivist attitude of "well, this might be a useful tool for some purposes." Hence their clinging to the absurd "ideal" of perfect competition, etc.—and in many other ways.

This same grave philosophical confusion permits them to suddenly slip their own ethical judgments into the book, undefended and practically unannounced. Suddenly, they say that the outlawing of basing-point pricing was a great "social victory." I said that this was *gall* because they had never bothered to construct or present a cogent ethical system on which to make such a remark. Similarly, they feel free, while cloaking themselves in the robes of scientists, to say suddenly that of course there has to be compulsory egalitarianism, with the government enforcing some equality through taxes and subsidies. Why? Simply because it seems evident to them that a little more equality would be better, and that we can't let the weak be "liquidated."

And they have even the further colossal gall to denounce "price discrimination" (e.g., doctors charging more to the rich than to the poor) because it is, for some reason, terribly unethical for private people to engage in their own strictly voluntary redistribution of wealth. Apparently, and they say so explicitly, it is *only* legitimate for the government to effect this redistribution by coercion. This ethical nonsense they don't feel they have to defend; it appears self-evident to them. It is this kind of slipshod, unphilosophic, sophomoric "ethics" that is again typical of the Chicago school in action.

The pervading positivist epistemology pervades the technical economic analysis as well. The usual fashionable jargon of the "short-run" cost curves of the firm, etc., are used, despite the recognition by the authors that it is all rather arbitrary; this they brush aside with the retort that it can have some "predictive value." The term that I think best describes the shoddiness and eclecticism induced by this philosophic approach is "irresponsibility." For if a theory or analysis doesn't have to be strictly true or coherently united to other theory, then almost anything goes—all to be justified with "predictive value" or some other such excuse.

Happily, I can illustrate what I mean in a little exchange of letters that I had last week with Jim Buchanan about one minor piece of technical analysis in this book. I was appalled by the construction of a so-called "fixed demand" curve, which was clearly thrown in so as to have something geometrically symmetric with the standard, and perfectly proper, fixed-supply curve for the immediate market. The authors said that a fixed, vertical demand curve is illustrated by the government's demand for soldiers, and that if not enough people volunteer, the government will draft the rest. Now this is pure nonsense, since drafting cannot be illustrated by a demand curve. But what struck me is that even on the authors' own terms, the analysis is nonsense, since, if say the government wants 100,000 men in the army and its "demand curve" is therefore vertical at this amount, but if so many people are 4-F or exempt that only 60,000 can possibly be hired or drafted, we then have a vertical supply and vertical demand curve which never intersect. On the authors' own premises, then, *no one* would be in the army, which is clearly absurd.

So I wrote to Jim Buchanan asking him to clear up this point, and saying that maybe I was overlooking the happy and obvious solution. What interests us here, as revelatory of Buchanan's philosophical irresponsibility, was his reply. The reply *conceded* my point in full. Yes, his model *does* lead to absurd conclusions. Here is Buchanan's justification:

> Your letter points up the limitations of applying too literally many of our analytical tools. You are quite right in saying that the solution ... under your assumptions is absurd. But this is really the same in all of those cases in which we make rather extreme assumptions. ... At best, the fixed demand and fixed supply models are useful in that they isolate certain forces, and in few cases, the models themselves are useful for predictive purposes.

He goes on to say that he tried to find a case of fixed demand as a counterpart to the usual fixed supply case, and could only think of the draft example as remotely suitable.

Now, it seems to me that this kind of philosophy, this positivistic approach to economic theory, corrupts it, if I may use so strong a term, at the very core, and that no theory of lasting merit can emerge from this sort of cauldron. And this book of Allen, Buchanan, and Colberg is a particularly clear example of how this positivistic "corruption" ruins almost every key section of the book.

CHAPTER 27

Israel Kirzner
and the Economic Man

Economics has long been considered the dismal science by most edu-
cated men. Much of this negative attitude stems from a firm belief that
economics (1) deals solely with the grubby business of acquiring material wealth, of money-making; and (2) postulates a coldly rational, coolly
calculating, economic man, a man without sentiment or compassion, a man
who would refuse a few coppers to his sick old mother because his only
value in life is to "buy on the cheapest market and sell on the dearest."

Much of this picture of economics was always a caricature. To the
extent that it was ever relevant, it was relevant only to British classical
economics of the nineteenth century, and largely because these economists were not properly equipped to analyze the actions of consumers.
Despairing of bringing the consumer into their theoretical framework, the
classical economists concentrated on the businessmen and his drive for
pecuniary profit. Now, generally, it is the consumer who has values, and
guides the profit-seeking businessmen in the paths of production that will
fulfill these values. The classical omission, coupled with John Stuart Mill's
unfortunate—and positivistic—championing of the concept of the *homo
oeconomicus*, gave enough room for the enemies of the hard realities of the
economic discipline to heap scorn and abuse on the science as a whole.

Review of Israel Kirzner's *The Economic Point of View* (Princeton, N.J.: D. Van Nostrand,
1960); reprinted as "Economics as a Moral Science," *Modern Age* (Spring, 1961).

Economics has come a long way since the nineteenth century, although the story is not generally known. In this fine and scholarly work, Professor Israel Kirzner traces what has happened to the conception of the scope of economics since the early British classics. He shows how *economics* has broadened immeasurably through the years, until, in the remarkable achievement of Ludwig von Mises, it has become part of a general theoretical analysis of all human actions, of the science of "praxeology." And rather than being confined to certain specific goods or certain particular motives, economic analysis embraces all goods, material or immaterial, and all motives, and analyzes these actions from a certain particular aspect. The man who attends and enjoys a concert is engaging in an action analyzable by economics, even though his motive is "pure" and the good that he consumes is non-material. And not only interpersonal exchanges come under the praxeologic rubric, but also such purely personal actions as the deeds of Crusoe on his desert island. In brief, economics, or praxeology, deals with the logical implications of the universal, formal fact that human beings act, i.e., that they act purposively, employing means to achieve ends. Economics, therefore, in its profoundest sense, is not a quantitative, empirical statistical science as most people believe; it is a philosophical, qualitative, and deductive discipline.

It should be noted that economics is profoundly different from all other social or "behavioral" sciences. The latter, which try to develop scientific laws of the content of men's actions, are determinist, mechanistic, and therefore behaviorist: men are treated like stones to be "observed," charted, and "predicted." Genuine economics, especially economics as it has emerged in praxeology and as shown by Dr. Kirzner, is quite the opposite; instead of mechanistically substituting behavior for action, it grounds its deductions squarely on the axiom of action, which means in essence on the axiom of man's purposiveness and freedom of will. The conservative, properly suspicious of the anti-human essence of the "social science," should recognize that in economics, particularly economics in its most developed praxeological form, he has a staunch and extremely important ally. Praxeological economics rests squarely on the reality of the individual person, not on the collective; and instead of burying values and purpose, it portrays the individual as striving purposively to achieve his cherished ends. While, therefore, the actual construction of the edifice of economic law is strictly *Wertfrei*, in the deepest sense economics is not a "behavioral" nor even a "social" but—what Mill this time correctly called it—a moral science.

Section VI

Economic History

CHAPTER 28

Economic Determinism, Ideology, and the American Revolution

I t is part of the inescapable condition of the historian that he must make estimates and judgments about human motivation even though he cannot ground his judgments in absolute and apodictic certainty. If, for example, we find that Nelson Rockefeller made a secret gift of $650,000 to Dr. William J. Ronan, we can choose to interpret Rockefeller's motivation in one of at least two ways: we can conclude, as did that eminent student of contemporary politics Malcolm Wilson, that Nelson made this and similar gifts purely as "an act of love"; or we can conclude that some sort of political *quid pro quo* was involved in the transaction. In my view, the good historian (1) cannot escape making a judgment of motivation, and (2) will opt for the latter political judgment. Those historians who have made the realistic and what I hold to be the correct judgment have often been condemned as "materialists," "economic determinists," or even "Marxists," but I contend that what they have simply done was to use their common sense, their correct apprehension of reality.

In some matters, where the causal chain of economic interest to action is simple and direct, almost no one denies the overriding motive of economic interest. Thus, when the steel industry lobbies for a tariff or an import quota, and despite the fact that their *stated* motivations will include

---

A paper delivered at the Libertarian Scholars Conference, October 28, 1974, in New York City. Reprinted from *Libertarian Forum* 6, no. 11 (1974).

every bit of blather about the "public interest" or the "national security" that they can think of (even "an act of love" if they thought they could get away with it). It would be a rash historian indeed who did not conclude that the prime motivation of the steel industry was to gain higher profits and restrict foreign competition. Similarly with Nelson's "loving" largesse. There will be few charges of "Marxism" hurled in these situations. The problem comes when the actions involve longer and more complex causal chains: when, for example, we contemplate the reasons for the adoption of the American Constitution, or the Marshall Plan, or entry into World War I. It is in these matters that the focus on economic motives becomes somehow unpatriotic and disreputable.

And yet, the methodology in both sets of cases is the same. In each case, the actor himself tries his best to hide his economic motive and to trumpet his more abstract and ideological concerns. And, in each case, it is precisely because of the attempted cover-up (which, of course, is more successful in the longer causal chains) that the responsibility of the historian is to unearth the hidden motivations. There is no problem, for example, for the historian of the Marshall Plan to discover such ideological motivations as aid to the starving people of Europe or defense against Communism; these were trumpeted everywhere. But the goal of subsidizing American export industries was kept under wraps, and therefore requires more work by the historian in digging it up and spreading it on the record.

Neither is the Mises point that men are guided not by their economic interests but by ideas very helpful in discussing this problem: for the real question is *what* ideas are guiding them—ideas *about* their economic interests or ideas about religion, morality, or whatever? Ideas need not be a highly abstract level; it did not take profound familiarity with philosophy, for example, for the export manufacturers to realize that foreign aid would provide them a fat subsidy out of the pockets of the American taxpayer.

No "economic determinist" worth his salt, however, has ever held that economic motives are the sole or even always the dominant wellsprings of human action. Thus, no one who has ever studied the early Calvinists could ever deny that fiery devotion to their new religious creed was the overriding motivation for their conversion and even for their secular activities. Although even in the case of the Reformation, we cannot overlook the economic motivation, for example, for the German princes in siding with Luther or for Henry VIII's confiscation of the wealth of the

Roman Catholic monasteries. The point is in each case to give the economic motivation its due.

Can we, however, provide ourselves with a criterion, with a guide with which we can equip ourselves in at least our preliminary hypotheses about the weights of motivation? In short, can we formulate a theoretical guide which will indicate in advance whether or not an historical action will be predominantly for economic, or for ideological, motives? I think we can, although as far as I know we will be breaking new and untried ground.

Some years ago, an article in the *Journal of the History of Ideas*, in an attempt to score some points against the great "economic determinist" historian Charles A. Beard, charged that for Beard it was only his historical "bad guys" who were economically determined, whereas his "good guys" were governed largely by ideology. To the author, Beard's supposed "inconsistency" in this matter was enough to demolish the Beardian method. But my contention here is that in a sense, Beard wasn't so far wrong; and that, in fact, from the libertarian if not from the Beardian perspective, it is indeed true in a profound sense that the "bad guys" in history are largely economically motivated, and the "good guys" ideologically motivated. Note that the operative term here, of course, is "largely" rather than "exclusively."

Let us see why this should be so. The essence of the State through history is that a minority of the population, who constitute a "ruling class," govern, live off of, and exploit the majority, or the "ruled." Since a majority cannot live parasitically off a minority without the economy and the system breaking down very quickly, and since the majority can never act permanently by itself but must always be governed by an oligarchy, every State will persist by plundering the majority on behalf of a ruling minority. A further or corollary reason for the inevitability of minority rule is the pervasive fact of the division of labor; the majority of the public must spend most of its time about the business of making a daily living. Hence the actual rule of the State must be left to full-time professionals who are necessarily a minority of the society.

Throughout history, then, the State has consisted of a minority plundering and tyrannizing over a majority. This brings us to the great question, the great mystery if you will, of political philosophy: the mystery of civil obedience. From Etienne de La Boétie to David Hume to Ludwig von Mises, political philosophers have shown that no State—no minority—can continue long in power unless supported, even if passively, by the majority. Why then do the majority continue to accept or support the State when they are clearly acquiescing in their own exploitation and subjection? Why do the majority continue to obey the minority?

Here we arrive at the age-old role of the intellectuals, the opinion-moulding groups in society. The ruling class—be they warlords, nobles, feudal landlords, or monopoly merchants, or a coalition of several of these groups—must employ intellectuals to convince the majority of the public that their rule is beneficent, inevitable, necessary, and even divine. The dominant role of the intellectual through history is that of the Court Intellectual, who in return for a share, a junior partnership, in the power and pelf offered by the rest of the ruling class, spins the apologias for State rule with which to convince a deluded public. This is the age-old alliance of Church and State, of Throne and Altar, with the Church in modern times being largely replaced by "scientific" technocrats.

When the "bad guys" act, then, when they form a State or a centralizing Constitution, when they go to war or create a Marshall Plan or use and increase State power in any way, their *primary* motivation is economic: to increase their plunder at the expense of the subject and taxpayer. The ideology that they profess and that is formulated and spread through society by the Court Intellectuals is merely an elaborate rationalization for their venal economic interests. The ideology is the smokescreen for their loot, the fictitious clothes spun by the intellectuals to hide the naked plunder of the Emperor. The task of the historian, then, is to penetrate to the essence of the transaction, to strip the ideological garb from the Emperor State and to reveal the economic motive at the heart of the issue.

What then of the actions of the "good guys," i.e., those unfortunately infrequent but vital situations in history when the subjects rise up to diminish, or whittle away, or abolish State power? What, in short, of such historical events as the American Revolution or the classical liberal movements of the eighteenth and nineteenth centuries? It goes without saying, of course, that the economic motive for diminishing or throwing off State power is a "good" one from the libertarian point of view, in contrast to the "bad" economic motives of the statists. Thus, a move by the ruling class on behalf of higher taxation is a bad economic motive, a motive to increase their confiscation of the property of the producers, whereas the economic motive against taxation is the good one of defending private property against such unjust depredations. That is true, but that is not the major point I am trying to make here. My contention is that, in the nature of the case, the major motive of the opposition, or the revolutionaries, will be ideological rather than economic.

The basic reason is that the ruling class, being small and largely specialized, is motivated to think about its economic interests twenty-four hours a day. The steel manufacturers seeking a tariff, the bankers seeking taxes to repay their government bonds, the rulers seeking a strong state from which to obtain subsidies, the bureaucrats wishing to expand their empire, are all professionals in statism. They are constantly at work trying to preserve and expand their privileges. Hence the primacy of the economic motive in their pernicious actions. But the majority has allowed itself to be deluded largely because its immediate interests are diffuse and hard to observe, and because they are not professional "anti-statists" but people going about their business of daily living. What can the average person know of the arcane processes of subsidy or taxation or bond issue? Generally he is too wrapped up in his daily life, too habituated to his lot after centuries of State-guided propaganda, to give any thought to his unfortunate fate. Hence, an opposition or revolutionary movement, or indeed any mass movement from below, cannot be primarily guided by ordinary economic motives. For such a mass movement to form, the masses must be fired up, must be aroused to a rare and uncommon pitch of fervor against the existing system. But the only way for that to happen is for the masses to be fired up by ideology. It is only ideology, guided either by a new religious conversion, or by a passion for justice, that can arouse the interest of the masses (in the current jargon to "raise their consciousness") and lead them out of their morass of daily habit into an uncommon and militant activity in opposition to the State. This is not to say that an economic motive, a defense for example of their property, does not play an important role. But to form a mass movement in opposition means that they must shake off the habits, the daily mundane concerns of several lifetimes, and become politically aroused and determined as never before in their lives. Only a common and passionately believed in ideology can perform that role. Hence our strong hypothesis that such a mass movement as the American Revolution (or even in its sphere the Calvinist movement) must have been centrally motivated by a newly adopted and commonly shared ideology.

We turn now to the insight of such disparate political theorists as Marx and Mises, how do the masses of subjects *acquire* this guiding and determining ideology? By the very nature of the masses, it is impossible for them to arrive at such a revolutionary or opposition ideology on their own. Habituated as they are to their narrow and daily rounds, uninterested in ideology as they normally are, concerned with daily living, it is impossible for the masses to lift themselves up by their own bootstraps to hammer out an ideological movement in opposition to the existing State. Here we arrive at the vital role of the intellectuals. It is only intellectuals, the full-time professionals in ideas, who can have either the time, the ability, or the inclination to formulate the opposition ideology and then to spread the word to the mass of the subjects. In contrast to the statist Court Intellectual, whose role is a junior partner in rationalizing the economic interests of the ruling class, the radical or opposition intellectual's role is the centrally guiding one of formulating the opposition or revolutionary ideology and then to spread the ideology to the masses, thereby welding them into a revolutionary movement.

An important corollary point: in weighing the motivations of the intellectuals themselves or even of the masses, it is generally true that setting oneself up in opposition to an existing State is a lonely, thorny, and often dangerous road. It would usually be to the direct economic interests of the radical intellectuals to allow themselves to "sell out," to be coopted by the ruling State apparatus. Those intellectuals who choose the radical opposition path, then, can scarcely be dominated by economic motives; on the contrary, only a fiercely held ideology, centering on a passion for justice, can keep the intellectual to the rigorous path of truth. Hence, again, the inevitability of a dominant role for ideology in an opposition movement.

Thus, though perhaps not for Beardian reasons, it turns out to be true that the "bad guys," the statists, are governed by economic motivation with ideology serving as a smokescreen for such motives, whereas the "good guys," the libertarians or anti-statists, are ruled principally and centrally by ideology, with economic defense playing a subordinate role. Through this dichotomy we can at last resolve the age-old historiographical dispute over whether ideology or economic interests play the dominant role in historical motivation.

If it is the shame of the intellectuals that the Court Intellectual has been their dominant role over the course of world history, it is also the glory of the intellectuals that they played the central role in forming and guiding the mass movements of the modern world in opposition to the State: from the Calvinist upsurge of the Reformation to the classical liberal and radical movements of the seventeenth, eighteenth, and nineteenth centuries.

Let us now apply our framework to an analysis of the historiography of the American Revolution. In the long-standing controversy over the

Beard-Becker economic determinist school of American history dominant in the 1920s and 30s, it has generally been assumed that one must
either accept or reject this basic outlook wholesale, for each and every
period of American history. Yet our framework explains why the Beard-
Becker approach, so fruitful and penetrating when applied to the statist
drive for power which brought about the US Constitution, fails signally
when applied to the great anti-statist events of the American Revolution.

The Beard-Becker approach sought to apply an economic determinist framework to the American Revolution, and specifically a framework
of inherent conflict between various major economic classes. The vital
flaws in the Beard-Becker model were twofold. First, they did not understand the primary role of ideas in guiding any revolutionary or opposition movement. Second, and this is an issue we have not had time to deal
with, they did not understand that there are no inherent economic conflicts on the free market; without government intrusion, there is no reason
for merchants, farmers, landlords, *et al.* to be at loggerheads. Conflict is
only created between those classes which rule the State as against those
which are exploited by the State. Not understanding this crucial point, the
Beard-Becker historians framed their analysis in terms of the allegedly
conflicting class interests of, in particular, merchants and farmers. Since
the merchants clearly led the way in revolutionary agitation, the Beard-
Becker approach was bound to conclude that the merchants, in agitating for revolution, were aggressively pushing their class interests at the
expense of the deluded farmers.

But now the economic determinists were confronted with a basic
problem: if indeed the revolution was against the class interests of the
mass of the farmers, how come that the latter supported the revolutionary movement? To this key question, the determinists had two answers.
One was the common view—based on a misreading of a letter by John
Adams—that the Revolution was indeed supported by only a minority of
the population; in the famous formulation, one-third of the populace was
supposed to have supported the revolution, one-third opposed, and one-
third were neutral. This view flies in the face of our analysis of opposition
movements; for, it should be clear that any revolution, battling as it does
the professional vested interest of the State, and needing to lift the mass of
the people out of their accustomed inertia, must have the active support
of a large majority of the population in order to succeed. As confirmation,
it was one of the positive contributions of the later "consensus" school of
American history of such scholars as John Alden and Edmund Morgan, to

demonstrate conclusively that the Revolution had the active support of a large majority of the American public.

The Beard-Becker school had another answer to the puzzle of majority support of the Revolution: namely that the farmers were deluded into such support by the "propaganda" beamed at them by the upper classes. In effect, these historians transferred the analysis of the role of ideology as a rationalization of class interests from its proper use to explain *State* action to a fallacious use in trying to understand mass movements. In this approach, they relied on the jejune theory of "propaganda" common in the 1920s and 1930s under the inspiration of Harold Lasswell: namely, that no one sincerely holds any ideas or ideology, and that therefore no ideological statements whatever can be taken at face value, but must be considered only as insincere rhetoric for the purposes of "propaganda." Again, the Beard-Becker school was trapped by its failure to give *any* primary role to ideas in history.

The economic determinists were succeeded by the "consensus" school of American history, as part of the general "American celebration" among intellectuals after World War II. At its best, the consensus historians, notably Edmund Morgan and Bernhard Knollenberg, were able to show that the American Revolution was a genuine multi-class movement supported by the great majority of the American public. Furthermore, the economic determinists, in their eagerness to show the upper merchant class as duping the farmers into supporting the Revolution, emerged—in a curious kind of left-right alliance with the pro-British "Imperial" historians—as hostile to the American Revolution. The consensus historians restored the older view that the colonists were rebelling against genuine invasions of their liberties and property by the British Empire: that their grievances were real and compelling, and not simply a figment of upper class propaganda.

At its worst, however, and under the aegis of such major consensus theoreticians as the "neo-conservatives" Daniel Boorstin and Clinton Rossiter, the consensus school was moved to the truly absurd conclusion that the American Revolution, in contrast to all other revolutions in history, was not really a revolution at all, but a purely measured and conservative reflex against the restrictive measures of the Crown. Under the spell of the American celebration and of a Cold-War generated hostility to all modern revolutions, the consensus historians were constrained to deny any and all conflicts in American history, whether economic or ideological, and to absolve the American republic from the original sin of having been born via a revolution. Thus, the consensus historians were fully as hostile to ideology as a prime motive force in history as their enemies, the economic determinists. The difference is that where the determinists saw class conflict, the consensus school maintained that the genius of Americans has always been to be unfettered by abstract ideology, and that instead they have met every issue as *ad hoc* problem-solving pragmatists.

Thus, the consensus school, in its eagerness to deny the revolutionary nature of the American Revolution, failed to see that all revolutions against State power are necessarily radical and hence "revolutionary" acts, and further that they must be genuine mass movements guided by an informed and radical ideology. Furthermore, as Robert A. Nisbet has recently pointed out in his scintillating pamphlet, *The Social Impact of the Revolution*, the consensus view overlooks the truly revolutionary and libertarian consequences of the American Revolution in diminishing the role of government, in dismantling church establishments and winning religious freedom, in bringing about bills of rights for the individual's liberty and property, and in dismantling feudal land tenure in the colonies.

Nisbet's stress on the revolutionary and libertarian nature and consequences of the American Revolution brings us to the most recent and now dominant school of historiography on the Revolution: that of Professor Bernard Bailyn. Against the hostility of both of the older schools of historians, Bailyn has managed, in scarcely a decade, to win his way through to become the leading interpretation of the Revolution. Bailyn's great contribution was to discover for the first time the truly dominant role of ideology among the revolutionaries, and to stress that not only was the Revolution a genuine revolutionary and multi-class mass movement among the colonists, but that it was guided and impelled above all by the ideology of radical libertarianism; hence what Bailyn happily calls "the transforming libertarian radicalism of the Revolution." In a sense, Bailyn was harking back to an older generation of historians at the turn of the twentieth century, the so-called "Constitutionalists," who had also stressed the dominant role of ideas in the revolutionary movement. But Bailyn correctly saw that the mistake of the Constitutionalists was in ascribing the central and guiding role to sober and measured legalistic arguments about the British Constitution, and, secondarily, to John Locke's philosophy of natural rights and the right of revolution. Bailyn saw that the problem with this interpretation was to miss the major motive power of the Revolutionaries; Constitutional legalisms, as later critics pointed out, were dry-as-dust arguments that hardly stimulated the requisite revolutionary passions, and furthermore they neglected the important problem of economic depredations by Great Britain; while Locke's philosophy, though ultimately important, was too abstract to generate the passions or to stimulate widespread reading by the bulk of the colonists. Something, Bailyn rightly felt, was missing: the intermediate-level ideology that could stimulate revolutionary passions.

Guided by the extensive research into English libertarian writers by Caroline Robbins, Bailyn found the missing and vital ingredient: in the transforming of Lockean natural rights theory into a radical and passionate, and explicitly political and libertarian framework. This task was accomplished by radical English journalists who, in contrast to Locke, were read very widely in the colonies: notably, the newspaper essays of Trenchard and Gordon written during the 1720s. Trenchard and Gordon clearly and passionately set forth the libertarian theory of natural rights, went on to point out that government in general, and the British government specifically, was the great violator of such rights, and warned also that Power—government—stood ever ready to conspire to violate the liberties of the individual. To stop this crippling and destructive invasion of Liberty by Power, the people must be ever wary, ever vigilant, ever alert to the conspiracies by the rulers to expand their power and aggress against their subjects. It was this spirit that the American colonists eagerly imbibed, and which accounted for their "conspiracy view" of the English government. And while Bailyn himself, by concentrating solely on the ideology of the colonists, is ambivalent about whether such English conspiracies against liberty actually existed, the work of such historians as Bernhard Knollenberg has shown conclusively that the conspiracy was all too real, and that what some historians have derided as the "paranoia" of the colonists turned out to be an insightful apprehension of reality, an insight that was of course fueled by the colonists' understanding of the very nature and essence of State power itself.

While Bernard Bailyn has not continued his studies beyond the Revolution, his students Gordon Wood and Pauline Maier have done so, with unfortunate results. For how can one apply the concept of a "transforming libertarian radicalism," of a mass ideological hatred of the State and of the executive, to the movement for a Constitution which was the very antithesis of the libertarian and radical ideal? By trying to do so, Wood and Maier lose the idea of radical libertarianism altogether, and wind up in yet another form of consensus view of the Constitution. Yet the battle over the adoption of the Constitution was a fierce ideological and economic conflict; and in understanding that movement and that conflict we must turn to the neo-Beardian approach of such historians as Jackson Turner Main, E. James Ferguson, and Alfred Young, which stresses the economic and class interests behind this aggrandizement of a powerful central government. Furthermore, the Anti-Federalist resistance to the Constitution was fueled, not only by resistance to these economic depredations, but also and above all by the very ideology of Liberty versus Power that had sparked and guided the American Revolution. A glance at the eloquent speeches against the Constitution by Patrick Henry is enough to highlight the libertarian leitmotif of the anti-statist Revolution as well as the anti-statist resistance to the Constitution. Hence, the original insight of the Beardians was correct: that the Constitution was a reaction against the Revolution rather than its fulfillment.

The idea of economic motivation as the prime mover of statist actions through history, as contrasted to ideology as the major guide of anti-statist movements, is thus confirmed by analyzing the historiography of the American Revolution. Perhaps adoption of this basic framework will prove fruitful in the analysis of other important events and movements in human history.

CHAPTER 29

The Progressive Movement

The Federal Reserve Act of December 23, 1913, was part and parcel of the wave of Progressive legislation, on local, state, and federal levels of government, that began about 1900. Progressivism was a bipartisan movement which, in the course of the first two decades of the twentieth century, transformed the American economy and society from one of roughly laissez-faire to one of centralized statism.

Until the 1960s, historians had established the myth that Progressivism was a virtual uprising of workers and farmers who, guided by a new generation of altruistic experts and intellectuals, surmounted fierce big business opposition in order to curb, regulate, and control what had been a system of accelerating monopoly in the late nineteenth century. A generation of research and scholarship, however, has now exploded that myth for all parts of the American polity, and it has become all too clear that the truth is the reverse of this well-worn fable. In contrast, what actually happened was that business became increasingly competitive during the late nineteenth century, and that various big-business interests, led by the powerful financial house of J.P. Morgan and Company, had tried desperately to establish successful cartels on the free market. The first wave of

Excerpt from "The Origins of the Federal Reserve," in *A History of Money and Banking in the United States: The Colonial Era to World War II* (Auburn, Ala.: Mises Institute, [2002] 2005), pp. 183–85.

such cartels was in the first large-scale business, railroads, and in every case, the attempt to increase profits, by cutting sales with a quota system and thereby to raise prices or rates, collapsed quickly from internal competition within the cartel and from external competition by new competitors eager to undercut the cartel. During the 1890s, in the new field of large-scale industrial corporations, big-business interests tried to establish high prices and reduced production via mergers, and again, in every case, the mergers collapsed from the winds of new competition. In both sets of cartel attempts, J.P. Morgan and Company had taken the lead, and in both sets of cases, the market, hampered though it was by high protective tariff walls, managed to nullify these attempts at voluntary cartelization.

It then became clear to these big-business interests that the only way to establish a cartelized economy, an economy that would ensure their continued economic dominance and high profits, would be to use the powers of government to establish and maintain cartels by coercion. In other words, to transform the economy from roughly *laissez-faire* to centralized and coordinated statism. But how could the American people, steeped in a long tradition of fierce opposition to government-imposed monopoly, go along with this program? How could the public's consent to the New Order be engineered?

Fortunately for the cartelists, a solution to this vexing problem lay at hand. Monopoly could be put over *in the name* of opposition to monopoly! In that way, using the rhetoric beloved by Americans, the *form* of the political economy could be maintained, while the *content* could be totally reversed. Monopoly had always been defined, in the popular parlance and among economists, as "grants of exclusive privilege" by the government. It was now simply redefined as "big business" or business competitive practices, such as price-cutting, so that regulatory commissions, from the Interstate Commerce Commission to the Federal Trade Commission to state insurance commissions, were lobbied for and staffed by big-business men from the regulated industry, all done in the name of curbing "big business monopoly" on the free market. In that way, the regulatory commissions could subsidize, restrict, and cartelize in the name of "opposing monopoly," as well as promoting the general welfare and national security. Once again, it was railroad monopoly that paved the way.

For this intellectual shell game, the cartelists needed the support of the nation's intellectuals, the class of professional opinion molders in society. The Morgans needed a smoke screen of ideology, setting forth the rationale and the apologetics for the New Order. Again, fortunately for them, the intellectuals were ready and eager for the new alliance. The enormous growth of intellectuals, academics, social scientists, technocrats, engineers, social workers, physicians, and occupational "guilds" of all types in the late nineteenth century led most of these groups to organize for a far greater share of the pie than they could possibly achieve on the free market. These intellectuals needed the State to license, restrict, and cartelize their occupations, so as to raise the incomes for the fortunate people already in these fields. In return for their serving as apologists for the new statism, the State was prepared to offer not only cartelized occupations, but also ever increasing and cushier jobs in the bureaucracy to plan and propagandize for the newly statized society. And the intellectuals were ready for it, having learned in graduate schools in Germany the glories of statism and organicist socialism, of a harmonious "middle way" between dog-eat-dog *laissez-faire* on the one hand and proletarian Marxism on the other. Instead, big government, staffed by intellectuals and technocrats, steered by big business and aided by unions organizing a subservient labor force, would impose a cooperative commonwealth for the alleged benefit of all.

CHAPTER 30

Unhappiness with the National Banking System

The previous big push for statism in America had occurred during the Civil War, when the virtual one-party Congress after secession of the South emboldened the Republicans to enact their cherished statist program under cover of the war. The alliance of big business and big government with the Republican Party drove through an income tax, heavy excise taxes on such sinful products as tobacco and alcohol, high protective tariffs, and huge land grants and other subsidies to transcontinental railroads. The overbuilding of railroads led directly to Morgan's failed attempts at railroad pools, and finally to the creation, promoted by Morgan and Morgan-controlled railroads, of the Interstate Commerce Commission in 1887. The result of *that* was the long secular decline of the railroads beginning before 1900. The income tax was annulled by Supreme Court action, but was reinstated during the Progressive period.

The most interventionary of the Civil War actions was in the vital field of money and banking. The approach toward hard money and free banking that had been achieved during the 1840s and 1850s was swept away by two pernicious inflationist measures of the wartime Republican administration. One was fiat money greenbacks, which depreciated by half by the

Excerpt from "The Origins of the Federal Reserve," in *A History of Money and Banking in the United States: The Colonial Era to World War II* (Auburn, Ala.: Mises Institute, [2002] 2005), pp. 185–88.

middle of the Civil War, and were finally replaced by the gold standard after urgent pressure by hard-money Democrats, but not until 1879, some fourteen full years after the end of the war. A second, and more lasting, intervention were the National Banking Acts of 1863, 1864, and 1865, which destroyed the issue of bank notes by state-chartered (or "state") banks by a prohibitory tax, and then monopolized the issue of bank notes in the hands of a few large, federally chartered "national banks," mainly centered on Wall Street. In a typical cartelization, national banks were compelled by law to accept each other's notes and demand deposits at par, negating the process by which the free market had previously been discounting the notes and deposits of shaky and inflationary banks.

In this way, the Wall Street–federal government establishment was able to control the banking system, and inflate the supply of notes and deposits in a coordinated manner.

But there were still problems. The national banking system provided only a halfway house between free banking and government central banking, and by the end of the nineteenth century, the Wall Street banks were becoming increasingly unhappy with the status quo. The centralization was only limited, and, above all, there was no governmental central bank to coordinate inflation, and to act as a lender of last resort, bailing out banks in trouble. No sooner had bank credit generated booms when they got into trouble and bank-created booms turned into recessions, with banks forced to contract their loans and assets and to deflate in order to save themselves. Not only that, but after the initial shock of the National Banking Acts, state banks had grown rapidly by pyramiding their loans and demand deposits on top of national bank notes. These state banks, free of the high legal capital requirements that kept entry restricted in national banking, flourished during the 1880s and 1890s and provided stiff competition for the national banks themselves. Furthermore, St. Louis and Chicago, after the 1880s, provided increasingly severe competition to Wall Street. Thus, St. Louis and Chicago bank deposits, which had been only 16 percent of the St. Louis, Chicago, and New York City total in 1880, rose to 33 percent of that total by 1912. All in all, bank clearings outside of New York City, which were 24 percent of the national total in 1882, had risen to 43 percent by 1913.

The complaints of the big banks were summed up in one word: "inelasticity." The national banking system, they charged, did not provide for the proper "elasticity" of the money supply; that is, the banks were not able to expand money and credit as much as they wished, particularly in times of recession. In short, the national banking system did not provide sufficient room for inflationary expansions of credit by the nation's banks.[1]

By the turn of the century the political economy of the United States was dominated by two generally clashing financial aggregations: the previously dominant Morgan group, which had begun in investment banking and expanded into commercial banking, railroads, and mergers of manufacturing firms; and the Rockefeller forces, which began in oil refining and then moved into commercial banking, finally forming an alliance with the Kuhn, Loeb Company in investment banking and the Harriman interests in railroads.[2]

Although these two financial blocs usually clashed with each other, they were as one on the need for a central bank. Even though the eventual major role in forming and dominating the Federal Reserve System was taken by the Morgans, the Rockefeller and Kuhn, Loeb forces were equally enthusiastic in pushing, and collaborating on, what they all considered to be an essential monetary reform.

---

[1]On the national banking system background and on the increasing unhappiness of the big banks, see Murray N. Rothbard, "The Federal Reserve as a Cartelization Device: The Early Years, 1913–1920," in *Money in Crisis*, Barry Siegel, ed. (San Francisco: Pacific Institute, 1984), pp. 89–94; Ron Paul and Lewis Lehrman, *The Case for Gold: A Minority Report on the U.S. Gold Commission* (Washington, D.C.: Cato Institute, 1982); and Gabriel Kolko, *The Triumph of Conservatism: A Reinterpretation of American History* (Glencoe, Ill.: Free Press, 1983), pp. 139–46.

[2]Indeed, much of the political history of the United States from the late nineteenth century until World War II may be interpreted by the closeness of each administration to one of these sometimes cooperating, more often conflicting, financial groupings: Cleveland (Morgan), McKinley (Rockefeller), Theodore Roosevelt (Morgan), Taft (Rockefeller), Wilson (Morgan), Harding (Rockefeller), Coolidge (Morgan), Hoover (Morgan), and Franklin Roosevelt (Harriman-Kuhn Loeb-Rockefeller).

Section VII

Political Philosophy and
the Libertarian Movement

CHAPTER 31

Property and Exchange

THE NONAGGRESSION AXIOM

The libertarian creed rests upon one central axiom: that no man or group of men may aggress against the person or property of anyone else. This may be called the "nonaggression axiom." "Aggression" is defined as the initiation of the use or threat of physical violence against the person or property of anyone else. Aggression is therefore synonymous with invasion.

If no man may aggress against another; if, in short, everyone has the absolute right to be "free" from aggression, then this at once implies that the libertarian stands foursquare for what are generally known as "civil liberties": the freedom to speak, publish, assemble, and to engage in such "victimless crimes" as pornography, sexual deviation, and prostitution (which the libertarian does not regard as "crimes" at all, since he defines a "crime" as violent invasion of someone else's person or property). Furthermore, he regards conscription as slavery on a massive scale. And since war, especially modern war, entails the mass slaughter of civilians, the libertarian regards such conflicts as mass murder and therefore totally illegitimate.

Reprinted from *For a New Liberty: The Libertarian Manifesto* (1973, 1978; Auburn, Ala.: Mises Institute, 2006), chap. 2.

All of these positions are now considered "leftist" on the contemporary ideological scale. On the other hand, since the libertarian also opposes invasion of the rights of private property, this also means that he just as emphatically opposes government interference with property rights or with the free-market economy through controls, regulations, subsidies, or prohibitions. For if every individual has the right to his own property without having to suffer aggressive depredation, then he also has the right to give away his property (bequest and inheritance) and to exchange it for the property of others (free contract and the free market economy) without interference. The libertarian favors the right to unrestricted private property and free exchange; hence, a system of "laissez-faire capitalism."

In current terminology again, the libertarian position on property and economics would be called "extreme right wing." But the libertarian sees no inconsistency in being "leftist" on some issues and "rightist" on others. On the contrary, he sees his own position as virtually the *only* consistent one, consistent on behalf of the liberty of every individual. For how can the leftist be opposed to the violence of war and conscription while at the same time supporting the violence of taxation and government control? And how can the rightist trumpet his devotion to private property and free enterprise while at the same time favoring war, conscription, and the outlawing of noninvasive activities and practices that he deems immoral? And how can the rightist favor a free market while seeing nothing amiss in the vast subsidies, distortions, and unproductive inefficiencies involved in the military-industrial complex?

While opposing any and all private or group aggression against the rights of person and property, the libertarian sees that throughout history and into the present day, there has been one central, dominant, and overriding aggressor upon all of these rights: the State. In contrast to all other thinkers, left, right, or in-between, the libertarian refuses to give the State the moral sanction to commit actions that almost everyone agrees would be immoral, illegal, and criminal if committed by any person or group in society. The libertarian, in short, insists on applying the general moral law to everyone, and makes no special exemptions for any person or group. But if we look at the State naked, as it were, we see that it is universally allowed, and even encouraged, to commit all the acts which even non-libertarians concede are reprehensible crimes. The State habitually commits mass murder, which it calls "war," or sometimes "suppression of subversion"; the State engages in enslavement into its military forces, which it calls "conscription"; and it lives and has its being in the practice of forcible theft, which it calls "taxation." The libertarian insists that whether or not such practices are supported by the majority of the population is not germane to their nature: that, regardless of popular sanction, War is Mass Murder, Conscription is Slavery, and Taxation is Robbery. The libertarian, in short, is almost completely the child in the fable, pointing out insistently that the emperor has no clothes.

Throughout the ages, the emperor has had a series of pseudo-clothes provided for him by the nation's intellectual caste. In past centuries, the intellectuals informed the public that the State or its rulers were divine, or at least clothed in divine authority, and therefore what might *look* to the naïve and untutored eye as despotism, mass murder, and theft on a grand scale was only the divine working its benign and mysterious ways in the body politic. In recent decades, as the divine sanction has worn a bit threadbare, the emperor's "court intellectuals" have spun ever more sophisticated apologias: informing the public that what the government does is for the "common good" and the "public welfare," that the process of taxation-and-spending works through the mysterious process of the "multiplier" to keep the economy on an even keel, and that, in any case, a wide variety of governmental "services" could not possibly be performed by citizens acting voluntarily on the market or in society. All of this the libertarian denies: he sees the various apologias as fraudulent means of obtaining public support for the State's rule, and he insists that whatever services the government actually performs could be supplied far more efficiently and far more morally by private and cooperative enterprise.

The libertarian therefore considers one of his prime educational tasks is to spread the demystification and desanctification of the State among its hapless subjects. His task is to demonstrate repeatedly and in depth that not only the emperor but even the "democratic" State has no clothes; that all governments subsist by exploitive rule over the public; and that such rule is the reverse of objective necessity. He strives to show that the very existence of taxation and the State necessarily sets up a class division between the exploiting rulers and the exploited ruled. He seeks to show that the task of the court intellectuals who have always supported the State has ever been to weave mystification in order to induce the public to accept State rule, and that these intellectuals obtain, in return, a share in the power and pelf extracted by the rulers from their deluded subjects.

Take, for example, the institution of taxation, which statists have claimed is in some sense really "voluntary." Anyone who truly believes in the "voluntary" nature of taxation is invited to refuse to pay taxes and to see what then happens to him. If we analyze taxation, we find that, among all the persons and institutions in society, only the government acquires its revenues through coercive violence. Everyone else in society acquires income *either* through voluntary gift (lodge, charitable society, chess club) *or* through the sale of goods or services voluntarily purchased by consumers. If anyone *but* the government proceeded to "tax," this would clearly be considered coercion and thinly disguised banditry. Yet the mystical trappings of "sovereignty" have so veiled the process that only libertarians are prepared to call taxation what it is: legalized and organized theft on a grand scale.

PROPERTY RIGHTS

If the central axiom of the libertarian creed is nonaggression against anyone's person and property, how is this axiom arrived at? What is its groundwork or support? Here, libertarians, past and present, have differed considerably. Roughly, there are three broad types of foundation for the libertarian axiom, corresponding to three kinds of ethical philosophy: the emotivist, the utilitarian, and the natural rights viewpoint. The emotivists assert that they take liberty or nonaggression as their premise purely on subjective, emotional grounds. While their own intense emotion might seem a valid basis for their own political philosophy, this can scarcely serve to convince anyone else. By ultimately taking themselves outside the realm of rational discourse, the emotivists thereby insure the lack of general success of their own cherished doctrine.

The utilitarians declare, from their study of the consequences of liberty as opposed to alternative systems, that liberty will lead more surely to widely approved goals: harmony, peace, prosperity, etc. Now no one disputes that relative consequences should be studied in assessing the merits or demerits of respective creeds. But there are many problems in confining ourselves to a utilitarian ethic. For one thing, utilitarianism assumes that we can weigh alternatives, and decide upon policies, on the basis of their good or bad *consequences*. But if it is legitimate to apply value judgments to the *consequences* of X, why is it not equally legitimate to apply such judgments to X *itself*? May there not be something about an act itself which, in its very nature, can be considered good or evil?

Another problem with the utilitarian is that he will rarely adopt a principle as an absolute and consistent yardstick to apply to the varied concrete situations of the real world. He will only use a principle, at best, as a vague guideline or aspiration, as a *tendency* which he may choose to override at any time. This was the major defect of the nineteenth-century English Radicals, who had adopted the *laissez-faire* view of the eighteenth-century liberals but had substituted a supposedly "scientific" utilitarianism for the supposedly "mystical" concept of natural rights as the groundwork for that philosophy. Hence the nineteenth-century laissez-faire liberals came to use laissez-faire as a vague tendency rather than as an unblemished yardstick, and therefore increasingly and fatally compromised the libertarian creed. To say that a utilitarian cannot be "trusted" to maintain libertarian principle in every specific application may sound harsh, but it puts the case fairly. A notable contemporary example is the free-market economist Professor Milton Friedman who, like his classical economist forebears, holds to freedom as against State intervention as a general tendency, but in practice allows a myriad of damaging exceptions, exceptions which serve to vitiate the principle almost completely, notably in the fields of police and military affairs, education, taxation, welfare, "neighborhood effects," antitrust laws, and money and banking.

Let us consider a stark example: Suppose a society which fervently considers all redheads to be agents of the Devil and therefore to be executed whenever found. Let us further assume that only a small number of redheads exist in any generation—so few as to be statistically insignificant. The utilitarian-libertarian might well reason: "While the murder of isolated redheads is deplorable, the executions are small in number; the vast majority of the public, as non-redheads, achieves enormous psychic satisfaction from the public execution of redheads. The social cost is negligible, the social, psychic benefit to the rest of society is great; therefore, it is right and proper for society to execute the redheads." The natural-rights libertarian, overwhelmingly concerned as he is for the *justice* of the act, will react in horror and staunchly and unequivocally oppose the executions as totally unjustified murder and aggression upon nonaggressive persons. The *consequence* of stopping the murders—depriving the bulk of society of great psychic pleasure—would not influence such a libertarian, the "absolutist" libertarian, in the slightest. Dedicated to justice and to logical consistency, the natural-rights libertarian cheerfully admits to being "doctrinaire," to being, in short, an unabashed follower of his own doctrines.

Let us turn then to the natural-rights basis for the libertarian creed, a basis which, in one form or another, has been adopted by most of the libertarians, past and present. "Natural rights" is the cornerstone of a political philosophy which, in turn, is embedded in a greater structure of "natural law." Natural law theory rests on the insight that we live in a world of more than one—in fact, a vast number—of entities, and that each entity has distinct and specific properties, a distinct "nature," which can be investigated by man's reason, by his sense perception and mental faculties. Copper has a distinct nature and behaves in a certain way, and so do iron, salt, etc. The species man, therefore, has a specifiable nature, as does the world around him and the ways of interaction between them. To put it with undue brevity, the activity of each inorganic and organic entity is determined by its own nature and by the nature of the other entities with which it comes in contact. Specifically, while the behavior of plants and at least the lower animals is determined by their biological nature or perhaps by their "instincts," the nature of man is such that each individual person must, in order to act, choose his own ends and employ his own means in order to attain them. Possessing no automatic instincts, each man must learn about himself and the world, use his mind to select values, learn about cause and effect, and act purposively to maintain himself and advance his life. Since men can think, feel, evaluate, and act only as individuals, it becomes vitally necessary for each man's survival and prosperity that he be free to learn, choose, develop his faculties, and act upon his knowledge and values. This is the necessary path of human nature; to interfere with and cripple this process by using violence goes profoundly against what is necessary by man's nature for his life and prosperity. Violent interference with a man's learning and choices is therefore profoundly "antihuman"; it violates the natural law of man's needs.

Individualists have always been accused by their enemies of being "atomistic"—of postulating that each individual lives in a kind of vacuum, thinking and choosing without relation to anyone else in society. This, however, is an authoritarian straw man; few, if any, individualists have ever been "atomists." On the contrary, it is evident that individuals always learn from each other, cooperate and interact with each other; and that this, too, is required for man's survival. But the point is that each individual makes the final choice of which influences to adopt and which to reject, or of which to adopt first and which afterwards. The libertarian welcomes the process of voluntary exchange and cooperation between freely acting individuals; what he abhors is the use of violence to cripple such voluntary cooperation and force someone to choose and act in ways different from what his own mind dictates.

The most viable method of elaborating the natural-rights statement of the libertarian position is to divide it into parts, and to begin with the basic axiom of the "right to self-ownership." The right to self-ownership asserts the absolute right of each man, by virtue of his (or her) being a human being, to "own" his or her own body; that is, to control that body free of coercive interference. Since each individual must think, learn, value, and choose his or her ends and means in order to survive and flourish, the right to self-ownership gives man the right to perform these vital activities without being hampered and restricted by coercive molestation.

Consider, too, the consequences of *denying* each man the right to own his own person. There are then only two alternatives: either (1) a certain class of people, A, have the right to own another class, B; or (2) everyone has the right to own his own equal quotal share of everyone else. The first alternative implies that while Class A deserves the rights of being human, Class B is in reality subhuman and therefore deserves no such rights. But since they *are* indeed human beings, the first alternative contradicts itself in denying natural human rights to one set of humans. Moreover, as we shall see, allowing Class A to own Class B means that the former is allowed to exploit, and therefore to live parasitically, *at the expense* of the latter. But this parasitism itself violates the basic economic requirement for life: production and exchange.

The second alternative, what we might call "participatory communal-ism" or "communism," holds that every man should have the right to own his equal quotal share of everyone else. If there are two billion people in the world, then everyone has the right to own one two-billionth of every other person. In the first place, we can state that this ideal rests on an absurdity: proclaiming that every man is entitled to own a part of everyone else, yet is not entitled *to own himself*. Second, we can picture the viability of such a world: a world in which *no* man is free to take *any* action whatever without prior approval or indeed command by *everyone* else in society. It should be clear that in that sort of "communist" world, no one would be able to do anything, and the human race would quickly perish. But if a world of zero self-ownership and one hundred percent other ownership spells death for the human race, then any steps in that direction also contravene the natu-ral law of what is best for man and his life on earth.

Finally, however, the participatory communist world *cannot* be put into practice. For it is physically impossible for everyone to keep continual tabs on everyone else, and thereby to exercise his equal quotal share of partial ownership over every other man. In practice, then, the concept of universal and equal other-ownership is utopian and impossible, and supervision and therefore control and ownership of others necessarily devolves upon a specialized group of people, who thereby become a ruling class. Hence, in practice, any attempt at communist rule will automatically become class rule, and we would be back at our first alternative.

The libertarian therefore rejects these alternatives and concludes by adopting as his primary axiom the universal right of self-ownership, a right held by everyone by virtue of being a human being. A more difficult task is to settle on a theory of property in nonhuman objects, in the things of this earth. It is comparatively easy to recognize the practice when someone is aggressing against the property right of another's person: If A assaults B, he is violating the property right of B in his own body. But with nonhuman objects the problem is more complex. If, for example, we see X seizing a watch in the possession of Y we cannot automatically assume that X is aggressing against Y's right of property in the watch; for may not X have been the original, "true" owner of the watch who can therefore be said to be repossessing his own legitimate property? In order to decide, we need a theory of justice in property, a theory that will tell us whether X or Y or indeed someone else is the legitimate owner.

Some libertarians attempt to resolve the problem by asserting that whoever the existing government decrees has the property title should be considered the just owner of the property. At this point, we have not yet delved deeply into the nature of government, but the anomaly here should be glaring enough: it is surely odd to find a group eternally suspicious of virtually any and all functions of government suddenly leaving it to government to define and apply the precious concept of property, the base and groundwork of the entire social order. It is particularly the utilitarian laissez-fairists who believe it most feasible to begin the new libertarian world by confirming all existing property titles; that is, property titles and rights as decreed by the very government that is condemned as a chronic aggressor.

Let us illustrate with a hypothetical example. Suppose that libertarian agitation and pressure has escalated to such a point that the government and its various branches are ready to abdicate. But they engineer a cunning ruse. Just before the government of New York state abdicates it passes a law turning over the entire territorial area of New York to become the private property of the Rockefeller family. The Massachusetts legislature does the same for the Kennedy family. And so on for each state. The government could then abdicate and decree the abolition of taxes and coercive legislation, but the victorious libertarians would now be confronted with a dilemma. Do they recognize the new property titles as legitimately private property? The utilitarians, who have no theory of justice in property rights, would, if they were consistent with their acceptance of given property titles as decreed by government, have to accept a new social order in which fifty new satraps would be collecting taxes in the form of unilaterally imposed "rent." The point is that *only* natural-rights libertarians, only those libertarians who have a theory of justice in property titles that does not depend on government decree, could be in a position to scoff at the new rulers' claims to have private property in the territory of the country, and to rebuff these claims as invalid. As the great nineteenth-century liberal Lord Acton saw clearly, the natural law provides the only sure ground for a continuing critique of governmental laws and decrees.[1] What, specifically, the natural-rights position on property titles may be is the question to which we now turn.

We have established each individual's right to self-ownership, to a property right in his own body and person. But people are not floating wraiths; they are not self-subsistent entities; they can only survive and flourish by grappling with the earth around them. They must, for example, *stand* on land areas; they must also, in order to survive and maintain themselves, transform the resources given by nature into "consumer goods," into objects more suitable for their use and consumption. Food must be grown and eaten; minerals must be mined and then transformed into capital and then useful consumer goods, etc. Man, in other words, must own not only his own person, but also material objects for his control and use. How, then, should the property titles in these objects be allocated?

Let us take, as our first example, a sculptor fashioning a work of art out of clay and other materials; and let us waive, for the moment, the question of original property rights in the clay and the sculptor's tools. The question then becomes: *Who* owns the work of art as it emerges from the sculptor's fashioning? It is, in fact, the sculptor's "creation," not in the sense that he has created matter, but in the sense that he has transformed nature-given matter—the clay—into another form dictated by his own ideas and fashioned by his own hands and energy. Surely, it is a rare person who, with the case put thus, would say that the sculptor does not have the property right in his own product. Surely, if every man has the right to own his own body, and if he must grapple with the material objects of the world in order to survive, then the sculptor has the right to own the product he has

---

[1]See Gertrude Himmelfarb, *Lord Acton: A Study in Conscience and Politics* (Chicago: Phoenix Books, 1962), pp. 294–305. Compare also John Wild, *Plato's Modern Enemies and the Theory of Natural Law* (Chicago: University of Chicago Press, 1953), p. 176.

made, by his energy and effort, a veritable *extension* of his own personality. He has placed the stamp of his person upon the raw material, by "mixing his labor" with the clay, in the phrase of the great property theorist John Locke. And the product transformed by his own energy has become the material embodiment of the sculptor's ideas and vision. John Locke put the case this way:

> every man has a *property* in his own *person*. This nobody has any right to but himself. The *labour* of his body and the *work* of his hands, we may say, are properly his. Whatsoever, then, he removes out of the state that nature hath provided and left it in, he hath mixed his labour with it, and joined it to something that is his own, and thereby makes it his property. It being by him removed from the common state nature placed it in, it hath by this labour something annexed to it that excludes the common right of other men. For this labour being the unquestionable property of the labourer, no man but he can have a right to what that is once joined to.[2]

As in the case of the ownership of people's bodies, we again have three logical alternatives: (1) either the transformer, or "creator" has the property right in his creation; or (2) another man or set of men have the right in that creation, i.e., have the right to appropriate it by force without the sculptor's consent; or (3) every individual in the world has an equal, quotal share in the ownership of the sculpture—the "communal" solution. Again, put baldly, there are very few who would not concede the monstrous injustice of confiscating the sculptor's property, either by one or more others, or on behalf of the world as a whole. By what right do they do so? By what right do they appropriate to themselves the product of the creator's mind and energy? In this clear-cut case, the right of the creator to own what he has mixed his person and labor with would be generally conceded. (Once again, as in the case of communal ownership of persons, the world communal solution would, in practice, be reduced to an oligarchy of a *few* others expropriating the creator's work *in the name of* "world public" ownership.)

---

[2]John Locke, "An Essay Concerning the True Original Extent and End of Civil Government," in *Social Contract*, E. Barker, ed. (New York: Oxford University Press, 1948), pp. 17–18.

The main point, however, is that the case of the sculptor is not qualitatively different from all cases of "production." The man or men who had extracted the clay from the ground and had sold it to the sculptor may not be as "creative" as the sculptor, but they too are "producers," they too have mixed their ideas and their technological know-how with the nature-given soil to emerge with a useful product. They, too, are "producers," and they too have mixed their labor with natural materials to transform those materials into more useful goods and services. These persons, too, are entitled to the ownership of their products. Where then does the process begin?

If every man owns his own person and therefore his own labor, and if by extension he owns whatever property he has "created" or gathered out of the previously unused, unowned, "state of nature," then what of the last great question: the right to own or control the earth *itself*? In short, if the gatherer has the right to own the acorns or berries he picks, or the farmer the right to own his crop of wheat or peaches, *who* has the right to own the land on which these things have grown? It is at this point that Henry George and his followers, who have gone all the way so far with the libertarians, leave the track and deny the individual's right to own the piece of land itself, *the ground* on which these activities have taken place. The Georgists argue that, while every man should own the goods which he produces or creates, since Nature or God created the land itself, no individual has the right to assume ownership of that land. Yet, if the land is to be used at all as a resource in any sort of efficient manner, it must be owned or controlled by *someone* or some group, and we are again faced with our three alternatives: either the land belongs to the first user, the man who first brings it into production; *or* it belongs to a group of others; *or* it belongs to the world as a whole, with every individual owning a quotal part of every acre of land. George's option for the last solution hardly solves his moral problem: If the land itself should belong to God or Nature, then why as it more moral for every acre in the world to be owned by the world as a whole, than to concede individual ownership? In practice, again, it is obviously impossible for every person in the world to exercise effective ownership of his four-billionth portion (if the world population is, say, four billion) of every piece of the world's land surface. In practice, of course, a small oligarchy would do the controlling and owning, and not the world as a whole.

But apart from these difficulties in the Georgist position, the natural-rights justification for the ownership of ground land is the same as the justification for the original ownership of all other property. For, as we have seen, no producer *really* "creates" matter; he takes nature-given matter and transforms it by his labor energy in accordance with his ideas and vision. But *this* is precisely what the pioneer—the "homesteader"— does when he brings previously unused land into his own private owner- ship. Just as the man who makes steel out of iron ore transforms that ore out of his know-how and with his energy, and just as the man who takes the iron out of the ground does the same, so does the homesteader who clears, fences, cultivates, or builds upon the land. The homesteader, too, has transformed the character of the nature-given soil by his labor and his personality. The homesteader is just as legitimately the owner of the prop- erty as the sculptor or the manufacturer; he is just as much a "producer" as the others.

Furthermore, if the original land is nature- or God-given then so are the people's talents, health, and beauty. And just as all these attributes are given to specific individuals and not to "society," so then are land and nat- ural resources. All of these resources are given to individuals and not to "society," which is an abstraction that does not actually exist. There is no existing entity called "society"; there are only interacting individuals. To say that "society" should own land or any other property in common, then, must mean that a group of oligarchs—in practice, government bureau- crats—should own the property, and at the expense of expropriating the creator or the homesteader who had originally brought this product into existence.

Moreover, no one can produce *anything* without the cooperation of original land, if only as standing room. No man can produce or create any- thing by his labor alone; he must have the cooperation of land and other natural raw materials.

Man comes into the world with just himself and the world around him—the land and natural resources given him by nature. He takes these resources and transforms them by his labor and mind and energy into goods more useful to man. Therefore, if an individual cannot own original land, neither can he in the full sense own any of the fruits of his labor. The farmer cannot own his wheat crop if he cannot own the land on which the wheat grows. Now that his labor has been inextricably mixed with the land, he cannot be deprived of one without being deprived of the other.

Moreover, if a producer is *not* entitled to the fruits of his labor, who is? It is difficult to see why a newborn Pakistani baby should have a moral claim to a quotal share of ownership of a piece of Iowa land that someone has just transformed into a wheatfield—and vice versa of course for an Iowan baby and a Pakistani farm. Land in its original state is unused and unowned. Georgists and other land communalists may claim that the whole world population really "owns" it, but if no one has yet used it, it is in the real sense owned and controlled by no one. The pioneer, the homesteader, the first user and transformer of this land, is the man who first brings this simple valueless thing into production and social use. It is difficult to see the morality of depriving him of ownership in favor of people who have never gotten within a thousand miles of the land, and who may not even know of the existence of the property over which they are supposed to have a claim.

The moral, natural-rights issue involved here is even clearer if we consider the case of animals. Animals are "economic land," since they are original nature-given resources. Yet will anyone deny full title to a horse to the man who finds and domesticates it—is this any different from the acorns and berries that are generally conceded to the gatherer? Yet in land, too, some homesteader takes the previously "wild," undomesticated land, and "tames" it by putting it to productive use. Mixing his labor with land sites should give him just as clear a title as in the case of animals. As Locke declared: "As much land as a man tills, plants, improves, cultivates, and can use the product of, so much is his property. He by his labour does, as it were, enclose it from the common."[3]

---

[3]Locke, *Civil Government*, p. 20.

CHAPTER 32

War, Peace, and the State

The libertarian movement has been chided by William F. Buckley, Jr., for failing to use its "strategic intelligence" in facing the major problems of our time. We have, indeed, been too often prone to "pursue our busy little seminars on whether or not to demunicipalize the garbage collectors" (as Buckley has contemptuously written), while ignoring and failing to apply libertarian theory to the most vital problem of our time: war and peace. There is a sense in which Libertarians have been utopian rather than strategic in their thinking, with a tendency to divorce the ideal system which we envisage from the realities of the world in which we live. In short, too many of us have divorced theory from practice, and have then been content to hold the pure libertarian society as an abstract ideal for some remotely future time, while in the concrete world of today we follow unthinkingly the orthodox "conservative" line. To live liberty, to begin the hard but essential strategic struggle of changing the unsatisfactory world of today in the direction of our ideals, we must realize and demonstrate to the world that libertarian theory can be brought sharply to bear upon all of the world's crucial problems. By coming to grips with these problems, we can demonstrate that libertarianism is not just a beautiful ideal somewhere on

Reprinted from *Egalitarianism as a Revolt Against Nature and Other Essays* (Auburn, Ala.: Mises Institute, 2000), chap. 5.

Cloud Nine, but a tough-minded body of truths that enables us to take our stand and to cope with the whole host of issues of our day.

Let us then, by all means, use our strategic intelligence. Although, when he sees the result, Mr. Buckley might well wish that we had stayed in the realm of garbage collection. Let us construct a libertarian theory of war and peace.

The fundamental axiom of libertarian theory is that no one may threaten or commit violence ("aggress") against another man's person or property. Violence may be employed only against the man who commits such violence; that is, only defensively against the aggressive violence of another.[1] In short, no violence may be employed against a nonaggressor. Here is the fundamental rule from which can be deduced the entire *corpus* of libertarian theory.[2]

Let us set aside the more complex problem of the State for a while and consider simply relations between "private" individuals. Jones finds that he or his property is being invaded, aggressed against, by Smith. It is legitimate for Jones, as we have seen, to repel this invasion by defensive violence of his own. But now we come to a more knotty question: is it within the right of Jones to commit violence against innocent third parties as a corollary to his legitimate defense against Smith? To the Libertarian, the answer must be clearly, no. Remember that the rule prohibiting violence against the persons or property of innocent men is absolute: it holds regardless of the subjective *motives* for the aggression. It is wrong and criminal to violate the property or person of another, even if one is a Robin Hood, or starving, or is doing it to save one's relatives, *or* is defending oneself against a third man's attack. We may understand and sympathize with the motives in many of these cases and extreme situations. We may later mitigate the guilt if the criminal comes to trial for punishment, but we cannot evade the judgment that this aggression is still a criminal act, and one which

---

[1]There are some libertarians who would go even further and say that no one should employ violence even in defending himself against violence. However, even such Tolstoyans, or "absolute pacifists," would concede the defender's right to employ defensive violence and would merely urge him not to exercise that right. They, therefore, do not disagree with our proposition. In the same way, a Libertarian temperance advocate would not challenge a man's right to drink liquor, only his wisdom in exercising that right.

[2]We shall not attempt to justify this axiom here. Most Libertarians and even Conservatives are familiar with the rule and even defend it; the problem is not so much in arriving at the rule as in fearlessly and consistently pursuing its numerous and often astounding implications.

the victim has every right to repel, by violence if necessary. In short, A aggresses against B because C is threatening, or aggressing against, A. We may understand C's "higher" culpability in this whole procedure; but we must still label this aggression as a criminal act which B has the right to repel by violence.

To be more concrete, if Jones finds that his property is being stolen by Smith, he has the right to repel him and try to catch him; but he has *no* right to repel him by bombing a building and murdering innocent people or to catch him by spraying machine gun fire into an innocent crowd. If he does this, he is as much (or more of) a criminal aggressor as Smith is.

The application to problems of war and peace is already becoming evident. For while war in the narrower sense is a conflict between States, in the broader sense we may define it as the outbreak of open violence between people or groups of people. If Smith and a group of his henchmen aggress against Jones and Jones and his bodyguards pursue the Smith gang to their lair, we may cheer Jones on in his endeavor; and we, and others in society interested in repelling aggression, may contribute financially or personally to Jones's cause. But Jones has *no* right, any more than does Smith, to aggress against anyone else in the course of his "just war": to steal others' property in order to finance his pursuit, to conscript others into his posse by use of violence or to kill others in the course of his struggle to capture the Smith forces. If Jones should do any of these things, he becomes a criminal as *fully* as Smith, and he too becomes subject to whatever sanctions are meted out against criminality. In fact, if Smith's crime was theft, and Jones should use conscription to catch him, or should kill others in the pursuit, Jones becomes more of a criminal than Smith, for such crimes against another person as enslavement and murder are surely far worse than theft. (For while theft injures the extension of another's personality, enslavement injures, and murder obliterates, that personality itself.)

Suppose that Jones, in the course of his "just war" against the ravages of Smith, should kill a few innocent people, and suppose that he should declaim, in defense of this murder, that he was simply acting on the slogan, "Give me liberty or give me death." The absurdity of this "defense" should be evident at once, for the issue is not whether Jones was willing to risk death personally in his defensive struggle against Smith; the issue is whether he was willing to kill other people in pursuit of his legitimate end.

For Jones was in truth acting on the completely indefensible slogan: "Give me liberty or give *them* death" surely a far less noble battle cry.[3]

The Libertarian's basic attitude toward war must then be: it is legitimate to use violence against criminals in defense of one's rights of person and property; it is completely impermissible to violate the rights of *other* innocent people. War, then, is only proper when the exercise of violence is rigorously limited to the individual criminals. We may judge for ourselves how many wars or conflicts in history have met this criterion.

It has often been maintained, and especially by Conservatives, that the development of the horrendous modern weapons of mass murder (nuclear weapons, rockets, germ warfare, etc.) is only a difference of *degree* rather than *kind* from the simpler weapons of an earlier era. Of course, one answer to this is that when the degree is the number of human lives, the difference is a very big one.[4] But another answer that the Libertarian is particularly equipped to give is that while the bow and arrow and even the rifle can be pinpointed, if the will be there, against actual criminals, modern nuclear weapons cannot. Here is a crucial difference in kind. Of course, the bow and arrow could be used for aggressive purposes, but it could also be pinpointed to use only against aggressors. Nuclear weapons, even "conventional" aerial bombs, cannot be. These weapons are *ipso facto* engines of indiscriminate mass destruction. (The only exception would be the extremely rare case where a mass of people who were all criminals inhabited a vast geographical area.) We must, therefore, conclude that the use of nuclear or similar weapons, or the threat thereof, is a sin and a crime against humanity for which there can be no justification.

This is why the old cliché no longer holds that it is not the arms but the will to use them that is significant in judging matters of war and peace. For it is precisely the characteristic of modern weapons that they cannot be used selectively, cannot be used in a libertarian manner. Therefore, their very existence must be condemned, and nuclear disarmament becomes a

---

[3]Or, to bring up another famous antipacifist slogan, the question is not whether "we would be willing to use force to prevent the rape of our sister," but whether, to prevent that rape, we are willing to kill innocent people and perhaps even the sister herself.

[4]William Buckley and other Conservatives have propounded the curious moral doctrine that it is no worse to kill millions than it is to kill one man. The man who does either is, to be sure, a murderer; but surely it makes a huge difference how many people he kills. We may see this by phrasing the problem thus: after a man has already killed one person, does it make any difference whether he stops killing now or goes on a further rampage and kills many dozen more people? Obviously, it does.

good to be pursued for its own sake. And if we will indeed use our strategic intelligence, we will see that such disarmament is not only a good, but the highest political good that we can pursue in the modern world. For just as murder is a more heinous crime against another man than larceny, so mass murder—indeed murder so widespread as to threaten human civilization and human survival itself—is the worst crime that any man could possibly commit. And that crime is now imminent. And the forestalling of massive annihilation is far more important, in truth, than the demunicipalization of garbage disposal, as worthwhile as that may be. Or are Libertarians going to wax properly indignant about price control or the income tax, and yet shrug their shoulders at or even positively advocate the ultimate crime of mass murder?

If nuclear warfare is totally illegitimate even for individuals defending themselves against criminal assault, how much more so is nuclear or even "conventional" warfare between States!

It is time now to bring the State into our discussion. The State is a group of people who have managed to acquire a virtual monopoly of the use of violence throughout a given territorial area. In particular, it has acquired a monopoly of aggressive violence, for States generally recognize the right of individuals to use violence (though not against States, of course) in self-defense.[5] The State then uses this monopoly to wield power over the inhabitants of the area and to enjoy the material fruits of that power. The State, then, is the only organization in society that regularly and openly obtains its monetary revenues by the use of *aggressive* violence; all other individuals and organizations (except if delegated that right by the State) can obtain wealth only by peaceful production and by voluntary exchange of their respective products. This use of violence to obtain its revenue (called "taxation") is the keystone of State power. Upon this base the State erects a further structure of power over the individuals in its territory, regulating them, penalizing critics, subsidizing favorites, etc. The State also takes care to arrogate to itself the compulsory monopoly of various critical services needed by society, thus keeping the people in dependence upon the State for key services, keeping control of the vital

---

[5]Professor Robert L. Cunningham has defined the State as the institution with "a monopoly on initiating open physical coercion." Or, as Albert Jay Nock put it similarly if more caustically, "The State claims and exercises the monopoly of crime. ... It forbids private murder, but itself organizes murder on a colossal scale. It punishes private theft, but itself lays unscrupulous hands on anything it wants."

command posts in society and also fostering among the public the myth that only the State can supply these goods and services. Thus the State is careful to monopolize police and judicial service, the ownership of roads and streets, the supply of money, and the postal service, and effectively to monopolize or control education, public utilities, transportation, and radio and television.

Now, since the State arrogates to itself the monopoly of violence over a territorial area, so long as its depredations and extortions go unresisted, there is said to be "peace" in the area, since the only violence is one-way, directed by the State downward against the people. Open conflict within the area only breaks out in the case of "revolutions" in which people resist the use of State power against them. Both the quiet case of the State unresisted and the case of open revolution may be termed "vertical violence": violence of the State against its public or vice versa.

In the modern world, each land area is ruled over by a State organization, but there are a number of States scattered over the earth, each with a monopoly of violence over its own territory. No super-State exists with a monopoly of violence over the entire world; and so a state of "anarchy" exists between the several States. (It has always been a source of wonder, incidentally, to this writer how the same Conservatives who denounce as lunatic any proposal for eliminating a monopoly of violence over a given territory and thus leaving private individuals without an overlord, should be equally insistent upon leaving *States* without an overlord to settle disputes between them. The former is always denounced as "crackpot anarchism"; the latter is hailed as preserving independence and "national sovereignty" from "world government.") And so, except for revolutions, which occur only sporadically, the open violence and two-sided conflict in the world takes place *between* two or more States, that is, in what is called "international war" (or "horizontal violence").

Now there are crucial and vital differences between inter-State warfare on the one hand and revolutions against the State or conflicts between private individuals on the other. One vital difference is the shift in geography. In a revolution, the conflict takes place *within* the same geographical area: both the minions of the State and the revolutionaries inhabit the same territory. Inter-State warfare, on the other hand, takes place between two groups, each having a monopoly over its own geographical area; that is, it takes place between inhabitants of different territories. From this difference flow several important consequences: (1) in inter-State war the scope for the use of modern weapons of destruction is far greater. For if the "escalation" of weaponry in an intra-territorial conflict becomes too great, each side will blow itself up with the weapons directed against the other. Neither a revolutionary group nor a State combatting revolution, for example, can use nuclear weapons against the other. But, on the other hand, when the warring parties inhabit different territorial areas, the scope for modern weaponry becomes enormous, and the entire arsenal of mass devastation can come into play. A second consequence (2) is that while it is possible for revolutionaries to pinpoint their targets and confine them to their State enemies, and thus avoid aggressing against innocent people, pinpointing is far less *possible* in an inter-State war.[6] This is true even with older weapons; and, of course, with modern weapons there can be no pinpointing whatever. Furthermore, (3) since each State can mobilize all the people and resources in its territory, the other State comes to regard all the citizens of the opposing country as at least temporarily its enemies and to treat them accordingly by extending the war to them. Thus, all of the consequences of inter-territorial war make it almost inevitable that inter-State war will involve aggression by each side against the innocent civilians— the private individuals—of the other. This inevitability becomes absolute with modern weapons of mass destruction.

If one distinct attribute of inter-State war is inter-territoriality, another unique attribute stems from the fact that each State lives by taxation over its subjects. Any war against another State, therefore, involves the increase and extension of taxation—aggression over its own people.[7] Conflicts between private individuals can be, and usually are, voluntarily waged and financed by the parties concerned. Revolutions can be, and often are, financed and fought by voluntary contributions of the public. But State wars can only be waged through aggression against the taxpayer.

All State wars, therefore, involve increased aggression against the State's own taxpayers, and almost all State wars (*all*, in modern warfare) involve the maximum aggression (murder) against the innocent civilians

---

[6]An outstanding example of pinpointing by revolutionaries was the invariable practice of the Irish Republican Army, in its later years, of making sure that only British troops and British government property were attacked and that no innocent Irish civilians were injured. A guerrilla revolution not supported by the bulk of the people, of course, is far more likely to aggress against civilians.

[7]If it be objected that a war *could* theoretically be financed solely by a State's lowering of nonwar expenditures, then the reply still holds that taxation remains greater than it *could* be without the war effect. Moreover, the purport of this article is that Libertarians should be opposed to government expenditures *whatever* the field, war or nonwar.

ruled by the enemy State. On the other hand, revolutions are generally financed voluntarily and may pinpoint their violence to the State rulers, and private conflicts may confine their violence to the actual criminals. The Libertarian must, therefore, conclude that, while some revolutions and some private conflicts *may* be legitimate, State wars are *always* to be condemned.

Many Libertarians object as follows: "While we too deplore the use of taxation for warfare, and the State's monopoly of defense service, we have to recognize that these conditions exist, and while they do, we must support the State in just wars of defense." The reply to this would go as follows: "Yes, as you say, unfortunately States exist, each having a monopoly of violence over its territorial area." What then should be the attitude of the Libertarian toward conflicts between these States? The Libertarian should say, in effect, to the State: "All right, you exist, but as long as you exist at least confine your activities to the area which you monopolize." In short, the Libertarian is interested in reducing as much as possible the area of State aggression against all private individuals. The only way to do this, in international affairs, is for the people of each country to pressure their own State to confine its activities to the area which it monopolizes and not to aggress against other State-monopolists. In short, the objective of the Libertarian is to confine any existing State to as small a degree of invasion of person and property as possible. And this means the total avoidance of war. The people under each State should pressure "their" respective States not to attack one another, and, if a conflict should break out, to negotiate a peace or declare a cease-fire as quickly as physically possible.

Suppose further that we have that rarity—an unusually clear-cut case in which the State is actually trying to defend the property of one of its citizens. A citizen of country A travels or invests in country B, and then State B aggresses against his person or confiscates his property. Surely, our libertarian critic would argue, here is a clear-cut case where State A should threaten or commit war against State B in order to defend the property of "its" citizen. Since, the argument runs, the State has taken upon itself the monopoly of defense of its citizens, it then has the obligation to go to war on behalf of any citizen, and libertarians have an obligation to support this war as a just one.

But the point again is that each State has a monopoly of violence and, therefore, of defense only over its territorial area. It has no such monopoly; in fact, it has no power at all, over any other geographical area. Therefore, if an inhabitant of country A should move to or invest in country B, the libertarian must argue that he thereby takes his chances with the State monopolist of country B, and it would be immoral and criminal for State A to tax people in country A *and* kill numerous innocents in country B in order to defend the property of the traveler or investor.[8]

It should also be pointed out that there is no defense against nuclear weapons (the only current "defense" is the threat of mutual annihilation) and, therefore, that the State *cannot* fulfill any sort of defense function so long as these weapons exist.

The libertarian objective, then, should be, regardless of the specific causes of any conflict, to pressure States not to launch wars against other States and, should a war break out, to pressure them to sue for peace and negotiate a cease-fire and peace treaty as quickly as physically possible. This objective, incidentally, is enshrined in the international law of the eighteenth and nineteenth centuries, that is, the ideal that no State could aggress against the territory of another—in short, the "peaceful coexistence" of States.[9]

Suppose, however, that despite libertarian opposition, war has begun and the warring States are not negotiating a peace. What, then, should be the libertarian position? Clearly, to reduce the scope of assault of innocent civilians as much as possible. Old-fashioned international law had two excellent devices for this: the "laws of war," and the "laws of neutrality" or "neutrals' rights." The laws of neutrality are designed to keep any war that breaks out confined to the warring States themselves, without aggression against the States or particularly the peoples of the other nations. Hence the importance of such ancient and now forgotten American principles as "freedom of the seas" or severe limitations upon the rights of warring States to blockade neutral trade with the enemy country. In short, the libertarian tries to induce neutral States to remain neutral in any inter-State conflict and to induce the warring States to observe fully the rights of neutral

---

[8]There is another consideration which applies rather to "domestic" defense within a State's territory: the less the State can successfully defend the inhabitants of its area against attack by criminals, the more these inhabitants may come to learn the inefficiency of state operations, and the more they will turn to non-State methods of defense. Failure by the State to defend, therefore, has educative value for the public.

[9]The international law mentioned in this paper is the old-fashioned libertarian law as had voluntarily emerged in previous centuries and has nothing to do with the modern statist accretion of "collective security." Collective security forces a maximum escalation of every local war into a worldwide war—the precise reversal of the libertarian objective of *reducing* the scope of any war as much as possible.

citizens. The "laws of war" were designed to limit as much as possible the invasion by warring States of the rights of the civilians of the respective warring countries. As the British jurist F.J.P. Veale put it:

> The fundamental principle of this code was that hostilities between civilized peoples must be limited to the armed forces actually engaged. ... It drew a distinction between combatants and noncombatants by laying down that the sole business of the combatants is to fight each other and, consequently, that noncombatants must be excluded from the scope of military operations.[10]

In the modified form of prohibiting the bombardment of all cities not in the front line, this rule held in Western European wars in recent centuries until Britain launched the strategic bombing of civilians in World War II. Now, of course, the entire concept is scarcely remembered, the very nature of nuclear war resting on the annihilation of civilians.

In condemning all wars, regardless of motive, the Libertarian knows that there may well be varying degrees of guilt among States for any specific war. But the overriding consideration for the Libertarian is the condemnation of any State participation in war. Hence his policy is that of exerting pressure on all States not to start a war, to stop one that has begun and to reduce the scope of any persisting war in injuring civilians of either side or no side.

A neglected corollary to the libertarian policy of peaceful coexistence of States is the rigorous abstention from any foreign aid; that is, a policy of nonintervention between States (= "isolationism" = "neutralism"). For any aid given by State A to State B (1) increases tax aggression against the people of country A and (2) aggravates the suppression by State B of its own people. If there are any revolutionary groups in country B, then foreign aid intensifies this suppression all the more. Even foreign aid to a revolutionary group in B—more defensible because directed to a voluntary group opposing a State rather than a State oppressing the people—must be condemned as (at the very least) aggravating tax aggression at home.

Let us see how libertarian theory applies to the problem of *imperialism*, which may be defined as the aggression by State A over the people of country B, and the subsequent maintenance of this foreign rule. Revolution by the B people against the imperial rule of A is certainly legitimate,

---

[10]F.J.P. Veale, *Advance to Barbarism* (Appleton, Wis.: C.C. Nelson, 1953), p. 58.

provided again that revolutionary fire be directed only against the rulers. It has often been maintained—even by Libertarians—that Western imperialism over undeveloped countries should be supported as more watchful of property rights than any successor native government would be. The first reply is that judging what might follow the *status quo* is purely speculative, whereas existing imperialist rule is all too real and culpable. Moreover, the libertarian here begins his focus at the wrong end—at the alleged benefit of imperialism to the native. He should, on the contrary, concentrate first on the Western taxpayer, who is mulcted and burdened to pay for the wars of conquest, and then for the maintenance of the imperial bureaucracy. On this ground alone, the libertarian must condemn imperialism.[11]

Does opposition to all war mean that the libertarian can never countenance change—that he is consigning the world to a permanent freezing of unjust regimes? Certainly not. Suppose, for example, that the hypothetical state of "Waldavia" has attacked "Ruritania" and annexed the western part of the country. The Western Ruritanians now long to be reunited with their Ruritanian brethren. How is this to be achieved? There is, of course, the route of peaceful negotiation between the two powers, but suppose that the Waldavian imperialists prove adamant. Or, libertarian Waldavians can put pressure on their government to abandon its conquest in the name of justice. But suppose that this, too, does not work. What then? We must still maintain the illegitimacy of Ruritania's mounting a war against Waldavia. The legitimate routes are (1) revolutionary uprisings by the oppressed Western Ruritanian people, and (2) aid by private Ruritanian groups (or, for that matter, by friends of the Ruritanian cause in other countries) to the Western rebels—either in the form of equipment or of volunteer personnel.[12]

---

[11]Two other points about Western imperialism: first, its rule is not nearly so liberal or benevolent as many libertarians like to believe. The only property rights respected are those of the Europeans; the natives find their best lands stolen from them by the imperialists and their labor coerced by violence into working the vast landed estates acquired by this theft.

Second, another myth holds that the "gunboat diplomacy" of the turn of the century was a heroic libertarian action in defense of the property rights of Western investors in backward countries. Aside from our above strictures against going beyond any State's monopolized land area, it is overlooked that the bulk of gunboat moves were in defense, not of private investments, but of Western holders of government bonds. The Western powers coerced the smaller governments into increasing tax aggression on their own people, in order to pay off foreign bondholders. By no stretch of the imagination was this an action on behalf of private property—quite the contrary.

[12]The Tolstoyan wing of the libertarian movement could urge the Western Ruritanians to engage in *nonviolent* revolution, for example, tax strikes, boycotts, mass refusal to obey

We have seen throughout our discussion the crucial importance, in any present-day libertarian peace program, of the elimination of modern methods of mass annihilation. These weapons, against which there can be no defense, assure maximum aggression against civilians in any conflict with the clear prospect of the destruction of civilization and even of the human race itself. Highest priority on any libertarian agenda, therefore, must be pressure on all States to agree to general and complete disarmament down to police levels, with particular stress on nuclear disarmament. In short, if we are to use our strategic intelligence, we must conclude that the dismantling of the greatest menace that has ever confronted the life and liberty of the human race is indeed far more important than demunicipalizing the garbage service.

We cannot leave our topic without saying at least a word about the domestic tyranny that is the inevitable accompaniment of war. The great Randolph Bourne realized that "war is the health of the State."[13] It is in war that the State really comes into its own: swelling in power, in number, in pride, in absolute dominion over the economy and the society. Society becomes a herd, seeking to kill its alleged enemies, rooting out and suppressing all dissent from the official war effort, happily betraying truth for the supposed public interest. Society becomes an armed camp, with the values and the morale—as Albert Jay Nock once phrased it—of an "army on the march."

The root myth that enables the State to wax fat off war is the canard that war is a defense *by* the State *of* its subjects. The facts, of course, are precisely the reverse. For if war is the health of the State, it is also its greatest danger. A State can only "die" by defeat in war or by revolution. In war, therefore, the State frantically mobilizes the people to fight for *it* against another State, under the pretext that *it* is fighting for them. But all this should occasion no surprise; we see it in other walks of life. For which categories of crime does the State pursue and punish most intensely—those against private citizens or those against *itself?* The gravest crimes in the State's lexicon are almost invariably not invasions of person and property, but dangers to its own contentment: for example, treason, desertion of a

---

government orders or a general strike—especially in arms factories. Cf. the work of the revolutionary Tolstoyan, Bartelemy De Ligt, *The Conquest of Violence: An Essay On War and Revolution* (New York: Dutton, 1938).

[13]See Randolph Bourne, "Unfinished Fragment on the State," in *Untimely Papers* (New York: B.W. Huebsch, 1919).

soldier to the enemy, failure to register for the draft, conspiracy to overthrow the government. Murder is pursued haphazardly unless the victim be a *policeman*, or *Gott soll hüten*, an assassinated Chief of State; failure to pay a private debt is, if anything, almost encouraged, but income tax evasion is punished with utmost severity; counterfeiting the State's money is pursued far more relentlessly than forging private checks, etc. All this evidence demonstrates that the State is far more interested in preserving its own power than in defending the rights of private citizens.

A final word about conscription: of all the ways in which war aggrandizes the State, this is perhaps the most flagrant and most despotic. But the most striking fact about conscription is the absurdity of the arguments put forward on its behalf. A man must be conscripted to defend his (or someone else's?) liberty against an evil State beyond the borders. Defend his liberty? How? By being coerced into an army whose very *raison d'etre* is the expunging of liberty, the trampling on all the liberties of the person, the calculated and brutal dehumanization of the soldier and his transformation into an efficient engine of murder at the whim of his "commanding officer"?[14] Can any conceivable foreign State do anything worse to him than what "his" army is now doing for his alleged benefit? Who is there, O Lord, to defend him against his "defenders"?

---

[14]To the old militarist taunt hurled against the pacifist: "Would you use force to prevent the rape of your sister?" the proper retort is: "Would you rape your sister if ordered to do so by your commanding officer?"

CHAPTER 33

Notes on the Nintendo War

For the first two days and nights of the war, I, like many other people, stayed glued to my TV set, watching the war, concentrating on CNN but flipping in and out of the networks. Then, suddenly, it hit me: I wasn't getting any *news*. And it remains true. What we have been getting is:

1. Endless repetitions of the same few static shots: A plane landing or taking off on a darkened field. A missile thrusting upwards. The same damn bird covered with oil. (How many hundreds of times did we see that *one*? And that was a fake—a shot taken after some oil accident several days *before* Saddam's oil strike.) If you turn on five minutes of news per day, you get the full 24 hours.

2. Slides of maps, with radio voices cracking from Middle East spots. No news.

3. Press conferences, with Bush, Cheney, and various Pentagon biggies sounding off with braggadocio: We've got him; we've crushed him; we'll crush him again.

4. Press conferences where Bush and Pentagon biggies engage in schoolyard tantrums. After five months of routinely calling Saddam a monster, a madman, and a Hitler, every time Saddam does something, e.g., putting our pilot POWs on television, or unloosing all that oil, our

Written in March 1991 for the *Rothbard-Rockwell Report*; reprinted in *The Irrepressible Rothbard* (Auburn, Ala.: Mises Institute, 2000).

biggies invariably say: "That's it. Now we're *really* mad." But why is this fatheaded behavior taken seriously?

5. The rest of the airtime is filled with the talking heads of seemingly every retired colonel and general on the armed forces pension rolls. All these mavens invariably say one thing: We've got him; we've crushed him; we'll crush him again.

Several astute critics, notably Leslie Gelb in the *New York Times* and Howard Rosenberg in the *Los Angeles Times,* have pointed out that this first "television war" is not in any sense bringing us *the war*, but only a highly censored, sanitized high-tech computer Nintendo game, with US missiles going off, gallant Patriot (whichever PR man thought up *that* name should be getting a million bucks a year) missiles intercepting evil Scud (ditto for *that* PR man) missiles. It's a TV-high-tech phony war that the average Americano can really get behind, sending the Bush approval rating up to—what is it?—110 percent?

CIVILIAN CASUALTIES?

And yet, every once in a great while, some bit of truth manages to peek through the facade: Iraqi refugees in Jordan note that blood is running in the streets in residential neighborhoods in Baghdad; and Ramsey Clark reports that in the major Southern Iraqi city of Basra civilians are being targeted and killed in great numbers. Concerned that more of these reports might shake the "Nobody Dies" theme, the Pentagon has issued a preemptive strike against such revelations by assuring us that we never, ever, target civilians, that our pilots have gone out of their way and even sacrificed themselves to avoid hitting civilians, but that sometimes—even with "smart" precision bombs—there is unavoidable "collateral damage" (sort of like "side effect" in medicine?) to civilians, and anyway it's all that evil Saddam Hussein's fault for putting military targets near civilian areas. Oh. Like at Hiroshima and Nagasaki, right?

Even when a smart bomb killed 400 civilians, it was all Saddam's fault.

WHAT HAPPENED TO THE MAVENS?

Another curious aspect of the war is: what in blazes happened to the mavens, to all those military and strategic experts upon whom we all rely for sober judgment on world affairs? Before January 16, most of the mavens sounded pretty good: they warned sternly that launching a war would be decidedly inadvisable, and that a ground war would be even worse. Then, Bush blows the whistle on the Night of January 16, and the mavens totally flipflop. From then on, it's: Hey, hey, high-tech! Missiles! B-52s! Pounding! No living person can stand up to it! We'll win the war in ten days, two weeks at the outside!

There were two parts to this total switcheroo of the mavens. Partly it was the very same mavens changing their tune within a few hours. But partly, too, many of the old mavens were dumped and new ones—the B team—substituted. Suddenly, the sober and thoughtful Brzezinskis and Admiral Le Rocques and Carrolls were gone, and the second team of mindless retired colonels are trundled in to whoop it up for imminent victory. Is this a coincidence?

Also, what happened to that fascinating pre-war session on *Crossfire* when former Secretary of the Navy James Webb and the military expert from the *Chicago Tribune,* slated to debate the possibility of a draft, stunned both Pat Buchanan and Michael Kinsley by agreeing that the US Army and Air Force were not equipped to fight a Gulf war for longer than four weeks. After gaining a brief news flash, this item was dropped and never referred to again. What do these two say now? Inquiring minds would like to know.

Grinding It Out

It occurs to me that US military strategy, ever since U.S. Grant, has been dogged, plonky, and unimaginative. Mencken once wrote that the Americans love to boast about US military victories, but that we make sure, before launching any war, that we outnumber the enemy by at least five to one. And then, in every war, we amass the men and firepower, and just slog it out, wearing the enemy down—something like the hated New York Giants in football. With a few exceptions such as General Patton, brilliant surprises and strategy are left to the opposition.

In this war, so far all the surprises again have come from Saddam, who despite being vastly out-numbered—in fire-power, *but* not in men on the ground—is constantly keeping the US Behemoth nervous, puzzled on edge. "*Why* is he laying back?" or "*Why* didn't he fire all his Scud missiles or fly all of his planes at once? (so we can spot them)." "*Why* did he unloose all that oil? MiGod he's worse than Exxon!" (Maybe because we insisted on embargoing it. What *else* should he do with it than confuse us, slow us down, maybe even wipe out the desalinization plants in Saudi Arabia? Saddam's brain, after all, has not been addled by the Environmentalist Movement.)

But we have an all-too-effective PR reply to any surprises that Saddam can pull. The endless litany: "We're right on schedule. Everything's on schedule."

DRAMATIC NON-EVENTS OF THE WAR

1. **Gas Attacks.** With all the fuss and feathers about gas masks, issuing of gas masks, practicing in sealed rooms, constant agitation in Israel and in Saudi Arabia, *not one* gas attack has yet occurred. How about waiting until something happens before featuring it everywhere? Or is that asking too much of our Nintendo war?

2. **"Terrorism."** (Assaults upon Western or Israeli civilians, that is, *not* against Iraqi civilians.) The great Old Right journalist Garet Garrett analyzed US imperialism in the 1950s as a "complex of fear and vaunting." His analysis has been unfortunately confirmed in spades. On the one hand, endless bragging and blustering: Hey, hey, USA! We've got him, we'll crush him, we'll kick his ass! On the other hand, craven cowardice, endless whimpering about prospective "terrorism." Travel has plummeted, security measures have tightened everywhere. My God: if *you* were an Iraqi terrorist, with after all strictly limited resources, would *you* plan your first strike thus: "OK, let's get the Shubert Theatre in New York!" And all the nonsense about the Super Bowl! Hey people, do you think anyone outside the US gives a tinker's damn about football? They have more pressing things to think about or to target.

And in all the hot air and prattling about "Iraqi terrorism," there has not yet been one terrorist incident! ("Watch out! He's *holding back!*") In fact, the only authentic incident so far—the shelling of Number Ten Downing Street—was committed, not by the evil Arabs, but by the good old Irish Republican Army, who antedate Saddam by about seventy years. Again: how about waiting until one certified incident occurs before spreading this alleged problem all over the front pages?

Besides, do you realize that they *never caught* those once-famous "bearded Libyan hit men," who supposedly snuck onto our shores to get President Reagan? Where are they now?

AND WHATEVER HAPPENED TO THE "DRUG WAR"?

Answer: Who needs more than one war at a time?

One Small Plea

Please, please, won't someone, somewhere, do something, to get the ubiquitous man with the improbable name of "Wolf Blitzer" off the air? I know that it's a small thing to ask amidst the grand follies and tragedies of this war, but it would be so ... blissful.

Red-Baiting the Anti-war Movement

The conservative movement (apart from the paleos) reminds me of a punch-drunk boxer who has been in the ring several fights too many. When he hears the bell, all he can do is to look around wildly, swing aimlessly, and red-bait. *Human Events* recently tried to do this by pointing out darkly, and correctly, that Ramsey Clark's anti-war Coalition is dominated by the Workers' World Party, a Marxist-Leninist group. It darkly pointed out that the Coalition failed to condemn the invasion of Kuwait. It then tried to draw an analogy to the Marxist-Leninists who opposed the Vietnam War, hoping to bring about a Marxist-Leninist Asia, and eventually a Marxist-Leninist world.

Very feeble, guys. It's true that the Workers' World Party (WWP) which originated long ago during the beginnings of the Soviet-Chinese Communist split, are demon organizers and run the Clark Coalition. But so what? The WWP, a pro-Maoist splinter from Trotskyism, has about fifty members, and is a threat to no one. Its Maximum Leader, theoretician, and organizer is one Sam Marcy, and its crackerjack organizer and editor is Dierdre Griswold. They never had any clout within Trotskyism or Leninism, much less in America as a whole. Their effectiveness comes from the fact that they early decided to abandon abstruse theoretical argument and concentrate on practical organizing and street demonstrations against any and all US wars. But to see the imbecility of the analogy with Vietnam, ponder this: no one, but no one, not even Comrades Marcy or Griswold, is writing letters to each other signed, "Yours for a Baathist America." No one wants to model the US or the world after Saddam's polity. Get it?

Furthermore, a careful analysis of the left's reaction to this war cuts totally against this standard conservative reflex. As a matter of fact, one can almost use the position on the war to figure out who on the left has been in the Communist orbit all along, and who has been truly independent. Many prominent leftists have spouted what could only be called the Gorby-Soviet line, i.e., that Saddam must be stopped, that it's wonderful to have the UN back again battling for a New World Order, that there should have been sanctions against Iraq; but that Bush is being too jingoistic and going too far in the war. Take, for example, Alexander Cockburn, the last of the unreconstructed Old Left, whose writings on politics and US foreign policy before August 2, 1990, were radical, punchy, and delightfully satiric and hard core. But since August 2, Cockburn has suddenly turned Judicious, writing stodgy and tedious articles in the *Nation*, denouncing the "extreme left" for attacking Mr. Bush's War and US imperialism and for overlooking the vast complexities of the new era. In fact, one of the many causalities of the Gulf War has been Cockburn's once fascinating writing.

So what does that tell you where Marxists-Leninists stand? In contrast, it should now be clear, if it ever was murky, that such staunch anti-war leftists as Erwin Knoll, editor of the *Progressive*, or Ramsey Clark, should never have been red-baited, and are truly independent persons.

Yellow Ribbon Conspiracy?

Surely, one of the main beneficiaries of the war so far has been the yellow ribbon industry. Has any intrepid journalist looked into this question: who are the major yellow-ribbon manufacturers? Do they have any ties with the Trilateralists? The Bilderbergers? With Neil Bush or any of the other little Bushes? And how did this yellow stuff start anyway?

Color scientists: is there any color, on the color spectrum, that may be considered *anti*-yellow?

The Right to a Speedy Trial

And when, Oh when is General Manuel Noriega (remember him? He was *last year's* "Hitler") going to get his constitutional right to a public, speedy trial?

The War Hero as Permanent Problem

Among the baleful consequences of nearly every American military victory has been the War Hero who emerges from the war and then plagues us for years as president. The American Revolution brought us High Federalism and George Washington, the Mexican War gave us President General Zachary Taylor, the Civil War the rotten regime of President U.S. Grant, and World War II brought us Ike Eisenhower, who fastened the

New-Fair Deal upon the nation at a time when there was a good chance of getting rid of it. (World War I gave us no military heroes, but it did elevate Herbert Hoover to political fame and eventually his disastrous presidency. Hoover was the aptly-named Food Czar during the collectivized economy of World War I.)

If the US wins a short, casualty-free Glorious Victory in this war (or if just as effectively the Washington spin-doctors are able to persuade the dazzled media and the deluded masses that this Glorious Victory occurred), then *who* will be the War Heroes emerging from this war to torment us in the years to come?

George Bush, thank God, is too old, unless of course, the neocon political theorists manage to get rid of the anti-Third Term Amendment and he can be elected President for Life. General Kelly has too raspy a voice (being short in the intellect department is no longer a bar to the Highest Office). General Schwarzkopf is too fat and thuggish looking. Brent Scowcroft is too old, and besides, he lacks charisma. We are left with: Dick Cheney, who I am sure is willing to shoulder the burden, and General Colin Powell, who could be our first Affirmative Action President, an event that would send the entire Cultural Left, from left-liberals to neocons to left-libertarians, into ecstasy. What, you ask, are *his* views on anything? Surely you jest; no one ever asked that question of any of the other War Heroes. We know that he wears his uniform smartly and comes across well on television; what *else* would anyone want?

A NIGHTMARE SCENARIO FOR 1996

In case no one is worried about more proximate problems, here's a lulu for 1996: who should become George Bush's heir apparent, to run all of our lives from January 1997 to January 2005: Dan Quayle or General Colin Powell? Sorry: None of the Above is not a permitted option in our Glorious Democracy.

CHAPTER 34

Society Without A State

I

In attempting to outline how a "society without a State"—i.e., an anarchist society—might function successfully, I would first like to defuse two common but mistaken criticisms of this approach. First, is the argument that in providing for such defense or protection services as courts, police, or even law itself, I am simply smuggling the State back into society in another form, and that therefore the system I am both analyzing and advocating is not "really" anarchism. This sort of criticism can only involve us in an endless and arid dispute over semantics. Let me say from the beginning that I define the State as that institution which possesses one or both (almost always both) of the following properties: (1) it acquires its income by the physical coercion known as "taxation"; and (2) it asserts and usually obtains a coerced monopoly of the provision of defense service (police and courts) over a given territorial area. Any institution, not possessing either of these properties is not and cannot be, in accordance with my definition, a "State." On the other hand, I define anarchist society as one where there is no legal possibility for coercive aggression against the person or property of any individual. Anarchists oppose the State because it has its very being in such aggression, namely, the expropriation of private property through taxation, the coercive exclusion of other providers

A paper delivered before the American Society for Political and Legal Philosophy, Washington, D.C., on December 28, 1974. Reprinted in *Libertarian Review* 7, no. 1 (1975).

of defense service from its territory, and all of the other depredations and coercions that are built upon these twin foci of invasions of individual rights.

Nor is our definition of the State arbitrary, for these two characteristics have been possessed by what is generally acknowledged to be "States" throughout recorded history. The State, by its use of physical coercion, has arrogated to itself a compulsory monopoly of defense services over its territorial jurisdiction. But it is certainly conceptually possible for such services to be supplied by private, non-State institutions, and indeed such services have historically been supplied by other organizations than the State. To be opposed to the State is then not necessarily to be opposed to services that have often been linked with it; to be opposed to the State does not necessarily imply that we must be opposed to police protection, courts, arbitration, the minting of money, postal service, or roads and highways. *Some* anarchists have indeed been opposed to police and to all physical coercion *in defense* of person and property, but this is not inherent in and is fundamentally irrelevant to the anarchist position, which is precisely marked by opposition to all physical coercion invasive of, or aggressing against, person and property.

The crucial role of taxation may be seen in the fact that the State is the only institution or organization in society which regularly and systematically acquires its income through the use of physical coercion. All other individuals or organizations acquire their income voluntarily, either (a) through the voluntary sale of goods and services to consumers on the market, or (b) through voluntary gifts or donations by members or other donors. If I cease or refrain from purchasing Wheaties on the market, the Wheaties producers do not come after me with a gun or prison to force me to purchase; if I fail to join the American Philosophical Association, the association may not force me to join or prevent me from giving up my membership. Only the State can do so; only the State can confiscate my property or put me in jail if I do not pay its tax-tribute. Therefore, only the State regularly exists and has its very being by means of coercive depredations on private property.

Neither is it legitimate to challenge this sort of analysis by claiming that in some other sense, the purchase of Wheaties or membership in the APA is in some way "coercive"; there again, we can only be trapped in an endless semantic dispute. Apart from other rebuttals which cannot be considered here, I would simply say that anarchists are interested in the abolition of this type of action: e.g., aggressive physical violence against person and property, and that this is how we define "coercion." Anyone who is still unhappy with this use of the term "coercion" can simply eliminate the word from this discussion, and substitute for it "physical violence or the threat thereof", with the only loss being in literary style rather than in the substance of the argument. What anarchism proposes to do, then, is to abolish the State, i.e., to abolish the regularized institution of aggressive coercion.

It need hardly be added that the State habitually builds upon its coercive source of income by adding a host of other aggressions upon society: ranging from economic controls to the prohibition of pornography to the compelling of religious observance to the mass murder of civilians in organized warfare. In short, that the State, in the words of Albert Jay Nock, "claims and exercises a monopoly of crime" over its territorial area.

The second criticism I would like to defuse before beginning the main body of the paper is the common charge that anarchists "assume that all people are good," and that without the State no crime would be committed. In short, that anarchism assumes that with the abolition of the State a New Anarchist Man will emerge, cooperative, humane, and benevolent, so that no problem of crime will then plague the society. I confess that I do not understand the basis for this charge. Whatever other schools of anarchism profess—and I do not believe that they are open to this charge—I certainly do not adopt this view. I assume with most observers that mankind is a mixture of good and evil, of cooperative and criminal tendencies. In my view, the anarchist society is one which maximizes the tendencies for the good and the cooperative, while it minimizes both the opportunity and the moral legitimacy of the evil and the criminal. If the anarchist view is correct, and the State is indeed the great legalized and socially legitimated channel for all manner of antisocial crime—theft, oppression, mass murder—on a massive scale, then surely the abolition of such an engine of crime can do nothing but favor the good in man and discourage the bad.

A further point: in a profound sense, *no* social system, whether anarchist or statist, can work at all unless most people are "good" in the sense that they are not all hell-bent upon assaulting and robbing their neighbors. If everyone were so disposed, no amount of protection, whether State or private, could succeed in staving off chaos. Furthermore, the more that people are disposed to be peaceful and not aggress against their neighbors, the more successfully any social system will work, and the fewer resources will need to be devoted to police protection. The anarchist view holds that, given the "nature of man," given the degree of goodness or badness at any point of time, anarchism will maximize the opportunities for good and minimize the channels for the bad. The rest depends on the values held by the individual members of society. The only further point that need be made is that by eliminating the living example and the social legitimacy of the massive legalized crime of the State, anarchism will to a large extent promote peaceful values in the minds of the public.

We cannot of course deal here with the numerous arguments in favor of anarchism or against the State, moral, political, and economic. Nor can we take up the various goods and services now provided by the State, and show how private individuals and groups will be able to supply them far more efficiently on the free market. Here we can only deal with perhaps the most difficult area, the area where it is almost universally assumed that the State must exist and act, even if it is only a "necessary evil" instead of a positive good: the vital realm of defense or protection of person and property against aggression. Surely, it is universally asserted, the State is at least vitally necessary to provide police protection, the judicial resolution of disputes and enforcement of contracts, and the creation of the law itself that is to be enforced. My contention is that all of these admittedly necessary services of protection can be satisfactorily and efficiently supplied by private persons and institutions on the free market.

One important caveat before we begin the body of this paper: new proposals such as anarchism are almost always gauged against the implicit assumption that the present, or statist, system works to perfection. Any lacunae or difficulties with the picture of the anarchist society are considered net liabilities, and enough to dismiss anarchism out of hand. It is, in short, implicitly assumed that the State is doing its self-assumed job of protecting person and property to perfection. We cannot here go into the reasons why the State is bound to suffer inherently from grave flaws and inefficiencies in such a task. All we need do now is to point to the black and unprecedented record of the State through history: no combination of private marauders can possibly begin to match the State's unremitting record of theft, confiscation, oppression, and mass murder. No collection of Mafia or private bank robbers can begin to compare with all the Hiroshimas, Dresdens, and Lidices and their analogs through the history of mankind.

This point can be made more philosophically: it is illegitimate to compare the merits of anarchism and statism by starting with the present system as the implicit given and then critically examining only the anarchist alternative. What we must do is to begin at the zero point and then critically examine both suggested alternatives. Suppose, for example, that we were all suddenly dropped down on the earth *de novo*, and that we were all then confronted with the question of what societal arrangements to adopt. And suppose then that someone suggested: "We are all bound to suffer from those of us who wish to aggress against their fellow men. Let us than solve this problem of crime by handing all of our weapons to the Jones family, over there, by giving all of our ultimate power to settle disputes to that family. In that way, with their monopoly of coercion and of ultimate decision making, the Jones family will be able to protect each of us from each other." I submit that this proposal would get very short shrift, except perhaps from the Jones family themselves. And yet this is precisely the common argument for the existence of the State. When we start from the zero point, as in the case of the Jones family, the question of "who will guard the guardians?" becomes not simply an abiding lacuna in the theory of the State but an overwhelming barrier to its existence.

A final *caveat*: the anarchist is always at a disadvantage in attempting to forecast the shape of the future anarchist society. For it is impossible for observers to predict voluntary social arrangements, including the provision of goods and services, on the free market. Suppose, for example, that this were the year 1874, and someone predicted that eventually there would be a radio manufacturing industry. To be able to make such a forecast successfully, does he have to be challenged to state immediately how many radio manufacturers there would be a century hence, how big they would be, where they would be located, what technology and marketing techniques they would use, etc.? Obviously, such a challenge would make no sense, and in a profound sense the same is true of those who demand a precise portrayal of the pattern of protection activities on the market. Anarchism advocates the dissolution of the State into social and market arrangements, and these arrangements are far more flexible and less predictable than political institutions. The most that we can do, then, is to offer broad guidelines and perspectives on the shape of a projected anarchist society.

One important point to make here is that the advance of modern technology makes anarchistic arrangements increasingly feasible. Take, for example, the case of lighthouses, where it is often charged that it is unfeasible for private lighthouse operators to row out to each ship to charge it for use of the light. Apart from the fact that this argument ignores the successful existence of private lighthouses in earlier days, e.g., in England in the eighteenth century, another vital consideration is that modern electronic technology makes charging each ship for the light far more feasible.

Thus, the ship would have to have paid for an electronically controlled beam which could then be automatically turned on for those ships which had paid for the service.

II

Let us now turn to the problem of how disputes—in particular, disputes over alleged violations of person and property—would be resolved in an anarchist society. First, it should be noted that all disputes involve two parties: the plaintiff, the alleged victim of the crime or tort, and the defendant, the alleged aggressor. In many cases of broken contract, of course, each of the two parties alleging that the other is the culprit is at the same time a plaintiff and a defendant.

An important point to remember is that *any* society, be it statist or anarchist, has to have *some* way of resolving disputes that will gain a majority consensus in society. There would be no need for courts or arbitrators if everyone were omniscient, and knew instantaneously *which* persons were guilty of any given crime or violation of contract. Since none of us are omniscient, there has to be some method of deciding who is the criminal or lawbreaker which will gain legitimacy, in short whose decision will be accepted by the great majority of the public.

In the first place, a dispute may be resolved voluntarily between the two parties themselves, either unaided or with the help of a third mediator. This poses no problem, and will automatically be accepted by society at large. It is so accepted even now, much less in a society imbued with the anarchistic values of peaceful cooperation and agreement. Second and similarly, the two parties, unable to reach agreement, may decide to submit voluntarily to the decision of an arbitrator. This agreement may arise either after a dispute has arisen, or be provided for in advance in the original contract. Again, there is no problem in such an arrangement gaining legitimacy. Even in the present statist era, the notorious inefficiency and coercive and cumbersome procedures of the politically run government courts has led increasing numbers of citizens to turn to voluntary and expert arbitration for a speedy and harmonious settling of disputes.

Thus, William C. Wooldridge has written that

> arbitration has grown to proportions that make the courts
> a secondary recourse in many areas and completely super-
> fluous in others. The ancient fear of the courts that arbi-
> tration would "oust" them of their jurisdiction has been

fulfilled with a vengeance the common-law judges probably never anticipated. Insurance companies adjust over
fifty thousand claims a year among themselves through
arbitration, and the American Arbitration Association
(AAA), with headquarters in New York and twenty-five
regional offices across the country, last year conducted
over twenty-two thousand arbitrations. Its twenty-three
thousand associates available to serve as arbitrators may
outnumber the total number of judicial personnel ... in
the United States. ... Add to this the unknown number
of individuals who arbitrate disputes within particular
industries or in particular localities, without formal AAA
affiliation, and the quantitatively secondary role of official
courts begins to be apparent.[1]

Wooldridge adds the important point that, in addition to the speed
of arbitration procedures vis-à-vis the courts, the arbitrators can proceed as experts in disregard of the official government law; in a profound
sense, then, they serve to create a voluntary body of private law. "In other
words," states Wooldridge, "the system of extralegal, voluntary courts has
progressed hand in hand with a body of private law; the rules of the state
are circumvented by the same process that circumvents the forums established for the settlement of disputes over those rules. ... In short, a private
agreement between two people, a bilateral 'law,' has supplanted the official
law. The writ of the sovereign has ceased to run, and for it is substituted
a rule tacitly or explicitly agreed to by the parties." Wooldridge concludes
that "if an arbitrator can choose to ignore a penal damage rule or the stat-
ute of limitations applicable to the claim before him (and it is generally
conceded that he has that power), arbitration can be viewed as a practically revolutionary instrument for self-liberation from the law."[2]

It may be objected that arbitration only works successfully because the
courts enforce the award of the arbitrator. Wooldridge points out, however,
that arbitration was unenforceable in the American courts before 1920, but
that this did not prevent voluntary arbitration from being successful and
expanding in the United States and in England. He points, furthermore, to

---

[1]William C. Wooldridge, *Uncle Sam, the Monopoly Man* (New Rochelle, N.Y.: Arlington
House, 1970), p. 101.

[2]Ibid., pp. 103–04.

the successful operations of merchant courts since the Middle Ages, those courts which successfully developed the entire body of the law merchant. None of those courts possessed the power of enforcement. He might have added the private courts of shippers which developed the body of admiralty law in a similar way.

How then did these private, "anarchistic," and voluntary courts insure the acceptance of their decisions? By the method of social ostracism, and the refusal to deal any further with the offending merchant. This method of voluntary "enforcement," indeed, proved highly successful. Wooldridge writes that

> the merchants' courts were voluntary, and if a man ignored their judgment, he could not be sent to jail. ... Nevertheless, it is apparent that ... [their] decisions were generally respected even by the losers; otherwise people would never have used them in the first place. ... Merchants made their courts work simply by agreeing to abide by the results. The merchant who broke the understanding would not be sent to jail, to be sure, but neither would he long continue to be a merchant, for the compliance exacted by his fellows ... proved if anything more effective than physical coercion.[3]

Nor did this voluntary method fail to work in modern times: Wooldridge writes that it was precisely in the years before 1920, when arbitration awards could not be enforced in the courts,

> that arbitration caught on and developed a following in the American mercantile community. Its popularity, gained at a time when abiding by an agreement to arbitrate had to be as voluntary as the agreement itself, casts doubt on whether legal coercion was an essential adjunct to the settlement of most disputes. Cases of refusal to abide by an arbitrator's award were rare; one founder of the American Arbitration Association could not recall a single example. Like their medieval forerunners, merchants in the Americas did not have to rely on any sanctions other than those they could collectively impose on each other. One who refused to pay up might find access

---

[3]Ibid., pp. 95–96.

to his association's tribunal cut off in the future, or his name released to the membership of his trade association; these penalties were far more fearsome than the cost of the award with which he disagreed. Voluntary and private adjudications were voluntarily and privately adhered to, if not out of honor, out of the self-interest of businessmen who knew that the arbitral mode of dispute settlement would cease to be available to them very quickly if they ignored an award.[4]

It should also be pointed out that modern technology makes even more feasible the collection and dissemination of information about people's credit ratings and records of keeping or violating their contracts or arbitration agreements. Presumably, an anarchist society would see the expansion of this sort of dissemination of data and thereby facilitate the ostracism or boycotting of contract and arbitration violators.

How would arbitrators be selected in an anarchist society? In the same way as they are chosen now, and as they were chosen in the days of strictly voluntary arbitration: the arbitrators with the best reputation for efficiency and probity would be chosen by the various parties on the market. As in other processes of the market, the arbitrators with the best record in settling disputes will come to gain an increasing amount of business, and those with poor records will no longer enjoy clients, and have to shift to another line of endeavor. Here it must be emphasized that parties in dispute will seek out those arbitrators with the best reputation for both expertise and impartiality, and that inefficient or biased arbitrators will rapidly have to find another occupation.

Thus, the Tannehills emphasize:

> the advocates of government see initiated force (the legal force of government) as the only solution to social disputes. According to them, if everyone in society were not forced to use the same court system ... disputes would be insoluble. Apparently it doesn't occur to them that disputing parties are capable of freely choosing their own arbiters. ... They have not realized that disputants would, in fact, be far better off if they could choose among competing arbitration agencies so that they could reap the

---

[4]Ibid., pp. 100–01.

benefits of competition and specialization. It should be obvious that a court system which has a monopoly guaranteed by the force of statutory law will not give as good quality service as will free-market arbitration agencies which must compete for their customers ...

Perhaps the least tenable argument for government arbitration of disputes is the one which holds that governmental judges are more impartial because they operate outside the market and so have no vested interests.

Owing political allegiance to government is certainly no guarantee of impartiality! A governmental judge is always impelled to be partial—in favor of the government, from whom he gets his pay and his power! On the other hand, an arbiter who sells his services in a free market knows that he must be as scrupulously honest, fair, and impartial as possible or no pair of disputants will buy his services to arbitrate their dispute. A free-market arbiter depends for his livelihood on his skill and fairness at settling disputes. A governmental judge depends on political pull.[5]

If desired, furthermore, the contracting parties could provide in advance for a series of arbitrators:

It would be more economical and in most cases quite sufficient to have only one arbitration agency to hear the case. But if the parties felt that a further appeal might be necessary and were willing to risk the extra expense, they could provide for a succession of two or even more arbitration agencies. The names of these agencies would be written into the contract in order from the "first court of appeal" to the "last court of appeal." It would be neither necessary nor desirable to have one single, final court of appeal for every person in the society, as we have today in the United States Supreme Court.[6]

---

[5]Morris and Linda Tannehill, *The Market for Liberty* (Lansing, Mich.: privately printed, 1970), pp. 65–67.

[6]Ibid., p. 68.

Arbitration, then poses little difficulty for a portrayal of the free society. But what of torts or crimes of aggression where there has been no contract? Or suppose that the breaker of a contract defies the arbitration award? Is ostracism enough? In short, how can courts develop in the free-market, anarchist society which will have the power to enforce judgments against criminals or contract-breakers?

In the wide sense, defense service consists of guards or police who use force in defending person and property against attack, and judges or courts whose role is to use socially accepted procedures to determine who the criminals or tortfeasors are, as well as to enforce judicial awards, such as damages or the keeping of contracts. On the free market, many scenarios are possible on the relationship between the private courts and the police; they may be "vertically integrated," for example, or their services may be supplied by separate firms. Furthermore, it seems likely that police service will be supplied by insurance companies who will provide crime-insurance to their clients. In that case, insurance companies will pay off the victims of crime or the breaking of contracts or arbitration awards, and then pursue the aggressors in court to recoup their losses. There is a natural market connection between insurance companies and defense service, since they need pay out less benefits in proportion as they are able to keep down the rate of crime.

Courts might either charge fees for their services, with the losers of cases obliged to pay court costs, or else they may subsist on monthly or yearly premiums by their clients, who may be either individuals or the police or insurance agencies. Suppose, for example, that Smith is an aggrieved party, either because he has been assaulted or robbed, or because an arbitration award in his favor has not been honored. Smith believes that Jones is the party guilty of the crime. Smith then goes to a court. Court A, of which he is a client, and brings charges against Jones as a defendant. In my view, the hallmark of an anarchist society is one where no man may legally compel someone who is not a convicted criminal to do anything, since that would be aggression against an innocent man's person or property. Therefore, Court A can only invite rather than subpoena Jones to attend his trial. Of course, if Jones refuses to appear or send a representative, his side of the case will not be heard. The trial of Jones proceeds. Suppose that Court A finds Jones innocent. In my view, part of the generally accepted Law Code of the anarchist society (on which see further below), is that this must end the matter, unless Smith can prove charges of gross incompetence or bias on the part of the court.

Suppose, next, that Court A finds Jones guilty. Jones might accept the verdict, either because he too is a client of the same court, because he knows he is guilty, or for some other reason. In that case, Court A proceeds to exercise judgment against Jones. Neither of these instances pose very difficult problems for our picture of the anarchist society. But suppose, instead, that Jones contests the decision; he, then, goes to his court, Court B, and the case is retried there. Suppose that Court B, too, finds Jones guilty. Again, it seems to me that the accepted Law Code of the anarchist society will assert that this ends the matter; both parties have had their say in courts which each has selected, and the decision for guilt is unanimous.

Suppose, however, the most difficult case: That Court B finds Jones innocent. The two courts, each subscribed to by one of the two parties, have split their verdicts. In that case, the two courts will submit the case to an appeals court, or arbitrator, which the two courts agree upon. There seems to be no real difficulty about the concept of an appeals court. As in the case of arbitration contracts, it seems very likely that the various private courts in the society will have prior agreements to submit their dis- putes to a particular appeals court. How will the appeals judges be chosen? Again, as in the case of arbitrators or of the first judges on the free market, they will be chosen for their expertise and reputation for efficiency, hon- esty and integrity. Obviously, appeals judges who are inefficient or biased will scarcely be chosen by courts who will have a dispute. The point here is that there is no need for a legally-established or institutionalized single, monopoly appeals court system, as States now provide. There is no reason why there cannot arise a multitude of efficient and honest appeals judges who will be selected by the disputant courts, just as there are numerous private arbitrators on the market today. The appeals court renders its deci- sion, and the courts proceed to enforce it if, in our example, Jones is con- sidered guilty—unless, of course, Jones can prove bias in some other court proceedings.

No society can have unlimited judicial appeals, for in that case there would be no point to having judges or courts at all. Therefore, every soci- ety, whether statist or anarchist, will have to have some socially accepted cut-off point for trials and appeals. My suggestion is the rule that the agreement *of any two courts* be decisive. "Two" is not an arbitrary figure, for it reflects the fact that there are two parties, the plaintiff and the defen- dant, to any alleged crime or contract dispute.

If the courts are to be empowered to enforce decisions against guilty parties, does this not bring back the State in another form and thereby negate anarchism? No, for at the beginning of this paper I explicitly defined anarchism in such a way as not to rule out the use of defensive force—force in defense of person and property—by privately supported agencies. In the same way, it is not bringing back the State to allow persons to use force to defend themselves against aggression, or to hire guards or police agencies to defend them.

It should be noted, however, that in the anarchist society there will be no "district attorney" to press charges on behalf of "society." Only the victims will press charges as the plaintiffs. If, then, these victims should happen to be absolute pacifists who are opposed even to defensive force, then they will simply not press charges in the courts or otherwise retaliate against those who have aggressed against them. In a free society that would be their right. If the victim should suffer from murder, then his heir would have the right to press the charges.

What of the Hatfield-and-McCoy problem? Suppose that a Hatfield kills a McCoy, and that McCoy's heir does not belong to a private insurance, police agency, or court, and decides to retaliate himself? Since, under anarchism there can be no coercion of the non-criminal, McCoy would have the perfect right to do so. No one may be compelled to bring his case to a court. Indeed, since the right to hire police or courts flows from the right of self-defense against aggression, it would be inconsistent and in contradiction to the very basis of the free society to institute such compulsion. Suppose, then, that the surviving McCoy finds what he believes to be the guilty Hatfield and kills him in turn? What then? This is fine, except that McCoy may have to worry about charges being brought against him by a surviving Hatfield. Here it must be emphasized that in the law of the anarchist society based on defense against aggression, the courts would not be able to proceed against McCoy if in fact he killed the right Hatfield. His problem would arise if the courts should find that he made a grievous mistake, and killed the wrong man; in that case, he in turn would be found guilty of murder. Surely, in most instances, individuals will wish to obviate such problems by taking their case to a court and thereby gain social acceptability for their defensive retaliation—not for the act of retaliation but for the correctness of deciding who the criminal in any given case might be. The purpose of the judicial process, indeed, is to find a way of general agreement on who might be the criminal or contract-breaker in any given case. The judicial process is not a good in itself; thus, in the case of an assassination, such as Jack Ruby's murder of Oswald, on public television, there is no need for a complex judicial process since the name of the murderer is evident to all.

Will not the possibility exist of a private court that may turn venal and dishonest, or of a private police force that turns criminal and extorts money by coercion? Of course such an event may occur, given the propensities of human nature. Anarchism is not a moral cure-all. But the important point is that market forces exist to place severe checks on such possibilities, especially in contrast to a society where a State exists. For, in the first place, judges, like arbitrators, will prosper on the market in proportion to their reputation for efficiency and impartiality. Second, on the free market important checks and balances exist against venal, courts or criminal police forces. Namely, that there are competing courts and police agencies to whom the victims may turn for redress. If the "Prudential Police Agency" should turn outlaw and extract revenue from victims by coercion, the latter would have the option of turning to the. "Mutual" or "Equitable" Police Agency for defense and for pressing charges against Prudential. These are the *genuine* "checks and balances" of the free market, genuine in contrast to the phony checks and balances of a State system, where all the alleged "balancing" agencies are in the hands of one monopoly government. Indeed, given the monopoly "protection service" of a State, what is there to prevent a State from using its monopoly channels of coercion to extort money from the public? What are the checks and limits of the State? None, except for the extremely difficult course of revolution against a Power with all of the guns in its hands. In fact, the State provides an easy, legitimated channel for crime and aggression, since it has its very being in the crime of tax-theft, and the coerced monopoly of "protection." It is the State, indeed, that functions as a mighty "protection racket" on a giant and massive scale. It is the State that says: "Pay us for your 'protection' or else." In the light of the massive and inherent activities of the State, the danger of a "protection racket" emerging from one or more private police agencies is relatively small indeed.

Moreover, it must be emphasized that a crucial element in the power of the State is its legitimacy in the eyes of the majority of the public, the fact that after centuries of propaganda, the depredations of the State are looked upon rather as benevolent services. Taxation is generally not seen as theft, nor war as mass murder, nor conscription as slavery. Should a private police agency turn outlaw, should "Prudential" become a protection racket, it would then lack the social legitimacy which the State has managed to accrue to itself over the centuries. "Prudential" would be seen by all as bandits, rather than as legitimate or divinely appointed "sovereigns", bent on promoting the "common good" or the "general welfare." And lacking such legitimacy, Prudential would have to face the wrath of the public and the defense and retaliation of the other private defense agencies, the police and courts, on the free market. Given these inherent checks and limits, a successful transformation from a free society to bandit rule becomes most unlikely. Indeed, historically, it has been very difficult for a State to arise to supplant a stateless society; usually, it has come about through external conquest rather than by evolution from within a society.

Within the anarchist camp, there has been much dispute on whether the private courts would have to be bound by a basic, common Law Code. Ingenious attempts have been made to work out a system where the laws or standards of decision-making by the courts would differ completely from one to another.[7] But in my view all would have to abide by the basic Law Code, in particular, prohibition of aggression against person and property, in order to fulfill our definition of anarchism as a system which provides no legal sanction for such aggression. Suppose, for example, that one group of people in society hold that all redheads are demons who deserve to be shot on sight. Suppose that Jones, one of this group, shoots Smith, a redhead. Suppose that Smith or his heir presses charges in a court, but that Jones's court, in philosophic agreement with Jones, finds him innocent therefore. It seems to me that in order to be considered legitimate, any court would have to follow the basic libertarian law code of the inviolate right of person and property. For otherwise, courts might legally subscribe to a code which sanctions such aggression in various cases, and which to that extent would violate the definition of anarchism and introduce, if not the State, then a strong element of statishness or legalized aggression into the society.

But again I see no insuperable difficulties here. For in that case, anarchists, in agitating for their creed, will simply include in their agitation the idea of a general libertarian Law Code as part and parcel of the anarchist creed of abolition of legalized aggression against person or property in the society.

In contrast to the general law code, other aspects of court decisions could legitimately vary in accordance with the market or the wishes of the clients e.g., the language the cases will be conducted in, the number of judges to be involved, etc.

---

[7]E.g., David Friedman, *The Machinery of Freedom* (New York: Harper and Row, 1973).

There are other problems of the basic Law Code which there is no time to go into here: for example, the definition of just property titles or the question of legitimate punishment of convicted offenders—though the latter problem of course exists in statist legal systems as well.[8] The basic point, however, is that the State is not needed to arrive at legal principles or their elaboration: indeed, much of the common law, the law merchant, admiralty law, and private law in general, grew up apart from the State, by judges not making the law but finding it on the basis of agreed upon principles derived either from custom or reason.[9] The idea that the State is needed to *make* law is as much a myth as that the State is needed to supply postal or police service.

Enough has been said here, I believe, to indicate that an anarchist system for settling disputes would be both viable and self-subsistent: that once adopted, it could work and continue indefinitely. How *to arrive* at that system is of course a very different problem, but certainly at the very least it will not likely come about unless people are convinced of its workability, are convinced, in short, that the State is not a *necessary* evil.

---

[8]For an elaboration of these points, see Murray N. Rothbard, *For a New Liberty* (New York: Macmillan, 1973).

[9]Thus, see Bruno Leoni, *Freedom and the Law* (Princeton, N.J.: D. Van Nostrand, 1961).

CHAPTER 35

Why Be Libertarian?

W hy be libertarian, anyway? By this we mean: what's the point of the whole thing? Why engage in a deep and lifelong commitment to the principle and the goal of individual liberty? For such a commitment, in our largely unfree world, means inevitably a radical disagreement with, and alienation from, the *status quo*, an alienation which equally inevitably imposes many sacrifices in money and prestige. When life is short and the moment of victory far in the future, why go through all this?

Incredibly, we have found among the increasing number of libertarians in this country many people who come to a libertarian commitment from one or another extremely narrow and personal points of view. Many are irresistibly attracted to liberty as an intellectual system or as an aesthetic goal; but liberty remains for them a purely intellectual parlor game, totally divorced from what they consider the "real" activities of their daily lives. Others are motivated to remain libertarians solely from their anticipation of their own personal financial profit. Realizing that a free market would provide far greater opportunities for able, independent men to reap entrepreneurial profits, they become and remain libertarians solely to find

Reprinted from *Egalitarianism as a Revolt Against Nature and Other Essays* (Auburn, Ala.: Mises Institute, 2000), chap. 15.

larger opportunities for business profit. While it is true that opportunities for profit will be far greater and more widespread in a free market and a free society, placing one's *primary* emphasis on this motivation for being a libertarian can only be considered grotesque. For in the often tortuous, difficult, and gruelling path that must be trod before liberty can be achieved, the libertarian's opportunities for personal profit will far more often be negative than abundant.

The consequence of the narrow and myopic vision of both the gamester and the would-be profitmaker is that neither group has the slightest interest in the work of building a libertarian movement. And yet it is only through building such a movement that liberty may ultimately be achieved. Ideas, and especially radical ideas, do not advance in the world in and by themselves, as it were in a vacuum; they can only be advanced by *people* and, therefore, the development and advancement of such people—and therefore of a "movement"—becomes a prime task for the Libertarian who is really serious about advancing his goals.

Turning from these men of narrow vision, we must also see that utilitarianism—the common ground of free-market economists—is unsatisfactory for developing a flourishing libertarian movement. While it is true and valuable to know that a free market would bring far greater abundance and a healthier economy to everyone, rich and poor alike, a critical problem is whether this knowledge is enough to bring many people to a lifelong dedication to liberty. In short, how many people will man the barricades and endure the many sacrifices that a consistent devotion to liberty entails, merely so that umpteen percent more people will have better bathtubs? Will they not rather set up for an easy life and forget the umpteen percent bathtubs? Ultimately, then, utilitarian economics, while indispensable in the developed structure of libertarian thought and action, is almost as unsatisfactory a basic groundwork for the movement as those opportunists who simply seek a short-range profit.

It is our view that a flourishing libertarian movement, a lifelong dedication to liberty, can only be grounded on a passion for justice. Here must be the mainspring of our drive, the armor that will sustain us in all the storms ahead, not the search for a quick buck, the playing of intellectual games or the cool calculation of general economic gains. And, to have a passion for justice, one must have a *theory* of what justice and injustice are—in short, a set of ethical principles of justice and injustice which cannot be provided by utilitarian economics. It is because we see the world reeking with injustices piled one on another to the very heavens that we are impelled to do all that we can to seek a world in which these and other injustices will be eradicated. Other traditional radical goals—such as the "abolition of poverty"—are, in contrast to this one, truly utopian, for man, simply by exerting his will, cannot abolish poverty. Poverty can only be abolished through the operation of certain economic factors—notably the investment of savings in capital—which can only operate by transforming nature over a long period of time. In short, man's will is here severely limited by the workings of—to use an old-fashioned but still valid term— natural law. But *injustices* are deeds that are inflicted by one set of men on another; they are precisely the actions of men, and, hence, they and their elimination are subject to man's instantaneous will.

Let us take an example: England's centuries-long occupation and brutal oppression of the Irish people. Now if, in 1900, we had looked at the state of Ireland, and we had considered the poverty of the Irish people, we would have had to say: poverty could be improved by the English getting out and removing their land monopolies, but the ultimate elimination of poverty in Ireland, under the best of conditions, would take time and be subject to the workings of economic law. But the goal of ending English oppression—that could have been done by the instantaneous action of men's will: by the English simply deciding to pull out of the country. The fact that of course such decisions do not take place instantaneously is not the point; the point is that the very failure is an injustice that has been decided upon and imposed by the perpetrators of injustice—in this case, the English government. In the field of justice, man's will is all; men can move mountains, if only men so decide. A passion for instantaneous justice—in short, a radical passion—is therefore not utopian, as would be a desire for the instant elimination of poverty or the instant transformation of everyone into a concert pianist. For instant justice *could* be achieved if enough people so willed.

A true passion for justice, then, must be radical—in short, it must at least wish to attain its goals radically and instantaneously. Leonard E. Read, founding president of the Foundation for Economic Education, expressed this radical spirit very aptly when he wrote a pamphlet, *I'd Push the Button*. The problem was what to do about the network of price and wage controls then being imposed on the economy by the Office of Price Administration. Most economic Liberals were timidly or "realistically" advocating one or another form of gradual or staggered decontrols; at that point, Mr. Read took an unequivocal and radical stand on principle: "if there were a button on this rostrum," he began his address, "the pressing of which would release all wage and price controls instantaneously, I would put my finger on it and push!"[1] The true test, then, of the radical spirit, is the button-pushing test: if we could push the button for instantaneous abolition of unjust invasions of liberty, would we do it? If we would not do it, we could scarcely call ourselves Libertarians, and most of us would only do it if primarily guided by a passion for justice.

The genuine Libertarian, then, is, in all senses of the word, an "abolitionist"; he would, if he could, abolish instantaneously all invasions of liberty, whether it be, in the original coining of the term, slavery, or whether it be the manifold other instances of State oppression. He would, in the words of another libertarian in a similar connection, "blister my thumb pushing that button!" The libertarian must perforce be a "button-pusher" and an "abolitionist." Powered by justice, he cannot be moved by amoral utilitarian pleas that justice not come about until the criminals are "compensated." Thus, when in the early nineteenth century, the great abolitionist movement arose, voices of moderation promptly appeared counselling that it would only be fair to abolish slavery if the slave masters were financially compensated for their loss. In short, after centuries of oppression and exploitation, the slave masters were supposed to be further rewarded by a handsome sum muleted by force from the mass of innocent taxpayers! The most apt comment on this proposal was made by the English philosophical radical Benjamin Pearson, who remarked that "he had thought it was the slaves who should have been compensated"; clearly, such compensation could only justly have come from the slaveholders themselves.[2]

Antilibertarians, and antiradicals generally, characteristically make the point that such "abolitionism" is "unrealistic"; by making such a charge they are hopelessly confusing the desired goal with a strategic estimate of the probable outcome. In framing principle, it is of the utmost importance not to mix in strategic estimates with the forging of desired goals. First, goals must be formulated, which, in this case, would be the instant abolition of slavery or whatever other statist oppression we are considering. And we must first frame these goals without considering the probability of attaining them. The libertarian goals are "realistic" in the sense that they *could* be achieved if enough people agreed on their desirability, and that, if achieved, they would bring about a far better world. The "realism"

---

[1]Leonard E. Read, *I'd Push the Button* (New York: Joseph D. McGuire, 1946), p. 3.

[2]William D. Grampp, *The Manchester School of Economics* (Stanford, Calif.: Stanford University Press, 1960), p. 59.

of the goal can only be challenged by a critique of the goal *itself*, not in the problem of how to attain it. Then, after we have decided on the goal, we face the entirely separate strategic question of how to attain that goal as rapidly as possible, how to build a movement to attain it, etc. Thus, William Lloyd Garrison was not being "unrealistic" when, in the 1830s, he raised the glorious standard of immediate emancipation of the slaves. His goal was the proper one, and his strategic realism came in the fact that he did not expect his goal to be quickly reached. Or, as Garrison himself distinguished:

> Urge immediate abolition as earnestly as we may, it will, alas! be gradual abolition in the end. We have never said that slavery would be overthrown by a single blow; that it ought to be, we shall always contend.[3]

Actually, in the realm of the strategic, raising the banner of pure and radical principle is generally the fastest way of arriving at radical goals. For if the pure goal is never brought to the fore, there will never be any momentum developed for driving toward it. Slavery would never have been abolished at all if the abolitionists had not raised the hue and cry thirty years earlier; and, as things came to pass, the abolition was at virtually a single blow rather than gradual or compensated.[4] But above and beyond the requirements of strategy lie the commands of justice. In his famous editorial that launched *The Liberator* at the beginning of 1831, William Lloyd Garrison repented his previous adoption of the doctrine of gradual abolition:

> I seize this opportunity to make a full and unequivocal recantation, and thus publicly to ask pardon of my God, of my country, and of my brethren, the poor slaves, for having uttered a sentiment so full of timidity, injustice and absurdity.

---

[3]Quoted in William H. and Jane H. Pease, eds., *The Antislavery Argument* (Indianapolis: Robbs-Merrill, 1965), p. xxxv.

[4]At the conclusion of a brilliant philosophical critique of the charge of "unrealism" and its confusion of the good and the currently probable, Professor Philbrook declares: "Only one type of serious defense of a policy is open to an economist or anyone else: he must maintain that the policy is good. True 'realism' is the same thing men have always meant by wisdom: to decide the immediate in the light of the ultimate." Clarence Philbrook, "'Realism' in Policy Espousal," *American Economic Review* (December 1953): 859.

Upon being reproached for the habitual severity and heat of his language, Garrison retorted: "I have need to be all on fire, for I have mountains of ice about me to melt." It is this spirit that must mark the man truly dedicated to the cause of liberty.[5]

[5]For the quotes from Garrison, see Louis Ruchames, ed., *The Abolitionists* (New York: Capricorn Books, 1964), p. 31, and Fawn M. Brodie, "Who Defends the Abolitionist?" in Martin Duberman, ed., *The Antislavery Vanguard* (Princeton, N.J.: Princeton University Press, 1965), p. 67. The Duberman work is a storehouse of valuable material, including refutations of the common effort by those committed to the status quo to engage in psychological smearing of radicals in general and abolitionists in particular. See especially Martin Duberman, "The Northern Response to Slavery," in ibid., pp. 406–13.

CHAPTER 36

In Praise of
Demagogues

For many years now, demagogues have been in great disfavor. They are not sober, they are not respectable, they are not "gentlemen." And yet there is a great and growing need for their services. What, exactly, have been the charges leveled against the demagogues? They are roughly three in number.

In the first place, they are disruptive forces in the body politic. They stir things up. Second, they supposedly fail to play the game in appealing to the base emotions, rather than to cool reason. From this stems the third charge: that they appeal to the unwashed masses with emotional, extreme, and, therefore, unsound views. Add to this the vice of ungentlemanly enthusiasm, and we have about catalogued the sins of the species demagogue.

The charge of emotionalism is surely an irrelevant one. The problem of an ideology is not whether it is put forth in an emotional, a matter-of-fact, or a dull manner. The question is whether or not the ideology is correct. Almost always, the demagogue is a man who finds that his ideas are held by only a small minority of people, a minority that is apt to be particularly small among the sober and respectable. Convinced of the truth and the importance of his ideas, he sees that the heavy weight of public opinion, and particularly of the respectable molders of this opinion, is either hostile

---

Written in 1954, this was first published as a *Mises Daily* on April 23, 2002.

or indifferent to this truth. Is it any wonder that such a situation will make a man emotional?

All demagogues are ideological nonconformists and therefore are bound to be emotional about the general and respectable rejection of what they consider to be vital truth. But not all ideological nonconformists become demagogues. The difference is that the demagogue possesses that quality of mass attraction that permits him to use emotion to stir up the masses. In going to the masses, he is going over the heads of the respectable intellectuals who ordinarily guide mass opinion. It is this electric, short-cut appeal direct to the masses that gives the demagogue his vital significance and that makes him such a menace to the dominant orthodoxy.

The demagogue is frequently accused by his enemies of being an insincere opportunist, a man who cynically uses certain ideas and emotions in order to gain popularity and power. It is almost impossible, however, to judge a person's motives, particularly in political life, unless one is a close friend. We have seen that the sincere demagogue is very likely to be emotional himself, while stirring others to emotion. Finally, if a man is really an opportunist, the easiest way to acclaim and power is to play ball with the ruling orthodoxy, and not the opposite. The way of the demagogue is the riskiest and has the least chance of success.

It is the fashionable belief that an idea is wrong in proportion to its "extremism" and right in proportion as it is a chaotic muddle of contradictory doctrines. To the professional middle-of-the-roader, a species that is always found in abundance, the demagogue invariably comes as a nasty shock. For it is one of the most admirable qualities of the demagogue that he forces men to think, some for the first time in their lives. Out of the muddle of current ideas, both fashionable and unfashionable, he extracts some and pushes them to their logical conclusions, i.e., "to extremes." He thereby forces people either to reject their loosely held views as unsound, or to find them sound and to pursue them to their logical consequences. Far from being an irrational force, then, the silliest of demagogues is a great servant of Reason, even when he is mostly in the wrong.

A typical example is the inflationist demagogue: the "monetary crank." The vast majority of respectable economists have always scoffed at the crank without realizing that they are not really able to answer his arguments. For what the crank has done is to take the inflationism that lies at the core of fashionable economics and push it to its logical conclusion. He asks; "If it is good to have an inflation of money of 10 percent per year, why isn't it still better to double the money supply every year?" Only a few economists have realized that in order to answer the crank reasonably instead of by ridicule, it is necessary to purge fashionable economics of its inflationist foundations.

Demagogues probably first fell into disrepute in the nineteenth century, when most of them were socialists. But their conservative opposition, as is typical of conservatives in every age, never came to grips with the logic of the demagogues' position. Instead, they contented themselves with attacking the emotionalism and extremism of the upstarts. Their logic unassailed, the socialist demagogues triumphed, as argument always will conquer pure prejudice in the long run. For it seemed as if the socialists had reason on their side.

Now socialism is the fashionable and respectable ideology. The old passionate arguments of the soap box have become the tired clichés of the cocktail party and the classroom. Any demagogy, any disruption of the apple cart, would almost certainly come from the individualist opposition. Furthermore, the State is now in command, and whenever this conditions prevails, the State is anxious to prevent disruption and ideological turmoil. In their wake, demagogues would bring "disunity," and people might be stirred to think for themselves instead of falling into a universal goose-step behind their anointed leaders. Furthermore, individualist demagogues would be more dangerous than ever, because they could now be equipped with rational arguments to refute the socialist clichés. The respectable statist Left, then, fears and hates the demagogue, and more than ever before, he is the object of attack.

It is true that, in the long run, we will never be free until the intellectuals—the natural molders of public opinions—have been converted to the side of freedom. In the short-run, however, the only route to liberty is by an appeal to the masses over the heads of the State and its intellectual bodyguard. And this appeal can be made most effectively by the demagogue—the rough, unpolished man of the people, who can present the truth in simple, effective, yes emotional, language. The intellectuals see this clearly, and this is why they constantly attack every indication of libertarian demagoguery as part of a "rising tide of anti-intellectualism." Of course, it is not anti-intellectualism; it is the saving of mankind from those intellectuals who have betrayed the intellect itself.

Section VIII

Movie Reviews

CHAPTER 37

The Godfather

The Godfather is one of the great movies of the last several years, and its enormous popularity is eminently well deserved. In the first place, it is a decidedly Old Culture movie, or "movie-movie"; it is gloriously *arrière-garde*, and there is not a trace of the *avant-garde* gimmicks and camera trickery that have helped to ruin so many films in recent years. It is a picture with heroes and villains, good guys and bad guys; there is not a trace of the recently fashionable concern with the "alienation" of shnooks and cretins searching endlessly for a purpose in life. The pace is terrific, the suspense and plot and direction and acting all excellent. Many of the lines are memorable, and "we're going to make him an offer he can't refuse" has already burned its way indelibly into American culture.

The key to the movie is the first scene, when an elderly undertaker, having gone to the police and to the courts for justice for his raped and beaten daughter, and failed abysmally to get it, at last turns to the Corleone Family for that precious quality, justice. Brando, as Don Vito Corleone, the "Godfather," berates the undertaker: "Why did you go to the courts for justice? Why didn't you come to me?" And it is further made gloriously evident that the Corleone Family's concept of justice is advanced indeed. When the undertaker asks Don Corleone to kill the assaulters of his daughter, Don Vito is shocked: "But that is not justice. They did not

Reprinted from *Libertarian Forum* 4, no. 6–7 (1972).

murder your daughter." With a keen sense of the concept of proportionate justice, of punishment fitting the crime, Don Vito agrees to make the rapists "suffer" as the daughter had suffered.

The central theme of the plot is the growth of son Michael Corleone; originally a college lad grown apart from the old Sicilian Family ways, Michael takes his stand with the family when his father is nearly murdered by other, aggressor Families, and toughens into the role of successor to Don Vito. (Actually, the word "godfather" is a weak translation of the Italian word *compare*, which also has connotations of: friend, best man, patron.)

A crucial political statement in the picture comes when Michael is trying to explain to his disapproving WASP girlfriend what the Family is all about: essentially their entrepreneurship of illegal goods and services, their necessity to enforce their own contracts, and (regrettably for the libertarian) their penchant for monopoly in which they are a pale reflection of "respectable" and "legitimate" government. Michael tells his girl that his father is a man of power and influence, and hence the methods he employs, "like the President of the United States." The girl replies: "But the President doesn't order anyone killed," to which Michael rebuts: "Now you're being naïve"—a masterpiece of political understatement.

But above all, a movie-movie in the grand tradition: a rugged, magnificent epic.

CHAPTER 38

The Godfather, Part II

The Oscars. From the beginning, it was clear that the Oscar race for best picture of 1974 was between two films: *Godfather, Part II* and *Chinatown*. As pointed out in these pages (*Libertarian Forum,* March, 1975), *Godfather,* a marvelous film, clearly deserved the award. In contrast, the morbid, cynical *Chinatown* (neatly skewered in *Libertarian Review* by Barbara Branden) was the darling of the *avant-garde* intellectuals, serving as it did as an "anti-hero" reversal of the great detective films of the 1940s.

Part of the excitement of Oscar night is to watch the race between the top pictures build up as the minor awards are allocated. From the beginning of the night, it became clear that *Chinatown* was losing out, as it was defeated in one minor award after another. Unfortunately, this meant that the cool, subtle, and nuanced performance of the beautiful Faye Dunaway in *Chinatown* lost out to Ellen Burstyn's hammy, tearful performance in *Alice Doesn't Live Here Anymore* as Best Actress, but the consolation was the clear meaning that *Chinatown* had had it. Sure enough, *Godfather, Part II* swept the boards, gaining its deserved triumph as Best Picture, and the directorial award for Francis Ford Coppola.

While justice triumphed splendidly in the Best Picture and Best Director awards, the splendid Al Pacino unfortunately lost out in the

Reprinted from *Libertarian Forum* 7, no. 4 (1975).

race for Best Actor; so too did the intellectuals, who were rooting for Jack Nicholson's anti-hero detective in *Chinatown*. Instead, the old Hollywood *penchant* for boozy sentimentality won out, with old favorite Art Carney winning the award for the piece of fluff, *Harry and Tonto*. Fortunately, however, the expected sentimentality did not triumph for the Best Supporting Actor award. Fred Astaire, who has *always* been a poor actor, was particularly weak and even grotesque in a minor role in *The Towering Inferno*; but the scuttlebutt had it that he would win anyway, in an orgy of collective Hollywood guilt for not having given him an Oscar in the 1930s for his glorious dancing in the famous Astaire movies of that era. However, justice again triumphed, as the award went to one of the finest young actors in recent years, Robert DeNiro's "proto-Brando" young godfather in *Godfather, Part II*. Sentimentality *did* triumph in the award to Ingrid Bergman for Best Supporting Actress in *Murder on the Orient Express*, in expiation of Hollywood's collective guilt for casting Miss Bergman into outer darkness thirty years ago for an act of personal "immorality" which would now be considered positively square and old-fashioned. However, in Miss Bergman's case, there was no harm done, since hers was probably the best performance out of a rather poor lot.

And so, the classical aesthetic has won out over its *avant-garde* enemies for the third straight year: in the awards to *Godfather* in 1973, in *The Sting* exorcising *The Exorcist* last year, and now in the victory of *Part II*. With luck, maybe we can enter the lists with a *Part III* for 1977.

CHAPTER 39

Blaxploitation

One of the most important movie phenomena of the last few years has been what the Left-liberal and Establishment critics bitterly deride as "blaxploitation" movies. These are exciting, often delightful films where black private eyes and black gunmen star in black versions of this familiar white style of motion pictures. Of varying quality, such films as *Shaft*, *Trouble Man*, and *Cotton Comes to Harlem* almost all convey a sense of drama and a keen appreciation of black argot and ghetto "street smarts." They are all, in short, fun pictures, and it is typical of the insufferably *serioso* left-critics to get on their neo-Puritan high horse and condemn them as "exploiting" black people by ... what? By giving them pictures which they intensely enjoy. Anyone who has seen a blaxploitation film will attest to the enjoyment and enthusiasm for these pictures by the virtually all-black audience. The audience identifies with the characters, shouts at the screen, applauds and hisses.

But, you see, according to our left-liberals, blacks must somehow be shielded from the supposedly "degrading" nature of street-private eye-police culture. Black audiences have to be fed "ennobling," if depressing and boring movies such as *Sounder*. How insufferably elitist can one get?[1]

---

[1] On the humorless Neo-Puritanism of our current Left, see the interesting article by George H. Douglas, "The New Puritanism of the Youth Culture," *Modern Age* (Spring, 1973).

Reprinted from *Libertarian Forum* 5, no. 5 (1973).

CHAPTER 40

The Tough Cop

The tough cop genre is definitely coming into its own. On TV, the new *Kojak* series, starring the tough and cynical Telly Savales, has become one of the best shows on television. In the movies, it is particularly significant that two of the great Western heroes have recently shifted to the tough cop role. As urban crime has become the concern of ever greater numbers of Americans, the tough crime fighter—in this case John Wayne and Clint Eastwood—has doffed his horse and ten gallon hat for the Magnum and the police badge.

John Wayne moves into the role of tough cop hero in *McQ*, directed by John Sturges. There is no such thing as a bad John Wayne picture, and it is good to have Big John, or Lt. McQ, on hand to carry on a one-man struggle against the rackets and against crooked colleagues. And yet, the picture is no better than workmanlike. It is surprisingly slow, for one thing, and the creaky action only highlights the age of Wayne and Eddie Albert. Also, the standard behavior of the females in falling all over the hero lacks a certain amount of credibility in the case of the aging Wayne. Al Lettieri makes a promising, shambling villain, but the female leads lend no help: Diana Muldaur seems to have only one expression: hangdog, while Colleen Dewhurst—billed on all sides as one of the great actresses of our

Reprinted from *Libertarian Forum* 6, no. 1 (1974).

epoch—croaks her way through a terrible performance. Warning to Warner Brothers: if *McQ* is going to stick around, you'd better come up with faster action and a better director.

The tough cop picture has done far better by Clint Eastwood. His first effort, in *Dirty Harry*, was one of the great films of the last several years. The leftist intellectuals virtually sputtered with fury over *Dirty Harry*, for here was Eastwood as Inspector Harry Callahan of San Francisco stalking a mad dog killer while being subverted and hobbled at every hand by liberals, politicians, and bleeding hearts. *Dirty Harry*, apart from being fast and exciting, was an explicitly right-wing, anti-criminal-coddling movie, and thus drove the liberal critics to inchoate rage. But it was not only the movie and its theme that aggravated them; it was also Eastwood himself. For of all the heroes in movies, Eastwood is the most ruthless, the most implacable, in his battle for the right and against criminal aggression. The critics who scorn Eastwood for his "lack of acting ability" don't understand the character that he is creating. For Eastwood's implacable calm is the result of his decisiveness, his ability to make instant—and correct—decisions in the midst of drama and danger, to make what he knows are the right decisions without moping or agonizing. Hence, Clint Eastwood is the polar opposite of the whining modern anti-hero beloved by the *avant-garde*. In a sense, the left intelligentsia were quite right in identifying Eastwood—or rather the Eastwood figure—as their deadly enemy. Hence their vituperation.

Now dirty Harry is back, in *Magnum Force*, directed by Ted Post. Like its predecessor, it is fast, tough, and exciting, beginning with a dramatic shot of Harry Callahan's Magnum revolver, and continuing to the final reel. If it is a bit less rightwing or less exciting than its predecessor, it remains one of the best movies of recent months.

The plot is particularly interesting in the light of the previous picture. At the end of *Dirty Harry*, Harry had tossed his badge into the river, the symbol of his disgust with the liberal, criminal-coddling System. At the beginning of *Magnum Force*, Harry is inexplicably back in the police force; early into the picture, he finds that the killers he seeks are a group of young police rookies organized into a paramilitary squad to wreak vengeance upon criminals whom the courts let loose. Harry rejects what seem to be youthful disciples of his own creed, and defends law and order against them. Why does he do so? Unfortunately, Harry doesn't seem to be able to articulate his own position, confining himself to: "You guys misunderstood me," and "I hate the System too, but you've got to stay within it until a better one comes along." Has Harry gone liberal? I think we can reassure Harry fans that it ain't so. If Harry could spell out his own position, perhaps he would say that he exacted vengeance on his own against a mad-dog monster, and not against mere racketeers; also his was an individual response, and not an organized gang—a gang, by the way, that committed unforgivable excesses, including the murder of fellow policemen. No, Harry has not gone liberal; his is the optimum degree of "dirt," neither bleeding-heart nor fascist. Long may he prosper.

CHAPTER 41

Death Wish

*D*eath Wish is a superb movie, the best hero-and-vengeance picture since *Dirty Harry*. Bronson, an architect whose young family has been destroyed by muggers, drops his namby-pamby left-liberalism, and begins to pack a gun, defending himself brilliantly and uncompromisingly against a series of muggers who infest New York City. Yet he never kills the innocent, or commits excesses. Naturally, even though he is only defending himself against assault, the police, who have failed to go after the muggers and who acknowledge the fall in the crime rate due to Bronson's activities, devote their resources to pursuing him instead of the criminals who terrorize New York. It is a great and heroic picture, a picture demonstrating one man's successful fight for justice.

As might be expected, *Death Wish* has been subjected to hysterical attacks by the left-liberal critics who acknowledge the power and technical qualities of the picture, which they proceed to denounce for its "fascist ideology" (self-defense by victims against crime) and its "pornography of violence" (in a just cause). Bronson is attacked for his "wooden acting," although this is by far his best acting performance in years, far better than in *The Mechanic*, where the violence was hailed by the critics precisely because it was meaningless and *not* in defense against aggression. Don't miss *Death Wish*; it says more about "the urban problem" than a dozen "message" documentaries, and it helps bring back heroism to the movies.

Reprinted from *Libertarian Forum* 6, no. 8 (1974).

CHAPTER 42

Cinema Paradiso

L ong-time readers know that I am decidedly not a fan of foreign language movies: not because it is a chore to read subtitles, but because
they are invariably horrible examples of aggressively *avant-garde*,
anti-bourgeois cinema. Hating as "commercial" movies that appeal to
the average movie-goer, the foreign movie-maker proclaims his superior
aesthetic sensibility by scorning interesting plot, tight writing and directing, meaningful dialogue, glamorous photography, or colorful settings.
Instead, the typical foreign movie has zero plot, minimal dialogue, and
wastes enormous amounts of time on close-ups of the brooding actors'
gloomy faces, all seemingly photographed in the midst of some dark and
dank box. The ineffable and pointless boredom of these motion pictures
are apparently supposed to embody the alleged boredom of bourgeois life.
In actuality, it is not life, but these infernal movies, that both embody and
induce boredom.

The trouble, however, is not with foreigners *per se*. Italians and
Frenchmen, for example, would rather and do spend their time watching *Dallas* and Clint Eastwood than waste their time and money watching
their compatriots' crummy movies. Moreover, it was not always thus. Jean
Renoir, the wonderful 1930s French movies featuring Raimu, and much

Written in July 1990 for the *Rothbard-Rockwell Report*; reprinted in *The Irrepressible Rothbard* (2000).

of the modern work of Eric Rohmer demonstrate that the problem is not with the nationality or language, but with the depraved riffraff who make today's foreign movies.

But once in a while there comes a shining exception to the rule. In addition to granting *Driving Miss Daisy* its Best Picture award for 1989, the Motion Picture Academy gave its foreign-language movie Oscar to Guiseppe Tornatore's lovely, charming, funny, and heart-warming (as well as heart-breaking) *Cinema Paradiso*. Disappearing fairly quickly from the screen the first time around, it came back in wake of the award. Go see it: it's the best foreign-language movie in many a year, and splendid in its own right.

Cinema Paradiso is a heart-felt autobiographical valentine by director and screen-writer Tornatore to the small town in Sicily in which he grew up during and after World War II. The movie is a rich tapestry of life in the Sicilian town, a town without cars or means of entertainment except the local cinema, where everyone crowds in to see the latest Italian or Hollywood product. The central character Salvatore, marvelously played for most of the film by a child actor, is fascinated by the life of the projectionist, the center of movie magic. The projectionist, Alfredo, magnificently played by the great French actor Philippe Noiret, reluctantly becomes a mentor to the boy, whose father had been killed in the war. The local priest views all the movies first, censoring out the—horrors!—kissing scenes, which Alfredo lovingly clips out and saves.

When, over a decade later, the movie theater burns down, a large shining new theater is built, funded by a Neapolitan who had just won the lottery. (As one local complains: "Those Northerners have all the luck!") In the new dispensation, the local priest no longer has censoring rights, and the local youth go bananas at the love scenes: "Kissing! After thirty years!" Loving the now grown boy, and blinded during the fire, Alfredo orders Salvatore to leave the stifling atmosphere of the Sicilian town, which has allowed him no real life and to go seek his life and fortune in Rome, never to look back.

The death of Alfredo, however, inexorably draws Salvatore, thirty years later and famous as a movie director in Rome, back to his home town for his funeral. He finds enormous change; the town, now packed with automobiles and TV sets, has no more use for the movie theater, which is being torn down for a parking lot. I won't give away the climactic discovering of Alfredo's carefully wrought final present for Salvatore, but suffice it to say that it's at least a two-handkerchief (decidedly non-*avant-garde*) ending. Don't miss it!

Index

THE MISES INSTITUTE

Made in the USA
San Bernardino, CA
29 July 2016